Collects
and Post Comm
in Traditional L

for

¶ *Lesser Festivals*

¶ *Common of the Saints*

¶ *Special Occasions*

Church House Publishing

Published by Church House Publishing
Church House
Great Smith Street
London SW1P 3NZ

Telephone 020 7898 1451
Fax 020 7898 1449

ISBN 0 7151 2089 1

Printed and bound by ArklePrint Ltd, Northampton
on 80 gsm Dutchman Ivory

Designed and typeset by John Morgan studio

The material in this booklet is extracted from the President's edition of *Common Worship*.

Contents

Notes

1 Collects and Post Communions in Traditional Language for Sundays, Principal Holy Days and Festivals are published in *Common Worship: Services and Prayers for the Church of England.*

2 Normally on any occasion only one Collect is used.

3 At Evening Prayer on Saturdays other than Easter Eve, Christmas Eve or Principal Feasts or Festivals, the Collect appointed for the ensuing Sunday shall be used. When Evening Prayer on the day before a Festival makes use of the lessons relating to that Festival, the Collect of that Festival shall be used.

4 Where a Collect ends 'Through Jesus Christ…now and for ever', the minister may use the shorter ending, 'Through Jesus Christ our Lord' to which the people respond 'Amen' and omit the longer Trinitarian ending. The longer ending is to be preferred at Holy Communion.

¶ *Lesser Festivals*

2 January **Basil the Great and Gregory of Nazianzus** *White*

Bishops, Teachers of the Faith, 379 and 389

Collect

Almighty God,
whose servants Basil and Gregory
proclaimed the mystery of thy Word made flesh,
that thy Church might be built up in wisdom and strength:
grant that we,
rejoicing in his presence among us,
may with them be brought to know the power
 of thine unending love;
through Jesus Christ thy Son our Lord,
who liveth and reigneth with thee,
in the unity of the Holy Spirit,
one God, now and for ever.

Post Communion

The Post Communion of Teachers of the Faith is used (page 66).

12 January **Aelred of Hexham** *White*

Abbot of Rievaulx, 1167

Collect

Almighty God,
who didst endow the blessed abbot Aelred
with the gift of Christian friendship
and the wisdom to lead others into the way of holiness:
grant to thy people that same spirit of mutual affection,
that in loving one another
we may know the love of Christ
and rejoice in the eternal possession
    of thine unsurpassable goodness;
through Jesus Christ thy Son our Lord,
who liveth and reigneth with thee,
in the unity of the Holy Spirit,
one God, now and for ever.

Post Communion

The Post Communion of Members of Religious Communities is used *(page 68).*

13 January **Hilary** *White*

Bishop of Poitiers, Teacher of the Faith, 367

Collect

Everlasting God,
whose servant Hilary
steadfastly confessed thy Son Jesus Christ
    to be both human and divine:
grant us his gentle courtesy
to bring to all the message of redemption
    in the incarnate Christ,
who liveth and reigneth with thee,
in the unity of the Holy Spirit,
one God, now and for ever.

Post Communion

The Post Communion of Teachers of the Faith is used *(page 66).*

17 January **Antony of Egypt** *White*

Hermit, Abbot, 356

Collect

Most gracious God,
who didst call thy servant Antony to sell all that he had
and to serve thee in the solitude of the desert:
grant that we, following his example,
may learn to deny ourselves
and to love thee before all things;
through Jesus Christ thy Son our Lord,
who liveth and reigneth with thee,
in the unity of the Holy Spirit,
one God, now and for ever.

Post Communion

The Post Communion of Members of Religious Communities is used *(page 68).*

19 January **Wulfstan** *White*

Bishop of Worcester, 1095

Collect

O Lord God,
who didst raise up Wulfstan to be a bishop among thy people
  and a leader in thy Church:
give us grace, after his example,
  to live simply,
  to work diligently,
  and to make thy kingdom known;
through Jesus Christ thy Son our Lord,
who liveth and reigneth with thee,
in the unity of the Holy Spirit,
one God, now and for ever.

Post Communion

The Post Communion of Bishops is used *(page 67).*

21 January **Agnes** *Red*

Child Martyr at Rome, 304

Collect

Eternal God, Shepherd of thy sheep,
by whose grace thy child Agnes was strengthened to bear witness,
in her life and in her death,
to the true love of her redeemer:
grant us the power to understand, with all thy saints,
what is the breadth and length and height and depth
and to know the love that passeth all knowledge,
even Jesus Christ thy Son our Lord,
who liveth and reigneth with thee,
in the unity of the Holy Spirit,
one God, now and for ever.

Post Communion

One of the Post Communions of Martyrs is used (page 65).

24 January **Francis de Sales** *White*

Bishop of Geneva, Teacher of the Faith, 1622

Collect

God of all holiness,
who didst call thy bishop Francis de Sales
to bring many to Christ through his devout life,
and to renew thy Church with patience and understanding,
grant that we may, by word and example,
reflect thy gentleness and love to all those whom we meet;
through Jesus Christ our Saviour,
who liveth and reigneth with thee,
in the unity of the Holy Spirit,
one God, now and for ever.

Post Communion

The Post Communion of Teachers of the Faith is used (page 66).

26 January **Timothy and Titus** *White*

Companions of Paul

Collect

Heavenly Father,
who didst send thine apostle Paul to preach the gospel,
and gavest him Timothy and Titus
to be his companions in the faith:
grant that our fellowship in the Holy Spirit
may bear witness to the name of Jesus,
who liveth and reigneth with thee,
in the unity of the Holy Spirit,
one God, now and for ever.

Post Communion

The Post Communion of Missionaries is used *(page 69).*

28 January **Thomas Aquinas** *White*

Priest, Philosopher, Teacher of the Faith, 1274

Collect

Everlasting God,
who didst enrich thy Church with the learning and holiness
of thy servant Thomas Aquinas:
grant to all who seek thee
a humble mind and a pure heart
that they may know thy Son Jesus Christ
to be the way, the truth and the life;
who liveth and reigneth with thee,
in the unity of the Holy Spirit,
one God, now and for ever.

Post Communion

The Post Communion of Teachers of the Faith is used *(page 66).*

30 January **Charles** *Red*

King and Martyr, 1649

Collect

King of kings and Lord of lords,
whose faithful servant Charles
prayed for his persecutors
and died in the living hope of thine eternal kingdom:
grant us, by thy grace, so to follow his example
that we may love and bless our enemies,
through the intercession of thy Son, our Lord Jesus Christ,
who liveth and reigneth with thee,
in the unity of the Holy Spirit,
one God, now and for ever.

Post Communion

One of the Post Communions of Martyrs is used (page 65).

3 February **Anskar** *White*

Archbishop of Hamburg,
Missionary in Denmark and Sweden, 865

Collect

Almighty and gracious God,
who didst send thy servant Anskar
to spread the gospel among the Nordic people:
raise up in this our generation, we beseech thee,
messengers of thy good tidings
and heralds of thy kingdom,
that the world may come to know
the immeasurable riches of our Saviour Jesus Christ,
who liveth and reigneth with thee,
in the unity of the Holy Spirit,
one God, now and for ever.

Post Communion

The Post Communion of Missionaries is used (page 69).

14 February **Cyril and Methodius** *White*

Missionaries to the Slavs, 869 and 885

Collect

O Lord of all,
who gavest to thy servants Cyril and Methodius
the gift of tongues to proclaim the gospel to the Slavic people:
we pray that thy whole Church may be one as thou art one,
that all who confess thy name may honour one another,
and that from east and west all may acknowledge
 one Lord, one faith, one baptism,
and thee, the God and Father of all;
through Jesus Christ thy Son our Lord,
who liveth and reigneth with thee,
in the unity of the Holy Spirit,
one God, now and for ever.

Post Communion

The Post Communion of Missionaries is used *(page 69).*

17 February **Janani Luwum** *Red*

Archbishop of Uganda, Martyr, 1977

Collect

O God of truth,
whose servant Janani Luwum walked in the light,
and in his death defied the powers of darkness:
free us, we beseech thee, from fear of those who kill the body,
that we also may walk as children of light,
through him who overcame darkness by the power of the cross,
Jesus Christ thy Son our Lord,
who liveth and reigneth with thee,
in the unity of the Holy Spirit,
one God, now and for ever.

Post Communion

One of the Post Communions of Martyrs is used *(page 65).*

23 February

Polycarp

Red

Bishop of Smyrna, Martyr, c.155

Collect

Almighty God,
who gavest to thy servant Polycarp
boldness to confess the name of our Saviour Jesus Christ
before the rulers of this world
and courage to suffer death for his faith:
grant that we too may be ready
to give an answer for the faith that is in us
and to suffer gladly for the sake of our Lord Jesus Christ,
who liveth and reigneth with thee,
in the unity of the Holy Spirit,
one God, now and for ever.

Post Communion

One of the Post Communions of Martyrs is used (page 65).

27 February

George Herbert

White

Priest, Poet, 1633

Collect

King of glory, king of peace,
who didst call thy servant George Herbert
from the pursuit of worldly honours
to be a priest in the temple of his God and king:
grant us also the grace to offer ourselves
with singleness of heart in humble obedience to thy service;
through Jesus Christ thy Son our Lord,
who liveth and reigneth with thee,
in the unity of the Holy Spirit,
one God, now and for ever.

Post Communion

The Post Communion of Pastors is used (page 67).

1 March **David** *White*

Bishop of Menevia, Patron Saint of Wales, c.601

Collect

Almighty God,
who didst call thy servant David
to be a faithful and wise steward of thy mysteries
for the people of Wales:
in thy mercy, grant that,
following his purity of life and zeal for the gospel of Christ,
we may with him receive the crown of everlasting life;
through Jesus Christ our Lord,
to whom with thee and the Holy Spirit
be all honour and glory,
world without end.

Post Communion

The Post Communion of Bishops is used (page 67).

2 March **Chad** *White*

Bishop of Lichfield, Missionary, 672

Collect

Almighty God,
who, from the first fruits of the English nation
that turned to Christ,
didst call thy servant Chad
to be an evangelist and bishop of his own people:
grant us grace so to follow his peaceable nature,
humble spirit and prayerful life,
that we may truly commend to others
the faith which we ourselves profess;
through Jesus Christ thy Son our Lord,
who liveth and reigneth with thee,
in the unity of the Holy Spirit,
one God, now and for ever.

Post Communion

The Post Communion of Missionaries is used (page 69).

7 March

Perpetua, Felicity and their Companions

Red

Martyrs at Carthage, 203

Collect

O holy God,
who gavest great courage to Perpetua,
Felicity and their companions:
grant that we may be worthy to climb the ladder of sacrifice
and be received into the garden of peace;
through Jesus Christ thy Son our Lord,
who liveth and reigneth with thee,
in the unity of the Holy Spirit,
one God, now and for ever.

Post Communion

One of the Post Communions of Martyrs is used (page 65).

8 March

Edward King

White

Bishop of Lincoln, 1910

Collect

O God of peace,
who gavest such grace to thy servant Edward King
that all whom he met he drew to Christ:
fill us, we pray, with tender sympathy and joyful faith,
that we too may draw others
to know the love which passeth knowledge;
through him who is the shepherd and guardian of our souls,
Jesus Christ thy Son our Lord,
who liveth and reigneth with thee,
in the unity of the Holy Spirit,
one God, now and for ever.

Post Communion

The Post Communion of Bishops is used (page 67).

17 March **Patrick** *White*

Bishop, Missionary, Patron Saint of Ireland, c.460

Collect

Almighty God,
who in thy providence chose thy servant Patrick
to be the apostle of the people of Ireland:
keep alive in us the fire of faith which he kindled,
and in this our earthly pilgrimage
strengthen us to gain the light of everlasting life;
through Jesus Christ thy Son our Lord,
who liveth and reigneth with thee,
in the unity of the Holy Spirit,
one God, now and for ever.

Post Communion

The Post Communion of Missionaries is used *(page 69).*

20 March **Cuthbert** *White*

Bishop of Lindisfarne, Missionary, 687

Collect

Almighty God,
who didst call thy servant Cuthbert from following the flock
to follow thy Son and to be a shepherd of thy people:
in thy mercy, grant that we may so follow his example
that we may bring those who are lost home to thy fold;
through Jesus Christ thy Son our Lord,
who liveth and reigneth with thee,
in the unity of the Holy Spirit,
one God, now and for ever.

Post Communion

The Post Communion of Missionaries is used *(page 69).*

21 March **Thomas Cranmer** *Red*

Archbishop of Canterbury, Reformation Martyr, 1556

Collect

Father of all mercies,
who through the work of thy servant Thomas Cranmer
didst renew the worship of thy Church
and through his death
didst reveal thy strength in human weakness:
strengthen us by thy grace so to worship thee in spirit and in truth
that we may come to the joys of thine everlasting kingdom;
through Jesus Christ, our Mediator and Advocate,
who liveth and reigneth with thee,
in the unity of the Holy Spirit,
one God, now and for ever.

Post Communion

One of the Post Communions of Martyrs is used (page 65).

10 April **William Law** *White*

Priest, Spiritual Writer, 1761

Collect

Almighty God,
who didst call thy servant William Law
to a devout and holy life:
grant that by thy spirit of love
and through faithfulness in prayer
we may find the way to divine knowledge
and so come to see the hidden things of God;
through Jesus Christ thy Son our Lord,
who liveth and reigneth with thee,
in the unity of the Holy Spirit,
one God, now and for ever.

Post Communion

The Post Communion of Teachers of the Faith is used (page 66).

19 April **Alphege** *Red*

Archbishop of Canterbury, Martyr, 1012

Collect

O merciful God,
who didst raise up thy servant Alphege
to be a pastor of thy people
and gavest him grace to suffer for justice and true religion:
grant that we who celebrate his martyrdom
may know the power of the risen Christ in our hearts
and share his peace in lives offered to thy service;
through Jesus Christ thy Son our Lord,
who liveth and reigneth with thee,
in the unity of the Holy Spirit,
one God, now and for ever.

Post Communion

One of the Post Communions of Martyrs is used (page 65).

21 April **Anselm** *White*

Abbot of Le Bec, Archbishop of Canterbury,
Teacher of the Faith, 1109

Collect

O everlasting God,
who gavest to thy servant Anselm
singular gifts as a pastor and teacher:
grant that we, like him,
may desire thee with our whole heart
and, so desiring, may seek thee
and, seeking, may find thee;
through Jesus Christ thy Son our Lord,
who liveth and reigneth with thee,
in the unity of the Holy Spirit,
one God, now and for ever.

Post Communion

The Post Communion of Teachers of the Faith is used (page 66).

29 April **Catherine of Siena** White

Teacher of the Faith, 1380

Collect

O merciful God,
who gavest to thy servant Catherine of Siena
a wondrous love of the passion of Christ:
grant that we thy people may be united to him in his majesty
and rejoice for ever in the revelation of his glory;
who liveth and reigneth with thee,
in the unity of the Holy Spirit,
one God, now and for ever.

Post Communion

The Post Communion of Teachers of the Faith is used (page 66).

2 May **Athanasius** White

Bishop of Alexandria, Teacher of the Faith, 373

Collect

Ever-living God,
whose servant Athanasius bore witness
to the mystery of the Word made flesh for our salvation:
give us grace, with all thy saints,
to contend for the truth
and to grow into the likeness of thy Son,
Jesus Christ our Lord,
who liveth and reigneth with thee,
in the unity of the Holy Spirit,
one God, now and for ever.

Post Communion

The Post Communion of Teachers of the Faith is used (page 66).

English Saints and Martyrs of the Reformation Era

White

Collect

O merciful God,
who, when thy Church on earth was torn apart
    by the ravages of sin,
didst raise up men and women in this land
who witnessed to their faith with courage and constancy:
give unto thy Church that peace which is thy will,
and grant that those who have been divided on earth
    may be reconciled in heaven
and be partakers together in the vision of thy glory;
through Jesus Christ thy Son our Lord,
who liveth and reigneth with thee,
in the unity of the Holy Spirit,
one God, now and for ever.

Post Communion

O God, the source of all holiness and giver of all good things:
grant that we, who have shared at this table
    as strangers and pilgrims here on earth,
may with all thy saints be welcomed
    to the heavenly feast in the day of thy kingdom;
through Jesus Christ our Lord.

8 May **Julian of Norwich** *White*

Spiritual Writer, c.1417

Collect

Most holy God, the ground of our beseeching,
who through thy servant Julian
didst reveal the wonders of thy love:
grant that as we are created in thy nature
    and restored by thy grace,
our wills may be so made one with thy will,
and that we may come to see thee face to face
and gaze on thee for ever;
through Jesus Christ thy Son our Lord,
who liveth and reigneth with thee,
in the unity of the Holy Spirit,
one God, now and for ever.

Post Communion

The Post Communion of Members of Religious Communities is used (page 68).

19 May **Dunstan** *White*

Archbishop of Canterbury, Restorer of Monastic Life, 988

Collect

Almighty God,
who didst raise up Dunstan
to be a true shepherd of the flock,
a restorer of monastic life
and a faithful counsellor to kings:
grant, we beseech thee, to all pastors
the like gifts of thy Holy Spirit
that they may be true servants of Christ
    and of all his people;
through Jesus Christ thy Son our Lord,
who liveth and reigneth with thee,
in the unity of the Holy Spirit,
one God, now and for ever.

Post Communion

The Post Communion of Bishops is used (page 67).

20 May

Alcuin of York

White

Deacon, Abbot of Tours, 804

Collect

O God of wisdom, eternal light,
who didst shine in the heart of thy servant Alcuin,
revealing to him thy power and pity:
scatter the darkness of our ignorance
that, with all our heart and mind and strength,
we may seek thy face
and be brought with all thy saints
  into thy holy presence;
through Jesus Christ thy Son our Lord,
who liveth and reigneth with thee,
in the unity of the Holy Spirit,
one God, now and for ever.

Post Communion

The Post Communion of Members of Religious Communities is used (page 68).

24 May

John and Charles Wesley

White

Evangelists, Hymn Writers, 1791 and 1788

Collect

Merciful God,
who didst inspire John and Charles Wesley
  with zeal for thy gospel:
grant to all people boldness to proclaim thy word
and a heart ever to rejoice in singing thy praises;
through Jesus Christ thy Son our Lord,
who liveth and reigneth with thee,
in the unity of the Holy Spirit,
one God, now and for ever.

Post Communion

The Post Communion of Pastors is used (page 67).

25 May

The Venerable Bede

Monk at Jarrow, Scholar, Historian, 735

White

Collect

Almighty God, maker of all things,
whose Son Jesus Christ gave to thy servant Bede
grace to drink in with joy
the word which leadeth us to know thee and to love thee:
in thy goodness
grant that we also may come at length to thee,
the source of all wisdom,
and stand before thy face;
through Jesus Christ thy Son our Lord,
who liveth and reigneth with thee,
in the unity of the Holy Spirit,
one God, now and for ever.

Post Communion

The Post Communion of Members of Religious Communities is used (page 68).

26 May

Augustine of Canterbury

First Archbishop of Canterbury, 605

White

Collect

Almighty God,
whose servant Augustine was sent as the apostle
of the English people:
mercifully grant that, as he laboured in the Spirit
to preach Christ in this land,
so all who hear thy gospel
may strive to make thy truth known in all the world;
through Jesus Christ thy Son our Lord,
who liveth and reigneth with thee,
in the unity of the Holy Spirit,
one God, now and for ever.

Post Communion

The Post Communion of Bishops is used (page 67).

30 May

Josephine Butler

Social Reformer, 1906

White

Collect

O God of compassion and love,
by whose grace thy servant Josephine Butler
followed in the way of thy Son
in caring for those in need:
help us, after her example, to work with strength
for the restoration of all to the dignity
    and freedom of those created in thine image;
through Jesus Christ our Saviour,
who liveth and reigneth with thee,
in the unity of the Holy Spirit,
one God, now and for ever.

Post Communion

O God our redeemer,
who didst inspire Josephine Butler to witness to thy love
and to labour for the coming of thy kingdom:
grant that we, who in this sacrament share the bread of heaven,
may be fired by thy Spirit
    to proclaim the gospel in our daily lives
and never to rest content until thy kingdom come,
on earth as it is in heaven;
through Jesus Christ our Lord.

Or another Post Communion of 'Any Saint' (pages 71–72) is used.

1 June **Justin** *Red*

Martyr at Rome, c.165

Collect

O God our redeemer,
who through the folly of the cross
didst teach thy martyr Justin
the surpassing knowledge of Jesus Christ:
free us, we beseech thee, from every kind of error,
that we, like him, may be firmly grounded in the faith,
and make thy name known to all peoples;
through Jesus Christ thy Son our Lord,
who liveth and reigneth with thee,
in the unity of the Holy Spirit,
one God, now and for ever.

Post Communion

One of the Post Communions of Martyrs is used *(page 65).*

5 June **Boniface (Wynfrith) of Crediton** *Red*

Bishop, Apostle of Germany, Martyr, 754

Collect

O God our redeemer,
who didst call thy servant Boniface
to preach the gospel among the German people
and to build up thy Church in holiness:
grant that we may hold fast in our hearts
that faith which he taught with his words
and sealed with his blood,
and profess it in lives dedicated to thy Son,
Jesus Christ our Lord,
who liveth and reigneth with thee,
in the unity of the Holy Spirit,
one God, now and for ever.

Post Communion

One of the Post Communions of Martyrs is used *(page 65).*

8 June **Thomas Ken** *White*

Bishop of Bath and Wells, Nonjuror, Hymn Writer, 1711

Collect

O God, from whom all blessings flow,
by whose providence we are kept
and by whose grace we are directed:
assist us, through the example of thy servant Thomas Ken,
faithfully to keep thy word,
humbly to accept adversity
and steadfastly to worship thee;
through Jesus Christ thy Son our Lord,
who liveth and reigneth with thee,
in the unity of the Holy Spirit,
one God, now and for ever.

Post Communion

The Post Communion of Bishops is used (page 67).

9 June **Columba** *White*

Abbot of Iona, Missionary, 597

Collect

Almighty God,
who didst fill the heart of Columba
with the joy of the Holy Spirit,
and with deep love for those in his care:
grant to thy pilgrim people grace to follow him,
strong in faith, sustained by hope,
and made one in the love that binds us to thee;
through Jesus Christ thy Son our Lord,
who liveth and reigneth with thee,
in the unity of the Holy Spirit,
one God, now and for ever.

Post Communion

The Post Communion of Missionaries is used (page 69).

16 June **Richard** *White*

Bishop of Chichester, 1253

Collect

Most merciful redeemer,
who gavest to thy bishop Richard
a love of learning, a zeal for souls
and a devotion to the poor:
grant that, encouraged by his example,
we may know thee more clearly,
 love thee more dearly,
 and follow thee more nearly,
day by day;
who livest and reignest with the Father,
in the unity of the Holy Spirit,
ever one God, world without end.

Post Communion

The Post Communion of Bishops is used (page 67).

22 June **Alban** *Red*

First Martyr of Britain, c.250

Collect

O eternal Father,
who, when the gospel of Christ first came to our land,
didst gloriously confirm the faith of Alban
by making him the first to win the martyr's crown:
grant that, following his example in the fellowship of the saints,
we may worship thee, the living God,
and faithfully witness to Jesus Christ thy Son our Lord,
who liveth and reigneth with thee,
in the unity of the Holy Spirit,
one God, now and for ever.

Post Communion

One of the Post Communions of Martyrs is used (page 65).

23 June **Etheldreda** *White*

Abbess of Ely, c.678

Collect

O eternal God,
who didst bestow such grace on thy servant Etheldreda
that she gave herself wholly to the life of prayer
 and to the service of thy true religion:
grant that we may in like manner
seek thy kingdom in our earthly lives,
that by thy guidance
we may be united in the glorious fellowship of thy saints;
through Jesus Christ thy Son our Lord,
who liveth and reigneth with thee,
in the unity of the Holy Spirit,
one God, now and for ever.

Post Communion

The Post Communion of Members of Religious Communities is used *(page 68).*

28 June **Irenæus** *White*

Bishop of Lyons, Teacher of the Faith, c.200

Collect

O God of peace,
who through the ministry of thy servant Irenæus
didst strengthen the true faith and bring harmony to thy Church:
keep us steadfast in thy true religion
and renew us in faith and love,
that we may ever walk in the way
 that leadeth to everlasting life;
through Jesus Christ thy Son our Lord,
who liveth and reigneth with thee,
in the unity of the Holy Spirit,
one God, now and for ever.

Post Communion

The Post Communion of Teachers of the Faith is used *(page 66).*

11 July **Benedict of Nursia** *White*

Abbot of Monte Cassino,
Father of Western Monasticism, c.550

Collect

O eternal God,
who made Benedict a wise master
in the school of thy service,
and a guide to many called into the common life
to follow the rule of Christ:
grant that we may put thy love above all things,
and seek with joy the way of thy commandments;
through Jesus Christ thy Son our Lord,
who liveth and reigneth with thee,
in the unity of the Holy Spirit,
one God, now and for ever.

Post Communion

The Post Communion of Members of Religious Communities is used *(page 68).*

14 July **John Keble** *White*

Priest, Tractarian, Poet, 1866

Collect

Father of the eternal Word,
in whose encompassing love
all things in peace and order move:
grant that, as thy servant John Keble
adored thee in all creation,
so we may have a humble heart of love
for the mysteries of thy Church
and know thy love to be new every morning,
in Jesus Christ thy Son our Lord,
who liveth and reigneth with thee,
in the unity of the Holy Spirit,
one God, now and for ever.

Post Communion

The Post Communion of Pastors is used *(page 67).*

15 July **Swithun** *White*

Bishop of Winchester, c.862

Collect

Almighty God,
by whose grace we celebrate again
the feast of thy servant Swithun:
grant that, as he governed with gentleness
    the people committed to his care,
so we, rejoicing in our inheritance in Christ,
may ever seek to build up thy Church in unity and love;
through Jesus Christ thy Son our Lord,
who liveth and reigneth with thee,
in the unity of the Holy Spirit,
one God, now and for ever.

Post Communion

The Post Communion of Bishops is used (page 67).

19 July **Gregory and Macrina** *White*

Gregory, Bishop of Nyssa, and his sister Macrina, Deaconess,
Teachers of the Faith, c.394 and c.379

Collect

O Lord of eternity, creator of all things,
who in thy Son Jesus Christ
    dost open for us the way to resurrection
that we may enjoy thy bountiful goodness:
grant that we, who celebrate thy servants Gregory and Macrina,
may press onwards in faith to thine unbounded love
and ever wonder at the miracle of thy presence among us;
through Jesus Christ thy Son our Lord,
who liveth and reigneth with thee,
in the unity of the Holy Spirit,
one God, now and for ever.

Post Communion

The Post Communion of Teachers of the Faith is used (page 66).

Anne and Joachim

White

Parents of the Blessed Virgin Mary

Collect

O Lord God of Israel,
who didst bestow such grace on Anne and Joachim
that their daughter Mary grew up obedient to thy word
and was made ready to be the mother of thy Son:
strengthen us to commit ourselves in all things to thy keeping
and grant us the salvation which thou hast promised to thy people;
through Jesus Christ thy Son our Lord,
who liveth and reigneth with thee,
in the unity of the Holy Spirit,
one God, now and for ever.

Post Communion

O God our Father,
from whom every family in heaven and on earth is named,
whose servants Anne and Joachim revealed thy goodness
in a life of tranquillity and service:
grant that we who have gathered in faith around this table
may like them know the love of Christ
that surpasses knowledge
and be filled with all thy fullness;
through Jesus Christ our Lord.

Or another Post Communion of 'Any Saint' (pages 71–72) is used.

29 July **Mary, Martha and Lazarus** *White*

Companions of Our Lord

Collect

O God our Father,
whose Son delighted in the love of his friends,
  Mary, Martha and Lazarus,
in learning, argument and hospitality:
grant to us so to rejoice in thy love
that the world may come to know
  the depths of thy wisdom, the wonder of thy compassion,
  and thy power to bring life out of death;
through the merits of Jesus Christ,
our friend and brother,
who liveth and reigneth with thee,
in the unity of the Holy Spirit,
one God, now and for ever.

Post Communion

O God our Father,
from whom every family in heaven and on earth is named,
whose servants Mary, Martha and Lazarus revealed thy goodness
  in a life of tranquillity and service:
grant that we who have gathered in faith around this table
may like them know the love of Christ
  that surpasses knowledge
and be filled with all thy fullness;
through Jesus Christ our Lord.

Or another Post Communion of 'Any Saint' (pages 71–72) is used.

William Wilberforce

Social Reformer, 1833

Collect

O God our deliverer,
who didst send thy Son Jesus Christ
to set thy people free from the slavery of sin:
grant that, as thy servant William Wilberforce
toiled against the sin of slavery,
so we may bring compassion to all,
and work for the liberty of all the children of God;
through Jesus Christ thy Son our Lord,
who liveth and reigneth with thee,
in the unity of the Holy Spirit,
one God, now and for ever.

Post Communion

O God our redeemer,
who didst inspire William Wilberforce to witness to thy love
and to labour for the coming of thy kingdom:
grant that we, who in this sacrament share the bread of heaven,
may be fired by thy Spirit
to proclaim the gospel in our daily lives
and never to rest content until thy kingdom come,
on earth as it is in heaven;
through Jesus Christ our Lord.

Or another Post Communion of 'Any Saint' (pages 71–72) is used.

5 August **Oswald** *Red*

King of Northumbria, Martyr, 642

Collect

O Lord God almighty,
who didst so kindle the faith of thy servant King Oswald
with thy Spirit
that he set up the sign of the cross in his kingdom
and turned his people to the light of Christ:
grant that we, being fired by the same Spirit,
may ever bear our cross before the world
and be found faithful servants of the gospel;
through Jesus Christ thy Son our Lord,
who liveth and reigneth with thee,
in the unity of the Holy Spirit,
one God, now and for ever.

Post Communion

One of the Post Communions of Martyrs is used (page 65).

8 August **Dominic** *White*

Priest, Founder of the Order of Preachers, 1221

Collect

Almighty God,
whose servant Dominic grew in the knowledge of thy truth,
and formed an order of preachers to proclaim the faith of Christ:
by thy grace grant to all thy people a love for thy word
and a longing to share the gospel,
that the whole world may be filled with the knowledge of thee
and of thy Son Jesus Christ our Lord,
who liveth and reigneth with thee,
in the unity of the Holy Spirit,
one God, now and for ever.

Post Communion

The Post Communion of Members of Religious Communities is used (page 68).

9 August **Mary Sumner** *White*

Founder of the Mothers' Union, 1921

Collect

O faithful and loving God,
who didst call Mary Sumner
to strive for the renewal of family life:
grant to us the gift of thy Holy Spirit,
that through word and prayer and deed
thy family may be strengthened and thy people served:
through Jesus Christ thy Son our Lord,
who liveth and reigneth with thee,
in the unity of the Holy Spirit,
one God, now and for ever.

Post Communion

O God our Father,
from whom every family in heaven and on earth is named,
whose servant Mary Sumner revealed thy goodness
in a life of tranquillity and service:
grant that we who have gathered in faith around this table
may like her know the love of Christ that surpasses knowledge
and be filled with all thy fullness;
through Jesus Christ our Lord.

Or another Post Communion of 'Any Saint' (pages 71–72) is used.

10 August **Laurence** *Red*

Deacon at Rome, Martyr, 258

Collect

Almighty God,
who didst make Laurence
a loving servant of thy people
and a wise steward of the treasures of thy Church:
inflame us, by his example, to love as he loved
and to walk in the way that leads to everlasting life;
through Jesus Christ thy Son our Lord,
who liveth and reigneth with thee,
in the unity of the Holy Spirit,
one God, now and for ever.

Post Communion

One of the Post Communions of Martyrs is used (page 65).

11 August **Clare of Assisi** *White*

Founder of the Minoresses (Poor Clares), 1253

Collect

O God of peace,
who in the poverty of the blessed Clare
gavest us a clear light to shine in the darkness of this world:
give us grace so to follow in her footsteps
that we may, at the last, rejoice with her in thine eternal glory;
through Jesus Christ thy Son our Lord,
who liveth and reigneth with thee,
in the unity of the Holy Spirit,
one God, now and for ever.

Post Communion

The Post Communion of Members of Religious Communities is used (page 68).

13 August **Jeremy Taylor** *White*

Bishop of Down and Connor, Teacher of the Faith, 1667

Collect

O holy and loving God,
who dwellest in the human heart
and makest us partakers of the divine nature
in Christ our great high priest:
grant that we,
having in remembrance thy servant Jeremy Taylor,
may put our trust in thy heavenly promises,
and follow a holy life in virtue and true godliness;
through Jesus Christ thy Son our Lord,
who liveth and reigneth with thee,
in the unity of the Holy Spirit,
one God, now and for ever.

Post Communion

The Post Communion of Teachers of the Faith is used *(page 66).*

20 August **Bernard** *White*

Abbot of Clairvaux, Teacher of the Faith, 1153

Collect

O merciful redeemer,
who, by the life and preaching of thy servant Bernard,
didst rekindle the radiant light of thy Church:
grant that we in our generation
may be inflamed with the same spirit of discipline and love
and ever walk before thee as children of light;
through Jesus Christ thy Son our Lord,
who liveth and reigneth with thee,
in the unity of the Holy Spirit,
one God, now and for ever.

Post Communion

The Post Communion of Teachers of the Faith is used *(page 66).*

27 August

Monica

White

Mother of Augustine of Hippo, 387

Collect

O faithful God,
who didst strengthen Monica, the mother of Augustine,
with wisdom,
and by her steadfast endurance
didst draw him to seek after thee:
grant us to be constant in prayer
that those who stray from thee may be brought to faith
in thy Son Jesus Christ our Lord,
who liveth and reigneth with thee,
in the unity of the Holy Spirit,
one God, now and for ever.

Post Communion

O God our Father,
from whom every family in heaven and on earth is named,
whose servant Monica revealed thy goodness
in a life of tranquillity and service:
grant that we who have gathered in faith around this table
may like her know the love of Christ that surpasses knowledge
and be filled with all thy fullness;
through Jesus Christ our Lord.

Or another Post Communion of 'Any Saint' (pages 71–72) is used.

28 August

Augustine of Hippo

White

Bishop of Hippo, Teacher of the Faith, 430

Collect

O merciful Lord,
who didst turn Augustine from his sins
to be a faithful bishop and teacher:
grant that we may follow him in penitence and godly discipline,
till our restless hearts find their rest in thee;
through Jesus Christ thy Son our Lord,
who liveth and reigneth with thee,
in the unity of the Holy Spirit,
one God, now and for ever.

Post Communion

The Post Communion of Teachers of the Faith is used (page 66).

29 August

The Beheading of John the Baptist

Red

Collect

Almighty God,
who didst call thy servant John the Baptist
to be in birth and death the forerunner of thy blessed Son:
strengthen us by thy grace
that, as he suffered for the truth,
so may we boldly withstand corruption and vice
and receive with him the unfading crown of glory;
through Jesus Christ thy Son our Lord,
who liveth and reigneth with thee,
in the unity of the Holy Spirit,
one God, now and for ever.

Post Communion

O merciful Lord,
whose prophet John the Baptist
proclaimed thy Son to be the Lamb of God
    who taketh away the sin of the world:
grant that we who in this sacrament
    have known thy pardon and thy life-giving love,
may ever tell of thy mercy and thy peace;
through Jesus Christ our Lord.

30 August **John Bunyan** *White*

Spiritual Writer, 1688

Collect

O God of peace,
who didst call thy servant John Bunyan
to be valiant for truth:
grant that as strangers and pilgrims
we may at the last
    rejoice with all Christian people in thy heavenly city;
through Jesus Christ thy Son our Lord,
who liveth and reigneth with thee,
in the unity of the Holy Spirit,
one God, now and for ever.

Post Communion

The Post Communion of Teachers of the Faith is used (page 66).

31 August

Aidan

Bishop of Lindisfarne, Missionary, 651

White

Collect

O everlasting God,
who didst send thy gentle bishop Aidan
to proclaim the gospel in this land:
grant that we may live after his teaching
in simplicity, humility and love for the poor;
through Jesus Christ thy Son our Lord,
who liveth and reigneth with thee,
in the unity of the Holy Spirit,
one God, now and for ever.

Post Communion

The Post Communion of Missionaries is used *(page 69).*

3 September

Gregory the Great

Bishop of Rome, Teacher of the Faith, 604

White

Collect

O merciful Father,
who didst choose thy bishop Gregory
to be a servant of the servants of God:
grant that, like him, we may ever desire to serve thee
by proclaiming thy gospel to the nations,
and may ever rejoice to sing thy praises;
through Jesus Christ thy Son our Lord,
who liveth and reigneth with thee,
in the unity of the Holy Spirit,
one God, now and for ever.

Post Communion

The Post Communion of Teachers of the Faith is used *(page 66).*

The Birth of the Blessed Virgin Mary

White

Collect

Almighty and everlasting God,
who stooped to raise fallen humanity
through the child-bearing of blessed Mary:
grant that we, who have seen thy glory
revealed in our human nature
and thy love made perfect in our weakness,
may daily be renewed in thine image
and conformed to the pattern of thy Son
Jesus Christ our Lord,
who liveth and reigneth with thee,
in the unity of the Holy Spirit,
one God, now and for ever.

Post Communion

O God most high,
whose handmaid bore the Word made flesh:
we give thee thanks that in this sacrament of our redemption
thou dost visit us with thy Holy Spirit
and dost overshadow us with thy power;
strengthen us to walk with Mary
in the joyful path of obedience,
that we may bring forth the fruits of holiness;
through Jesus Christ our Lord.

13 September **John Chrysostom** *White*

Bishop of Constantinople, Teacher of the Faith, 407

Collect

O God of truth and love,
who gavest to thy servant John Chrysostom
eloquence to declare thy righteousness in the great congregation
and courage to bear reproach for the honour of thy name:
mercifully grant to the ministers of thy word
such excellence in preaching
that all people may share with them
in the glory that shall be revealed;
through Jesus Christ thy Son our Lord,
who liveth and reigneth with thee,
in the unity of the Holy Spirit,
one God, now and for ever.

Post Communion

The Post Communion of Teachers of the Faith is used (page 66).

15 September **Cyprian** *Red*

Bishop of Carthage, Martyr, 258

Collect

O holy God,
who didst bring Cyprian to faith in Christ
and didst make him a bishop in the Church,
crowning his witness with a martyr's death:
grant that, following his example,
we may love the Church and her doctrine,
find thy forgiveness within her fellowship,
and so come to share the heavenly banquet
which thou hast prepared for us;
through Jesus Christ thy Son our Lord,
who liveth and reigneth with thee,
in the unity of the Holy Spirit,
one God, now and for ever.

Post Communion

One of the Post Communions of Martyrs is used (page 65).

16 September

Ninian

White

Bishop of Galloway, Apostle of the Picts, c.432

Collect

Almighty and everlasting God,
who didst call thy servant Ninian to preach the gospel
  to the people of northern Britain:
raise up, we beseech thee, in this and every land,
heralds and evangelists of thy kingdom,
that thy Church may make known the immeasurable riches
  of thy Son our Saviour Jesus Christ,
who liveth and reigneth with thee,
in the unity of the Holy Spirit,
one God, now and for ever.

Post Communion

The Post Communion of Missionaries is used *(page 69).*

17 September

Hildegard

White

Abbess of Bingen, Visionary, 1179

Collect

Most glorious and holy God,
whose servant Hildegard, strong in the faith,
was caught up in the vision of thy heavenly courts:
by the breath of thy Spirit
open our eyes to glimpse thy glory
and our lips to sing thy praises with all the angels;
through Jesus Christ thy Son our Lord,
who liveth and reigneth with thee,
in the unity of the Holy Spirit,
one God, now and for ever.

Post Communion

The Post Communion of Members of Religious Communities is used *(page 68).*

20 September **John Coleridge Patteson** *Red*

First Bishop of Melanesia, and his Companions, Martyrs, 1871

Collect

O God of all tribes and peoples and tongues,
who didst call thy servant John Coleridge Patteson
to witness in life and death to the gospel of Christ
amongst the peoples of Melanesia:
grant us to hear thy call to service
and to respond with trust and joy
to Jesus Christ our redeemer,
who liveth and reigneth with thee,
in the unity of the Holy Spirit,
one God, now and for ever.

Post Communion

One of the Post Communions of Martyrs is used (page 65).

25 September **Lancelot Andrewes** *White*

Bishop of Winchester, Spiritual Writer, 1626

Collect

O Lord God,
who didst give Lancelot Andrewes many gifts
    of thy Holy Spirit,
making him a man of prayer and a pastor of thy people:
perfect in us that which is lacking in thy gifts,
    of faith, to increase it,
    of hope, to establish it,
    of love, to kindle it,
that we may live in the light of thy grace and glory;
through Jesus Christ thy Son our Lord,
who liveth and reigneth with thee,
in the unity of the Holy Spirit,
one God, now and for ever.

Post Communion

The Post Communion of Bishops is used (page 67).

27 September **Vincent de Paul** *White*

Founder of the Congregation of the Mission (Lazarists), 1660

Collect

O merciful God,
whose servant Vincent de Paul,
by his ministry of preaching and pastoral care,
brought thy love to the sick and the poor:
grant to all thy people a heart of compassion,
that by serving the needs of others
they may serve thee in word and deed;
through Jesus Christ thy Son our Lord,
who liveth and reigneth with thee,
in the unity of the Holy Spirit,
one God, now and for ever.

Post Communion

The Post Communion of Members of Religious Communities is used (page 68).

4 October **Francis of Assisi** *White*

Friar, Deacon, Founder of the Friars Minor, 1226

Collect

O God,
who ever delightest to reveal thyself
to the childlike and lowly of heart,
grant that, following the example of the blessed Francis,
we may count the wisdom of this world as foolishness
and know only Jesus Christ and him crucified,
who liveth and reigneth with thee,
in the unity of the Holy Spirit,
one God, now and for ever.

Post Communion

The Post Communion of Members of Religious Communities is used (page 68).

6 October **William Tyndale** *Red*

Translator of the Scriptures, Reformation Martyr, 1536

Collect

O Lord, grant to thy people
grace to hear and keep thy word
that, after the example of thy servant William Tyndale,
we may both profess thy gospel
and also be ready to suffer and die for it,
to the honour of thy name;
through Jesus Christ thy Son our Lord,
who liveth and reigneth with thee,
in the unity of the Holy Spirit,
one God, now and for ever.

Post Communion

One of the Post Communions of Martyrs is used (page 65).

10 October **Paulinus** *White*

Bishop of York, Missionary, 644

Collect

O God our Saviour,
who didst send thy servant Paulinus to preach and to baptize,
and so to build up thy Church in this land:
grant that, being inspired by his example,
we may proclaim to the whole world thy truth,
that with him we may receive the reward
  thou hast prepared for all thy faithful servants;
through Jesus Christ thy Son our Lord,
who liveth and reigneth with thee,
in the unity of the Holy Spirit,
one God, now and for ever.

Post Communion

The Post Communion of Missionaries is used (page 69).

Wilfrid of Ripon

White

Bishop, Missionary, 709

Collect

Almighty God,
who didst call our forebears to the light of the gospel
    by the preaching of thy servant Wilfrid:
grant us, who keep his life and labour in remembrance,
to glorify thy name
    by following the example of his zeal and perseverance;
through Jesus Christ thy Son our Lord,
who liveth and reigneth with thee,
in the unity of the Holy Spirit,
one God, now and for ever.

Post Communion

The Post Communion of Missionaries is used (page 69).

Edward the Confessor

White

King of England, 1066

Collect

O Sovereign God,
who didst set thy servant Edward
upon the throne of an earthly kingdom
and didst inspire him with zeal for the kingdom of heaven:
grant that we may so confess the faith of Christ
by word and deed,
that we may, with all thy saints, inherit thine eternal glory;
through Jesus Christ thy Son our Lord,
who liveth and reigneth with thee,
in the unity of the Holy Spirit,
one God, now and for ever.

Post Communion

O God our redeemer,
who didst inspire Edward to witness to thy love
and to labour for the coming of thy kingdom:
grant that we, who in this sacrament share the bread of heaven,
may be fired by thy Spirit
to proclaim the gospel in our daily lives
and never to rest content until thy kingdom come,
on earth as it is in heaven;
through Jesus Christ our Lord.

Or another Post Communion of 'Any Saint' (pages 71–72) is used.

15 October **Teresa of Avila** *White*

Teacher of the Faith, 1582

Collect

Merciful God,
who by thy Spirit didst raise up thy servant Teresa of Avila
to reveal to thy Church the way of perfection:
grant that her teaching
may awaken in us a longing for holiness
until we attain to the perfect union of love
in Jesus Christ thy Son our Lord,
who liveth and reigneth with thee,
in the unity of the Holy Spirit,
one God, now and for ever.

Post Communion

The Post Communion of Teachers of the Faith is used (page 66).

17 October **Ignatius** *Red*

Bishop of Antioch, Martyr, c.107

Collect

Feed us, O Lord, with the living bread
and make us drink deep of the cup of salvation
that, following the teaching of thy bishop Ignatius,
and rejoicing in the faith
 with which he embraced the death of a martyr,
we may be nourished for that eternal life
 which he ever desired;
through Jesus Christ thy Son our Lord,
who liveth and reigneth with thee,
in the unity of the Holy Spirit,
one God, now and for ever.

Post Communion

One of the Post Communions of Martyrs is used (page 65).

19 October **Henry Martyn** *White*

Translator of the Scriptures,
Missionary in India and Persia, 1812

Collect

Almighty God,
who by thy Holy Spirit didst grant to Henry Martyn
a longing to proclaim the gospel of Christ
and skill to translate the Scriptures:
by the same Spirit, give us grace to offer our gifts to thee
wheresoever thou leadest, not counting the cost;
through Jesus Christ thy Son our Lord,
who liveth and reigneth with thee,
in the unity of the Holy Spirit,
one God, now and for ever.

Post Communion

The Post Communion of Missionaries is used (page 69).

26 October **Alfred the Great** *White*

King of the West Saxons, Scholar, 899

Collect

O God our maker and redeemer,
we beseech thee of thy great mercy
and by the power of thy holy cross
to guide us by thy will and to shield us from our foes,
that, following the example of thy servant Alfred,
we may inwardly love thee above all things;
through Jesus Christ thy Son our Lord,
who liveth and reigneth with thee,
in the unity of the Holy Spirit,
one God, now and for ever.

Post Communion

O God our redeemer,
who didst inspire Alfred to witness to thy love
and to labour for the coming of thy kingdom:
grant that we, who in this sacrament share the bread of heaven,
may be fired by thy Spirit
to proclaim the gospel in our daily lives
and never to rest content until thy kingdom come,
on earth as it is in heaven;
through Jesus Christ our Lord.

Or another Post Communion of 'Any Saint' (pages 71–72) is used.

29 October **James Hannington** *Red*

Bishop in Eastern Equatorial Africa,
Martyr in Uganda, 1885

Collect

Most merciful God,
who didst strengthen thy Church
by the steadfast courage of thy martyr James Hannington:
grant that we also,
thankfully remembering his victory of faith,
may overcome all that is evil,
and ever glorify thy holy name;
through Jesus Christ thy Son our Lord,
who liveth and reigneth with thee,
in the unity of the Holy Spirit,
one God, now and for ever.

Post Communion

One of the Post Communions of Martyrs is used (page 65).

Commemoration of the Faithful Departed

Purple

Collect

Everlasting God, our maker and redeemer,
grant us, with all the faithful departed,
the sure benefits of thy Son's saving passion
 and glorious resurrection,
that, in the last day,
when thou dost gather up all things in Christ,
we may with them enjoy the fullness of thy promises;
through Jesus Christ thy Son our Lord,
who liveth and reigneth with thee,
in the unity of the Holy Spirit,
one God, now and for ever.

Post Communion

O God of love,
grant that the death and resurrection of Christ
which we have celebrated in this sacrament
may bring us, with all the faithful departed,
into the peace of thine eternal home;
through Jesus Christ, our rock and our salvation,
to whom be glory for time and for eternity.

3 November **Richard Hooker** *White*

Priest, Anglican Apologist, Teacher of the Faith, 1600

Collect

O God of peace, the bond of all love,
who in thy Son Jesus Christ hast made for all people
thine inseparable dwelling place:
give us grace that,
after the example of thy servant Richard Hooker,
we thy servants may ever rejoice
in the true inheritance of thine adopted children
and show forth thy praises now and for ever;
through Jesus Christ thy Son our Lord,
who liveth and reigneth with thee,
in the unity of the Holy Spirit,
one God, now and for ever.

Post Communion

The Post Communion of Teachers of the Faith is used (page 66).

7 November **Willibrord of York** *White*

Bishop, Apostle of Frisia, 739

Collect

O God the Saviour of all,
who didst send thy bishop Willibrord from this land
to proclaim the gospel to many peoples
and confirm them in their faith:
strengthen us, we beseech thee,
to witness to thy steadfast love by word and deed
so that thy Church may increase and grow strong in holiness;
through Jesus Christ thy Son our Lord,
who liveth and reigneth with thee,
in the unity of the Holy Spirit,
one God, now and for ever.

Post Communion

The Post Communion of Missionaries is used (page 69).

The Saints and Martyrs of England

White

Collect

O God,
whom the glorious company of the redeemed adore,
gathered from all times and places of thy dominion:
we praise thee for the saints of our own land,
and for the lamps that were lit by their holiness;
and we beseech thee that, at the last,
we too may be numbered among those who have done thy will
and declared thy righteousness;
through Jesus Christ thy Son our Lord,
who liveth and reigneth with thee,
in the unity of the Holy Spirit,
one God, now and for ever.

Post Communion

O God,
the source of all holiness and giver of all good things:
grant that we, who have shared at this table
as strangers and pilgrims here on earth,
may with all thy saints be welcomed
to the heavenly feast in the day of thy kingdom;
through Jesus Christ our Lord.

10 November **Leo the Great** *White*

Bishop of Rome, Teacher of the Faith, 461

Collect

O God our Father,
who madest thy servant Leo strong in the defence of the faith:
we humbly beseech thee
so to fill thy Church with the spirit of truth
that, being guided by humility and governed by love,
she may prevail against the powers of evil;
through Jesus Christ thy Son our Lord,
who liveth and reigneth with thee,
in the unity of the Holy Spirit,
one God, now and for ever.

Post Communion

The Post Communion of Teachers of the Faith is used (page 66).

11 November **Martin of Tours** *White*

Bishop of Tours, c.397

Collect

Almighty God,
who didst call Martin from the armies of this world
to be a faithful soldier of Christ:
give us grace to follow him
in his love and compassion for those in need,
and empower thy Church to claim for all people
their inheritance as the children of God;
through Jesus Christ thy Son our Lord,
who liveth and reigneth with thee,
in the unity of the Holy Spirit,
one God, now and for ever.

Post Communion

The Post Communion of Bishops is used (page 67).

13 November **Charles Simeon** *White*

Priest, Evangelical Divine, 1836

Collect

O eternal God,
who didst raise up Charles Simeon
to preach the gospel of Jesus Christ
and inspire thy people in service and mission:
grant that we, with all thy Church, may worship the Saviour,
turn away in true repentance from our sins
and walk in the way of holiness;
through Jesus Christ thy Son our Lord,
who liveth and reigneth with thee,
in the unity of the Holy Spirit,
one God, now and for ever.

Post Communion

The Post Communion of Pastors is used *(page 67)*.

16 November **Margaret of Scotland** *White*

Queen of Scotland, Philanthropist,
Reformer of the Church, 1093

Collect

O God, the ruler of all,
who didst call thy servant Margaret to an earthly throne
and gavest to her both zeal for thy Church and love for thy people,
that she might advance thy heavenly kingdom:
mercifully grant that we who commemorate her example
may be fruitful in good works
and attain to the glorious crown of thy saints;
through Jesus Christ thy Son our Lord,
who liveth and reigneth with thee,
in the unity of the Holy Spirit,
one God, now and for ever.

Post Communion

O God our redeemer,
who didst inspire Margaret to witness to thy love
and to labour for the coming of thy kingdom:
grant that we, who in this sacrament share the bread of heaven,
may be fired by thy Spirit
  to proclaim the gospel in our daily lives
and never to rest content until thy kingdom come,
on earth as it is in heaven;
through Jesus Christ our Lord.

Or another Post Communion of 'Any Saint' (pages 71–72) is used.

17 November **Hugh** *White*
Bishop of Lincoln, 1200

Collect

O God,
who didst endow thy servant Hugh
with a wise and cheerful boldness
and didst teach him to commend to earthly rulers
  the discipline of a holy life:
give us grace like him to be bold in the service of the gospel,
putting our confidence in Christ alone,
who liveth and reigneth with thee,
in the unity of the Holy Spirit,
one God, now and for ever.

Post Communion

The Post Communion of Bishops is used (page 67).

18 November **Elizabeth of Hungary** *White*

Princess of Thuringia, Philanthropist, 1231

Collect

O Lord God,
who didst teach Elizabeth of Hungary
to recognize and to reverence Christ in the poor of this world:
grant that we, being strengthened by her example,
may so love and serve the afflicted and those in need
that we may honour thy Son, the servant king,
who liveth and reigneth with thee,
in the unity of the Holy Spirit,
one God, now and for ever.

Post Communion

Faithful God,
who didst call Elizabeth of Hungary to thy service
and gavest her joy in walking the path of holiness:
we pray that through this holy communion
in which the vision of thy glory is renewed within us,
we may all be strengthened to follow the way of perfection
until we come to see thee face to face;
through Jesus Christ our Lord.

Or another Post Communion of 'Any Saint' (pages 71–72) is used.

19 November **Hilda** *White*

Abbess of Whitby, 680

Collect

O eternal God,
who madest the abbess Hilda to shine as a jewel in our land
and through her holiness and leadership
    didst bless thy Church with newness of life and unity:
so assist us by thy grace
that we, like her, may yearn for the gospel of Christ
and bring reconciliation to those who are divided;
through Jesus Christ thy Son our Lord,
who liveth and reigneth with thee,
in the unity of the Holy Spirit,
one God, now and for ever.

Post Communion

The Post Communion of Members of Religious Communities is used (page 68).

20 November **Edmund** *Red*

King of the East Angles, Martyr, 870

Collect

O eternal God,
whose servant Edmund kept faith to the end,
both with thee and with his people,
and glorified thee by his death:
grant us the same steadfast faith,
that, together with the noble army of martyrs,
we may come to the perfect joy of the resurrection life;
through Jesus Christ thy Son our Lord,
who liveth and reigneth with thee,
in the unity of the Holy Spirit,
one God, now and for ever.

Post Communion

One of the Post Communions of Martyrs is used (page 65).

23 November **Clement** *Red*

Bishop of Rome, Martyr, c.100

Collect

Eternal Father, creator of all,
whose martyr Clement bore witness with his blood
to the love that he proclaimed and the gospel that he preached:
give us thankful hearts as we celebrate thy faithfulness,
revealed to us in the lives of thy saints,
and strengthen us in our pilgrimage as we follow thy Son,
Jesus Christ our Lord,
who liveth and reigneth with thee,
in the unity of the Holy Spirit,
one God, now and for ever.

Post Communion

One of the Post Communions of Martyrs is used (page 65).

6 December **Nicholas** *White*

Bishop of Myra, c.326

Collect

Almighty Father, lover of souls,
who didst choose thy servant Nicholas
to be a bishop in the Church,
that he might give freely out of the treasures of thy grace:
make us mindful of the needs of others
and, as we have received, so teach us also to give;
through Jesus Christ thy Son our Lord,
who liveth and reigneth with thee,
in the unity of the Holy Spirit,
one God, now and for ever.

Post Communion

The Post Communion of Bishops is used (page 67).

7 December **Ambrose** *White*

Bishop of Milan, Teacher of the Faith, 397

Collect

Lord God of hosts,
who didst call Ambrose from the governor's throne
to be a bishop in thy Church
and a courageous champion of thy faithful people:
mercifully grant that, as he fearlessly rebuked rulers,
so we may with like courage
    contend for the faith which we have received;
through Jesus Christ thy Son our Lord,
who liveth and reigneth with thee,
in the unity of the Holy Spirit,
one God, now and for ever.

Post Communion

The Post Communion of Teachers of the Faith is used *(page 66).*

The Conception of the Blessed Virgin Mary

White

Collect

Almighty and everlasting God,
who stooped to raise fallen humanity
through the child-bearing of blessed Mary:
grant that we, who have seen thy glory
revealed in our human nature
and thy love made perfect in our weakness,
may daily be renewed in thine image
and conformed to the pattern of thy Son
Jesus Christ our Lord,
who liveth and reigneth with thee,
in the unity of the Holy Spirit,
one God, now and for ever.

Post Communion

O God most high,
whose handmaid bore the Word made flesh:
we give thee thanks that in this sacrament of our redemption
thou dost visit us with thy Holy Spirit
and dost overshadow us with thy power;
strengthen us to walk with Mary
in the joyful path of obedience,
that we may bring forth the fruits of holiness;
through Jesus Christ our Lord.

13 December

Lucy

Red

Martyr at Syracuse, 304

Collect

O God our redeemer,
who gavest light to the world that was in darkness
by the healing power of the Saviour's cross:
we beseech thee to shed that light on us
that with thy martyr Lucy
we may, by the purity of our lives,
  reflect the light of Christ
and, by the merits of his passion,
  attain to the light of everlasting life;
through Jesus Christ thy Son our Lord,
who liveth and reigneth with thee,
in the unity of the Holy Spirit,
one God, now and for ever.

Post Communion

One of the Post Communions of Martyrs is used *(page 65).*

14 December

John of the Cross

White

Priest, Teacher of the Faith, 1591

Collect

O God, the judge of all,
who gavest to thy servant John of the Cross
a warmth of nature, a strength of purpose
  and a mystical faith
that sustained him even in the darkness:
shed thy light on all who love thee,
granting them union of body and soul
in thy Son Jesus Christ our Lord,
who liveth and reigneth with thee,
in the unity of the Holy Spirit,
one God, now and for ever.

Post Communion

The Post Communion of Teachers of the Faith is used *(page 66).*

29 December **Thomas Becket** *Red*

Archbishop of Canterbury, Martyr, 1170

Collect

O Lord God,
who gavest to thy servant Thomas Becket
grace to put aside all earthly fear
and be faithful even unto death:
grant that we, caring not for worldly esteem,
may fight against evil,
uphold thy rule,
and serve thee to our life's end;
through Jesus Christ thy Son our Lord,
who liveth and reigneth with thee,
in the unity of the Holy Spirit,
one God, now and for ever.

Post Communion

One of the Post Communions of Martyrs is used (page 65).

¶ *Common of the Saints*

The Blessed Virgin Mary *White*

Collect

Almighty and everlasting God,
who stooped to raise fallen humanity
through the child-bearing of blessed Mary:
grant that we, who have seen thy glory
revealed in our human nature
and thy love made perfect in our weakness,
may daily be renewed in thine image
and conformed to the pattern of thy Son
Jesus Christ our Lord,
who liveth and reigneth with thee,
in the unity of the Holy Spirit,
one God, now and for ever.

Post Communion

O God most high,
whose handmaid bore the Word made flesh:
we give thee thanks that in this sacrament of our redemption
thou dost visit us with thy Holy Spirit
and dost overshadow us with thy power;
strengthen us to walk with Mary
in the joyful path of obedience,
that we may bring forth the fruits of holiness;
through Jesus Christ our Lord.

Collect

O almighty God,
who hast built thy Church upon the foundation
of the apostles and prophets,
Jesus Christ himself being the head cornerstone:
grant us so to be joined together in unity of spirit
by their doctrine,
that we may be made an holy temple acceptable unto thee;
through Jesus Christ thy Son our Lord,
who liveth and reigneth with thee,
in the unity of the Holy Spirit,
one God, now and for ever.

Post Communion

Almighty God,
who on the day of Pentecost
didst send thy Holy Spirit to the apostles
with the wind from heaven and in tongues of flame,
filling them with joy and boldness to preach the gospel:
by the power of the same Spirit
strengthen us to bear witness to thy truth
and to draw everyone to the fire of thy love;
through Jesus Christ our Lord.

(or)

O Lord God, the source of truth and love,
keep us faithful to the apostles' teaching and fellowship,
united in prayer and the breaking of bread,
and one in joy and simplicity of heart,
in Jesus Christ our Lord.

Martyrs *Red*

Collect

Almighty God,
by whose grace and power thy holy martyr *N*
triumphed over suffering and was faithful unto death:
strengthen us with thy grace,
that we may endure reproach and persecution
and faithfully bear witness to the name
    of Jesus Christ thy Son our Lord,
who liveth and reigneth with thee,
in the unity of the Holy Spirit,
one God, now and for ever.

Post Communion

O eternal God,
who hast given us this holy meal
in which we have celebrated the glory of the cross
and the victory of thy martyr *N*:
by our communion with Christ
in his saving death and resurrection,
grant us with all thy saints the courage to overcome evil
and so to partake of the fruit of the tree of life;
through Jesus Christ our Lord.

(or)

O God our redeemer,
whose Church was strengthened by the blood of thy martyr *N*:
so bind us, in life and in death,
to the sacrifice of Christ
that, our lives being broken and offered with his,
we may carry his death
and proclaim his resurrection in the world;
through Jesus Christ our Lord.

Teachers of the Faith

Collect

O God,
who hast enlightened thy Church
by the teaching of thy servant *N*:
enrich it evermore, we beseech thee, with thy heavenly grace,
and raise up faithful witnesses,
who by their life and doctrine may set forth to all people
the truth of thy salvation;
through Jesus Christ thy Son our Lord,
who liveth and reigneth with thee,
in the unity of the Holy Spirit,
one God, now and for ever.

Post Communion

O God of truth,
whose Wisdom prepared her table
and invited us to eat the bread and drink the wine
of the kingdom:
help us to lay aside all folly
and to walk all our days in the way of discernment,
that we may come with *N* to the eternal heavenly feast;
through Jesus Christ our Lord.

Collect

Almighty and everlasting God,
who didst call thy servant *N* to proclaim thy glory
by a life of prayer and the zeal of a true pastor:
keep constant in faith the leaders of thy Church
and so bless thy people through their ministry
that the Church may grow into the full stature
of thy Son Jesus Christ our Lord,
who liveth and reigneth with thee,
in the unity of the Holy Spirit,
one God, now and for ever.

or, for a Bishop

Almighty God,
the light of the faithful and shepherd of souls,
who didst call thy servant *N* to be a bishop in the Church,
to feed thy sheep by the word of Christ
and to guide them by his godly example:
give us grace to abide by the faith of the Church
and to follow in the footsteps
of Jesus Christ thy Son our Lord,
who liveth and reigneth with thee,
in the unity of the Holy Spirit,
one God, now and for ever.

Post Communion

O God, the shepherd of thy people,
whose servant *N* showed forth the loving service of Christ
in *his/her* ministry as a pastor of thy people:
we pray that, by this sacrament in which we share,
thou wilt awaken within us the love of Christ
and keep us faithful to our calling in his name;
through him who laid down his life for us,
but liveth and reigneth with thee, now and for ever.

Members of Religious Communities

Collect

Almighty God,
by whose grace *N*,
enkindled with the fire of thy love,
became a burning and a shining light in the Church:
inflame us with the same spirit of discipline and love,
that we may ever walk before thee as children of light;
through Jesus Christ thy Son our Lord,
who liveth and reigneth with thee,
in the unity of the Holy Spirit,
one God, now and for ever.

Post Communion

Merciful God,
who gavest such grace to thy servant *N*
that *he/she* served thee with singleness of heart
and loved thee above all things:
help us, whose communion with thee
    has been renewed in this sacrament,
to forsake all that hinders us from following Christ
and to grow into his likeness from glory to glory;
through Jesus Christ our Lord.

Collect

O everlasting God,
whose servant *N* carried the gospel of thy Son
to the people of … :
mercifully grant that we who commemorate *his/her* service
may know the hope of the gospel in our hearts
and manifest its light in all our ways;
through Jesus Christ thy Son our Lord,
who liveth and reigneth with thee,
in the unity of the Holy Spirit,
one God, now and for ever.

Post Communion

Holy Father,
who didst gather us around the table of thy Son
that we, with all thy household,
might partake of this holy food:
in that new world
wherein the fullness of thy peace is revealed,
gather people of every race and tongue
to share with *N* and all thy saints
in the eternal banquet of Jesus Christ our Lord.

Collect (general)

Almighty Father,
who hast built up thy Church
through the love and devotion of thy saints:
inspire us to follow the example of *N*
whom we commemorate this day,
that we in our generation may rejoice with *him/her*
in the vision of thy glory;
through Jesus Christ thy Son our Lord,
who liveth and reigneth with thee,
in the unity of the Holy Spirit,
one God, now and for ever.

or (for Christian rulers)

Sovereign God,
who didst call *N* to be a ruler among *his/her* people
and gavest *him/her* grace to be their servant:
help us to follow our Saviour Christ
in the path of humble service,
that we may see his kingdom set forward on earth
and enjoy its fullness in heaven;
through Jesus Christ thy Son our Lord,
who liveth and reigneth with thee,
in the unity of the Holy Spirit,
one God, now and for ever.

or (for those working for the poor and underprivileged)

O merciful God,
who hast compassion on all that thou hast made,
and hast enfolded thy whole creation in thy love:
help us to stand firm for thy truth,
to strive against poverty,
and to share thy love with our neighbour,
that with thy servant *N* we may be instruments of thy peace;
through Jesus Christ thy Son our Lord,
who liveth and reigneth with thee,
in the unity of the Holy Spirit,
one God, now and for ever.

or (for men and women of learning)

O God our Father,
who gavest to thy servant *N* wisdom and discernment
that *he/she* might fathom the depths of thy love
and understand thy design for the world that thou hast made:
grant us the help of thy Holy Spirit,
that we also may come to a full knowledge of thy purposes
revealed in thy Son Jesus Christ, our Wisdom and our Life;
who liveth and reigneth with thee,
in the unity of the Holy Spirit,
one God, now and for ever.

or (for those whose holiness was revealed in marriage and family life)

O eternal God,
whose love is revealed in the mystery of the Trinity:
grant that we, like thy servant *N*,
may find in our human loving a mirror of thy divine love
and discern in all thy children our brothers and sisters in Christ,
who liveth and reigneth with thee,
in the unity of the Holy Spirit,
one God, now and for ever.

Post Communion

Faithful God,
who didst call *N* to thy service
and gavest *him/her* joy in walking the path of holiness:
we pray that through this holy communion,
in which the vision of thy glory is renewed within us,
we may all be strengthened to follow the way of perfection
until we come to see thee face to face;
through Jesus Christ our Lord.

(or)

O God our redeemer,
who didst inspire *N* to witness to thy love
and to labour for the coming of thy kingdom:
grant that we, who in this sacrament share the bread of heaven,
may be fired by thy Spirit
to proclaim the gospel in our daily lives
and never to rest content until thy kingdom come,
on earth as it is in heaven;
through Jesus Christ our Lord.

(or)

O God our Father,
from whom every family in heaven and on earth is named,
whose servant *N* revealed thy goodness
in a life of tranquillity and service:
grant that we who have gathered in faith around this table
may like *him/her* know the love of Christ
that surpasses knowledge
and be filled with all thy fullness;
through Jesus Christ our Lord.

(or)

O God,
the source of all holiness and giver of all good things:
grant that we, who have shared at this table
as strangers and pilgrims here on earth,
may with all thy saints be welcomed
to the heavenly feast in the day of thy kingdom;
through Jesus Christ our Lord.

¶ *Special Occasions*

The Guidance of the Holy Spirit *Red*

Collect

God, who dost teach the hearts of thy faithful people
by sending to them the light of thy Holy Spirit:
grant us by the same Spirit
to have a right judgement in all things
and evermore to rejoice in his holy comfort;
through the merits of Christ Jesus our Saviour,
who liveth and reigneth with thee,
in the unity of the same Spirit,
one God, now and for ever.

(or)

Almighty God,
who hast given thy Holy Spirit to the Church
to lead us into all truth:
bless with the Spirit's grace and presence
 the members of this *synod/PCC etc.;*
keep *us/them* steadfast in faith and united in love,
that *we/they* may manifest thy glory
and prepare the way of thy kingdom;
through Jesus Christ thy Son our Lord,
who liveth and reigneth with thee,
in the unity of the Holy Spirit,
one God, now and for ever.

Post Communion

God of all power and might,
by whose Holy Spirit thy people are made new
in the blessing and sharing of bread and wine:
grant that we may be transformed by the boldness of the Spirit,
guided by his gentleness,
and enabled by his gifts to serve and worship thee,
through Jesus Christ our Lord.

Collect

Almighty God,
by whose will both earth and sea bear their fruits in due season:
bless the labours of those who work on land and sea,
grant us a plenteous harvest
and the grace always to rejoice in thy fatherly care;
through Jesus Christ thy Son our Lord,
who liveth and reigneth with thee,
in the unity of the Holy Spirit,
one God, now and for ever.

(or)

Almighty God and Father,
who hast ordered our life
in common dependence one on another:
prosper those who work in commerce and industry
and direct their minds and their hands
that they may rightly use thy gifts in the service of others;
through Jesus Christ thy Son our Lord,
who liveth and reigneth with thee,
in the unity of the Holy Spirit,
one God, now and for ever.

(or)

O God our Father,
who dost never cease from the work that thou hast begun,
and dost prosper with thy blessing all human labour:
make us wise and faithful stewards of thy gifts,
that we may serve the common good,
maintain the fabric of the world
and seek that justice where all may share
the good things thou dost pour upon us;
through Jesus Christ thy Son our Lord,
who liveth and reigneth with thee,
in the unity of the Holy Spirit,
one God, now and for ever.

Post Communion

O God our creator,
who dost give seed for us to sow and bread for us to eat:
as thou hast blessed the fruit of our labour in this sacrament,
so give to all thy children their daily bread,
that the world may praise thee for thy goodness;
through Jesus Christ our Lord.

Harvest Thanksgiving *Green*

Harvest Thanksgiving may be celebrated on a Sunday and may replace the provision for that day, provided it does not supersede any Principal Feast or Festival.

Collect

O eternal God,
who crownest the year with thy goodness
and dost give us the fruits of the earth in their season:
give us grace that we may use them to thy glory,
for the relief of those in need and for our own well-being;
through Jesus Christ thy Son our Lord,
who liveth and reigneth with thee,
in the unity of the Holy Spirit,
one God, now and for ever.

Post Communion

Lord of the harvest,
as with joy we have offered our thanksgiving
    for thy love shown in creation
and have shared in the bread and the wine of the kingdom:
so by thy grace plant within us
a reverence for all that thou hast given us
and make us generous and wise stewards
    of those good things which we enjoy;
through Jesus Christ our Lord.

Mission and Evangelism

Colour of the Season

Collect

Almighty God,
who hast called thy Church to witness
that thou wast in Christ reconciling the world to thyself:
help us so to proclaim the good news of thy love
that all who hear it may be drawn to thee;
through him who was lifted up on the cross,
and reigneth with thee and the Holy Spirit,
one God, now and for ever.

Post Communion

Eternal God, giver of love and power,
whose Son Jesus Christ hast sent us into all the world
to preach the gospel of his kingdom:
so confirm us in this mission
that our lives may show forth the good news
which we proclaim;
through Jesus Christ our Lord.

The Unity of the Church

Colour of the Season

Collect

Heavenly Father,
who hast called us in the Body of thy Son Jesus Christ
to continue his work of reconciliation
and reveal thee to the world:
forgive us the sins which tear us apart;
give us the courage to overcome our fears
and to seek that unity which is thy gift and thy will;
through Jesus Christ thy Son our Lord,
who liveth and reigneth with thee,
in the unity of the Holy Spirit,
one God, now and for ever.

(or)

Lord Jesus Christ,
who didst say to thine apostles,
'Peace I leave with you, my peace I give unto you':
look not on our sins but on the faith of thy Church
and grant it the peace and unity of thy kingdom,
where thou livest and reignest with the Father
in the unity of the Holy Spirit,
ever one God, world without end.

Post Communion

Eternal God and Father,
whose Son at supper prayed that his disciples might be one,
as he is one with thee:
draw us closer to him,
that in mutual love and obedience to thee
we may be united to one another
in the fellowship of the one Spirit,
that the world may believe that he is Lord, to thine eternal glory;
through Jesus Christ our Lord.

The Peace of the World

Colour of the Season

Collect

Almighty God,
from whom all thoughts of truth and peace proceed:
kindle, we pray thee, in every heart
the true love of peace;
and guide with thy pure and peaceable wisdom
those who take counsel for the nations of the earth,
that in tranquillity thy kingdom may go forward,
till the earth is filled with the knowledge of thy love;
through Jesus Christ thy Son our Lord,
who liveth and reigneth with thee,
in the unity of the Holy Spirit,
one God, now and for ever.

Post Communion

O God our Father,
whose Son is our peace
and his cross the sign of reconciliation:
help us, who share the broken bread,
to draw together that which is scattered
and to bind up that which is wounded,
that Christ may bring in the everlasting kingdom of his peace;
who liveth and reigneth, now and for ever.

Social Justice and Responsibility

Colour of the Season

Collect

O eternal God,
in whose perfect realm
no sword is drawn but the sword of righteousness,
and no strength known but the strength of love:
so guide and inspire the work of those who seek thy kingdom
that all thy people may find their strength
in that love which casteth out fear
and in the fellowship revealed to us
in Jesus Christ our Saviour,
who liveth and reigneth with thee,
in the unity of the Holy Spirit,
one God, now and for ever.

(or)

Almighty and eternal God,
to whom we must all give account:
guide with thy Spirit the … of this *(city, society, etc.)*,
that *we/they* may be faithful to the mind of Christ
and seek in all *our/their* purposes to enrich our common life;
through Jesus Christ thy Son our Lord,
who liveth and reigneth with thee,
in the unity of the Holy Spirit,
one God, now and for ever.

Post Communion

Blessed God,
help us, whom thou hast fed and satisfied by this sacrament,
to hunger and thirst after righteousness;
help us that, having here rejoiced with great gladness,
we may stand with those who are reviled and persecuted;
help us that, having here received a glimpse of the life of heaven,
we may ever strive for thy righteous purposes
and for the coming of the kingdom of our Lord Jesus Christ,
who liveth and reigneth, now and for ever.

Ministry (including Ember Days)

Red or colour of the Season

Collect *(for the ministry of all Christian people)*

Almighty and everlasting God,
by whose Spirit the whole body of the Church
is governed and sanctified:
hear our prayer which we offer for all thy faithful people,
that in their vocation and ministry
each may serve thee in holiness and truth
to the glory of thy name;
through our Lord and Saviour Jesus Christ,
who liveth and reigneth with thee,
in the unity of the Holy Spirit,
one God, now and for ever.

or (for those to be ordained)

Almighty God, the giver of all good gifts,
who by thy Holy Spirit hast appointed
various orders of ministry in thy Church:
look with mercy on thy servants
now called to be deacons and priests;
so maintain them in truth and renew them in holiness,
that they may faithfully serve thee both in word and deed,
to the glory of thy name and the benefit of thy holy Church;
through the merits of our Saviour Jesus Christ,
who liveth and reigneth with thee,
in the unity of the Holy Spirit,
one God, now and for ever.

or (for vocations)

Almighty God,
who hast entrusted to thy Church
a share in the ministry of thy Son our great High Priest:
we pray that by the inspiration of thy Holy Spirit
the hearts of many may be moved to offer themselves
for the ministry of thy Church,
and that, strengthened by his power,
they may work for the increase of thy kingdom

and set forward the eternal praise of thy name;
through Jesus Christ thy Son our Lord,
who liveth and reigneth with thee,
in the unity of the Holy Spirit,
one God, now and for ever.

or (for the inauguration of a new ministry)

God our Father, Lord of all the world,
who through thy blessed Son hast called us
into the fellowship of thy universal Church:
hear our prayer for all thy faithful people
that in their vocation and ministry
each may be an instrument of thy love,
and grant to thy servant *N* now to be ... *(installed, inducted, etc.)*
the needful gifts of grace;
through our Lord and Saviour Jesus Christ,
who liveth and reigneth with thee,
in the unity of the Holy Spirit,
one God, now and for ever.

Post Communion

Heavenly Father,
whose ascended Son gave gifts of leadership and service
to the Church:
strengthen us who have received this holy food
to be good stewards of thy manifold grace;
through him who came not to be served but to serve,
and give his life as a ransom for many,
Jesus Christ our Lord.

(or)

Lord of the harvest,
who in this sacrament hast fed thy people
with the fruits of creation sanctified by thy Spirit:
by thy grace raise up among us faithful labourers
who shall sow thy word and reap the harvest of souls;
through Jesus Christ our Lord.

In Time of Trouble

Colour of the Season

Collect

Sovereign God,
who art the defence of those who trust in thee
and the strength of those who suffer:
mercifully look upon our affliction
and deliver us through the might of our Saviour Jesus Christ,
who liveth and reigneth with thee,
in the unity of the Holy Spirit,
one God, now and for ever.

Post Communion

Almighty God,
whose Son gave us in this meal a pledge of thy saving love
and a foretaste of thy just and peaceful kingdom:
strengthen thy people in their faith
that they may endure the sufferings of this present time
in expectation of the glory that shall be revealed;
through Jesus Christ our Lord.

For the Sovereign

Colour of the Season

Collect

Almighty God,
the fountain of all goodness,
we pray thee to bless our Sovereign Lady, *Queen Elizabeth*,
and all who are set in authority under her;
that they may order all things
in wisdom and equity, righteousness and peace,
to the honour and glory of thy name
and the good of thy Church and people;
through Jesus Christ thy Son our Lord,
who liveth and reigneth with thee,
in the unity of the Holy Spirit,
one God, now and for ever.

Post Communion

O God, the Father of our Lord Jesus Christ,
our only Saviour, the Prince of Peace:
give us grace seriously to lay to heart
the great dangers we are in by our unhappy divisions;
take away our hatred and prejudice
and whatsoever else may hinder us from godly union and concord,
that, as there is but one Body and one Spirit
and one hope of our calling,
one Lord, one faith, one baptism,
one God and Father of us all,
so we may henceforth be all of one heart and of one soul,
united in one holy bond of truth and peace, of faith and charity,
and may with one mind and one mouth glorify thee;
through Jesus Christ our Lord.

Authorization

¶ The *Common Worship* Collects and Post Communions are authorized pursuant to Canon B 2 of the Canons of the Church of England for use until further resolution of the General Synod. Use of the Collects and Post Communions in Traditional Language falls within the discretion canonically allowed to the minister under Canon B5.

Acknowledgements and Sources

The publisher gratefully acknowledges permission to reproduce copyright material in this book. Every effort has been made to trace and contact copyright holders. If there are any inadvertent omissions we apologize to those concerned and undertake to include suitable acknowledgements in all future editions.

*An asterisk * indicates that the prayer has been adapted.*

Published sources include the following:

The Archbishops' Council of the Church of England: *The Prayer Book as Proposed in 1928; The Alternative Service Book 1980; Common Worship: Initiation Services; The Christian Year: Calendar, Lectionary and Collects*, all of which are copyright © The Archbishops' Council of the Church of England.

Cambridge University Press: Extracts (and adapted extracts) from *The Book of Common Prayer*, the rights in which are vested in the Crown, are reproduced by permission of the Crown's Patentee, Cambridge University Press.

Thanks are also due to the following for permission to reproduce copyright material:

The Anglican Church in Aotearoa, New Zealand and Polynesia: the Post Communions for the Guidance of the Holy Spirit* (p. 73) and Rogation Days* (p. 74) Taken/adapted from *A New Zealand Prayer Book – He Karikia Mihinare O Aotearoa.*

The General Synod of the Anglican Church of Canada: the Post Communions for the Commemoration of the Faithful Departed (p. 50), Apostles and Evangelists (p. 64), Mission and Evangelism (p. 76). Adapted from (or excerpted from) *The Book of Alternative Services of the Anglican Church of Canada* © The General Synod of the Anglican Church of Canada 1985. Used by permission.

The Catholic Bishops' Conference of England and Wales: the Collects for Aelred of Hexham (p. 4), Columba (p. 23), Aidan (p. 38), Paulinus (p. 44), Willibrord of York (p. 51) and Hilda (p. 57). Used by permission.

Chichester Diocesan Board of Finance: the Collect for Wilfrid of Ripon* (p. 45).

The Dean and Chapter of Durham Cathedral: Collects for Cuthbert* (p. 13) and The Venerable Bede* (p. 20).

The International Commission on English in the Liturgy: the Collects for Elizabeth of Hungary* (p. 56), Clement* (p. 58) and the Unity of the Church* (p. 77); the Post Communions for Martyrs* (p. 65) are based on (or excerpted from) *The Roman Missal* © International Committee on English in the Liturgy 1973. Used by permission.

The Dean and Chapter of Lincoln Cathedral: the Collects for Edward King* (p. 12) and Hugh* (p. 55). Reproduced by kind permission.

The Cathedral and Abbey Church of Saint Alban: the Collect for Alban* (p. 24).

Church of the Province of Southern Africa: the Collects for Timothy and Titus (p. 7), Augustine of Hippo (p. 36), Bishops and Other Pastors (p. 67), Any Saint* (p. 70), Rogation Days (1) and (2) (p. 74), Harvest Thanksgiving (p. 75) and In Time of Trouble (p. 82) from *An Anglican Prayer Book*, 1989 © Provincial Trustees of the Church of the Province of Southern Africa. Used by permission.

Winchester Diocesan Board of Finance: Collect for Swithun (p. 27).

The Alcuin Club: the Collects for Ignatius* (p. 47), Nicholas* (p. 58) and Ambrose (p. 59) from Martin Draper (ed.), *The Cloud of Witnesses*, 1982. © G. B. Timms. Used with permission.

Church in Wales Publications: Collect for David (p. 11) from *The Book of Common Prayer for Use in the Church in Wales*, Vol. 1, 1984. Used with permission.

The Continuum International Publishing Group Ltd: the Post Communion for Ministry (including Ember Days)* (p. 80) from C. L. MacDonnell, *After Communion*, 1985 © Mowbray, an imprint of The Continuum International Publishing Group Ltd. Used by permission. The Collect for the Birth of the Blessed Virgin Mary (p. 39) from David Silk (ed.), *Prayers for Use at the Alternative Services*, 1980. © Mowbray, an imprint of The Continuum International Publishing Group Ltd. Used by permission.

Hodder and Stoughton Publishers: the Collect for Social Justice and Responsibility* (p. 79) from *Parish Prayers* © Frank Colquhoun 1967.

The Warden, Fellows and Scholars of Keble College: the Collect for John Keble* (p. 26).

The European Province of the Society of St Francis: the Collects for Hilary (p. 4), Antony of Egypt (p. 5), Agnes* (p. 6), Thomas Aquinas* (p. 7), Polycarp (p. 10), George Herbert* (p. 10), Chad (p. 11), Perpetua, Felicity and their Companions* (p. 12), William Law (p. 14), Anselm* (p. 15), Catherine of Siena (p. 16), Julian of Norwich (p. 18), Dunstan* (p. 18), John and Charles Wesley (p. 19), Augustine of Canterbury* (p. 20), Josephine Butler* (p. 21), Justin (p. 22), Boniface (Wynfrith) of Crediton (p. 22), Thomas Ken (p. 23), Irenaeus* (p. 25), Benedict of Nursia* (p. 26), William Wilberforce* (p. 30), Dominic* (p. 31), Laurence* (p. 33), Clare of Assisi* (p. 33), Bernard (p. 34), the Beheading of John the Baptist (p. 36), John Bunyan* (p. 37), Gregory the Great (p. 38), John Chrysostom* (p. 40), Vincent de Paul* (p. 43), Francis of Assisi (p. 43), William Tyndale* (p. 44), Teresa of Avila* (p. 47), James Hannington (p. 49), Leo the Great* (p. 53), Martin of Tours* (p. 53), Margaret of Scotland* (p. 54), Edmund* (p. 57), John of the Cross* (p. 61) and Thomas Becket (p. 62), from *Celebrating Common Prayer* © The Society of St Francis European Province 1992 and 1996.

The Very Revd Robert Jeffery: the Collect for Wulfstan* (p. 5).

The Rt Revd Dr Kenneth Stevenson: the Collect for Richard Hooker (p. 51).

SECR[illegible] A
GRAN[illegible] R

HOW TO BEAT MOST PEOPLE AND COMPUTERS AT CHESS

by

Kenneth Mark Colby

ISHI PRESS
INTERNATIONAL

Secrets of a Grandpatzer
How to Beat Most People and Computers at Chess

by Kenneth Mark Colby

First published in 1979
in England by Malibu Press

This Printing in March, 2011 by
Ishi Press in New York and Tokyo

with a new foreword by Michael R. Stewart
and a new introduction by Sam Sloan

ISBN 4-87187-887-2
978-4-87187-887-6

Ishi Press International
1664 Davidson Avenue, Suite 1B
Bronx NY 10453-7877
USA
1-917-507-7226
Printed in the United States of America

Introduction by Michael R. Stewart

Secrets of a Grandpatzer is the outstanding work by world renowned psychiatrist Kenneth Mark Colby. Mr Colby began this project by trying to help himself become a better player and to raise his United States Chess Federation rating.

Drawing from many different sources, such as the late USCF Senior Master Ken Smith, Colby put together a book that is designed to help a low rated player with a United States Chess Federation rating of 1799 and below, which is sometimes called a Patzer, raise their skill level and USCF rating to 1800 to 2200 which would be a Grand Patzer.

Colby covers all aspects of chess including the Opening, Middlegame, and Endgame which can be played against computers and even the mental ego game. He recommends that you play like a computer since a computer doesn't care who or what it plays since it is just the position on the board that counts.

Colby recommends playing openings that have similar middle games despite whether you are playing on the white or black side. By playing over hundreds of master games in this system you get a feel for the positions on the board. This is a time saver if you are playing the faster time controls they have today. In the Middle Game section, I would add the internet site Chessgames.com as a source of master games. The Endgame section is priceless by showing you which endgames to study. This would cut down on your study time.

I know Colby used this same information to raise his own USCF rating to 1983 which is a Class A GrandPatzer level.

Introduction by Michael R. Stewart

When I purchased this book in 1985, I had a USCF rating of 1990.By faithfully following the guidelines found in this book, I raised my rating to a personal best of 2308, a USCF National Master. Many long hours and a lot of hard work was part of that equation, but this book showed me the right material to study. The book Secrets of a GrandPatzer is as good today as when it was first published. My only regret is that Mr Colby passed away before I could say thank you!

Thank you, Kenneth Mark Colby.

Michael Stewart
National Chess Master

Introduction

Kenneth Mark Colby, M.D. (January 12, 1920 to April 20, 2001) was an American psychiatrist dedicated to the theory and application of computer science and artificial intelligence to psychiatry. Colby was a pioneer in the development of computer technology as a tool to try to understand cognitive functions and to assist both patients and doctors in the treatment process. He is perhaps best known for the development of a computer program called PARRY, which mimicked a paranoid schizophrenic and could "converse" with others. PARRY sparked serious debate about the possibility and nature of machine intelligence.

Colby began his career in psychoanalysis as a clinical associate at the San Francisco Institute of Psychoanalysis in 1951. During this time, he published A Primer for Psychotherapists, an introduction to psychodynamic psychotherapy. He joined the Department of Computer Science at Stanford University in the early sixties, beginning his pioneering work in the relatively new field of artificial intelligence. In 1967 the National Institute of Mental Health recognized his research potential when he was awarded a Career Research Scientist Award. Colby came to UCLA as a professor of psychiatry in 1974, and was jointly appointed professor in the Department of Computer Science a few years later. Over the course of his career, he wrote numerous books and articles on psychiatry, psychology, psychotherapy and artificial intelligence.

Early in his career, in 1955, Colby published Energy and Structure in Psychoanalysis, an effort to bring Freud's basic doctrines into line with modern concepts of physics and philosophy of science. This, however, would be one of the last attempts by Colby to reconcile psychoanalysis with what he saw as important developments in science and philosophical thought. Central to Freud's method is his employment of a hermeneutics of suspicion, a method of inquiry that refuses to take the subject at his or her word about internal processes. Freud sets forth explanations for a patient's mental state without regard for whether the patient agrees or not. If the patient does not agree, s/he has repressed the truth, that truth that the psychoanalyst alone can be entrusted with unfolding. The psychoanalyst's authority for deciding the nature or validity of a patient's state and the lack of empirical verifiability for making this decision was not acceptable to Colby.

Colby's disenchantment with psychoanalysis would be further expressed in several publications, including his 1958 book, A Skeptical Psychoanalyst. He began to vigorously criticize psychoanalysis for failing to satisfy the most fundamental requirement of a science, that being the generation of reliable data. In his 1983 book, Fundamental Crisis in Psychiatry, he wrote, "Reports of clinical findings are mixtures of facts, fabulations, and fictives so intermingled that one cannot tell where one begins and the other leaves off. …we never know how the reports are connected to the events that actually happened in the treatment sessions, and so they fail to qualify as acceptable scientific data.".

Likewise, in Cognitive Science and Psychoanalysis, he stated, "In arguing that psychoanalysis is not a science, we shall show that few scholars studying this question get to the bottom of the issue. Instead, they start by accepting, as do psychoanalytic theorists, that the reports of what happens in psychoanalytic treatment -- the primary source of the data -- are factual, and then they lay out their interpretations of the significance of facts for theory. We, on the other hand, question the status of the facts." [3] These issues would shape his approach to psychiatry and guide his research efforts.

In the 1960s Colby began thinking about the ways in which

computer theory and application could contribute to the understanding of brain function and mental illness. One early project involved an Intelligent Speech Prosthesis which allowed individuals suffering from aphasia to "speak" by helping them search for and articulate words using whatever phonemic or semantic clues they were able to generate.

Later, Colby would be one of the first to explore the possibilities of computer-assisted psychotherapy. In 1989, with his son Peter Colby, he formed the company Malibu Artificial Intelligence Works to develop and market a natural language version of cognitive behavioral therapy for depression, called Overcoming Depression. Overcoming Depression would go on to be used as a therapeutic learning program by the U.S. Navy and Department of Veteran Affairs and would be distributed to individuals who used it without supervision from a psychiatrist. Needless to say, this practice was challenged by the media. To one journalist Colby replied that the program could be better than human therapists because "After all, the computer doesn't burn out, look down on you or try to have sex with you."

In the 1960s at Stanford University, Colby embarked on the creation of software programs known as "chatterbots," which simulate conversations with people. One well known chatterbot at the time was ELIZA, a computer program developed by Joseph Weizenbaum in 1966 to parody a psychologist. ELIZA, by Weizenbaum's own admission, was developed more as a language-parsing tool than as an exercise in human intelligence. Named for the Eliza Doolittle character in "Pygmalion," it was the first conversational computer program, designed to imitate a psychotherapist asking questions instead of giving advice. It appeared to give conversational answers, although it could be led to lapse into obtuse nonsense.

In 1972, at the Stanford Artificial Intelligence Laboratory, Colby built upon the idea of ELIZA to create a natural language program called PARRY that simulated the thinking of a paranoid individual. This thinking entails the consistent misinterpretation of others' motives – others must be up to no good, they must have concealed motives that are dangerous, or their inquiries into certain areas must be deflected - which PARRY achieved via a complex system of assumptions, attributions, and "emotional responses" triggered by shifting weights assigned to verbal inputs.

Colby's aim in writing PARRY had been practical as well as theoretical. He thought of PARRY as a virtual reality teaching system for students before they were let loose on real patients. However, PARRY's design was driven by Colby's own theories about paranoia. Colby saw paranoia as a degenerate mode of processing symbols where the patient's remarks "are produced by an underlying organized structure of rules and not by a variety of random and unconnected mechanical failures." This underlying structure was an algorithm, not unlike a set of computer processes or procedures, which is accessible and can be reprogrammed, in other words "cured."

Shortly after it was introduced, PARRY would go on to create intense discussion and controversy over the possibility or nature of machine intelligence. PARRY was the first program to pass the "Turing Test," named for the British mathematician Alan Turing, who in 1950 suggested that if a computer could successfully impersonate a human by carrying on a typed conversation with a person, it could be called intelligent. PARRY succeeded in passing this test when human interrogators, interacting with the program via remote keyboard, were unable with more than random accuracy to distinguish PARRY from an actual paranoid individual.

As philosopher D.C. Dennett stated in Alan Turing:Life and Legacy of a Great Thinker, "To my knowledge, the only serious and interesting attempt by any program designer to win even a severely modified Turing test has been Kenneth Colby. He had genuine psychiatrists interview PARRY. He did not suggest that they might be talking or typing to a computer; rather he made up some plausible story about why they were communicating with a real live patient via teletype. Then he took the PARRY transcript, inserted it into a group of teletype transcripts and gave them to another group of experts—more psychiatrists —and said, 'One of these was a conversation with a computer. Can you figure out which one it was?' They couldn't."

Much of the criticism of ELIZA as a model for artificial intelligence focused on the program's lack of an internal world model that influenced and tracked the conversation. PARRY simulates paranoid behavior by tracking its own internal emotional state on a few different dimensions. To illustrate this, Colby created another program called RANDOM-PARRY which chose responses at random. Responses from RANDOM-PARRY did not model the human patients' responses as well as standard PARRY. Some have argued that PARRY fooled its judges because paranoid behavior makes inappropriate responses or non sequiturs appropriate. But there is still a certain logic to them that PARRY simulates effectively. It is simpler to simulate paranoid behavior, perhaps, but it is not trivial.

Colby would claim that PARRY mimics the natural process by which a person (in this case a paranoid schizophrenic) engages in conversation. The structure of the program that makes the linguistic decisions in PARRY is isomorphic to the 'deep structure' of the mind of the paranoiac. As Colby stated: "Since we do not know the structure of the 'real' simulative processes used by the mind-brain, our posited structure stands as an imagined theoretical analogue, a possible and plausible organization of processes analogous to the unknown processes and serving as an attempt to explain their workings".

Yet, some critics of PARRY expressed the concern that this computer program does not in actuality "understand" the way a person understands and continued to assert that the idiosyncratic, partial and idiolectic responses from PARRY cover up its limitations. Colby attempted to answer these and other criticisms in a 1974 publication entitled, "Ten Criticisms of Parry."

Colby also raised his own ethical concerns over the application of his work to real life situations. In 1984, he wrote, "With the great amount of attention now being paid by the media to artificial intelligence, it would be naive, shortsighted, and even self-deceptive to think that there will not be public interest in scrutinizing, monitoring, regulating, and even constraining our efforts. What we do can affect people's lives as they understand them. People are going to ask not only what we are doing but also whether it should be done. Some might feel we are meddling in areas best left alone. We should be prepared to participate in open discussion and debate on such ethical issues."

Still, PARRY has withstood the test of time and for many years has continued to be acknowledged by researchers in computer science for its apparent achievements. In a 1999 review of human-computer conversation, Yorick Wilks and Roberta Catizone from the University of Sheffield comment: "The best performance overall in HMC (Human-machine conversation) has almost certainly been Colby's PARRY program since its release on the net around 1973.

It was robust, never broke down, always had something to say and, because it was intended to model paranoid behaviour, its zanier misunderstandings could always be taken as further evidence of mental disturbance, rather than the processing failures they were."

During his career, Colby ventured into other, more esoteric areas of research including classifying dreams in "primitive tribes." His findings suggested that men and women of primitive tribes differ in their dream life, these differences possibly contributing an empirical basis to our theoretical constructs of masculinity and femininity.

Books

(1951) A Primer for Psychotherapists. (ISBN 978-0826020901)
(1955) Energy and Structure in Psychoanalysis.
* (1957) An exchange of views on psychic energy and psychoanalysis.
* (1958) A Skeptical Psychoanalyst.
* (1960) Introduction to Psychoanalytic Research
* (1973) Computer Models of Thought and Language.
* (1975) Artificial Paranoia : A Computer Simulation of Paranoid Processes (ISBN 9780080181622)
* (1983) Fundamental Crisis in Psychiatry: Unreliability of Diagnosis (ISBN 9780398047887)
* (1988) Cognitive Science and Psychoanalysis (ISBN 9780805801774)
* (1979) Secrets of a Grandpatzer: How to Beat Most People and Computers at Chess (ISBN 9784871878876)

Publications

* "Sex Differences in Dreams of Primitive Tribes" American Anthropologist, New Series, Vol. 65, No. 5, Selected Papers in Method and Technique (Oct., 1963), pp.

1116-1122

* "Computer Simulation of Change in Personal Belief Systems." Behavioral Science, 12 (1967), pp. 248-253

* "Dialogues Between Humans and an Artificial Belief System." IJCAI (1969), pp. 319-324

* "Experiments with a Search Algorithm for the Data Base of a Human Belief System." IJCAI (1969), pp. 649-654

* "Artificial Paranoia." Artif. Intell. 2(1) (1971), pp. 1-25

* "Turing-like Indistinguishability Tests for the Validation of a Computer Simulation of Paranoid Processes." Artif. Intell. 3(1-3) (1972), pp. 199-221

* "Idiolectic Language-Analysis for Understanding Doctor-Patient Dialogues." IJCAI (1973), pp. 278-284

* "Pattern-matching rules for the recognition of natural language dialogue expressions." Stanford University, Stanford, CA, 1974

* "Appraisal of four psychological theories of paranoid phenomena." Journal of Abnormal Psychology. Vol 86(1) (1977), pp. 54-59

* "Conversational Language Comprehension Using Integrated Pattern-Matching and Parsing." Artif. Intell. 9(2) (1977), pp. 111-134

* "Cognitive therapy of paranoid conditions: Heuristic suggestions based on a computer simulation model." Journal Cognitive Therapy and Research Vol 3 (1) (March 1979)

* "A Word-Finding Algorithm with a Dynamic Lexical-Semantic Memory for Patients with Anomia Using a Speech Prosthesis." AAAI (1980), pp. 289-291

* "Reloading a Human Memory: A New Ethical Question for Artificial Intelligence Technology." AI Magazine 6(4) (1986), pp. 63-64

Obituary of Kenneth Mark Colby

IN MEMORIAM

Kenneth Mark Colby
Professor of Psychiatry, Emeritus
Los Angeles
1920—2001

Fifty years ago there was only one psychiatrist thinking about the ways in which computers could contribute to the understanding of mental illness. Kenneth Mark Colby was that psychiatrist. Thus began a project that lasted until his death in 2001.

Kenneth Colby was born in Waterbury, Connecticut. He graduated from Yale University in 1941 and from Yale Medical School in 1943. He practiced psychoanalysis for the first several decades of his career, and was clinical associate at the San Francisco Institute of Psychoanalysis in 1951 when he published A Primer for Psychotherapists, a small book of elementary principles which many still regard as the finest introduction to psychodynamic psychotherapy ever published. But Colby became disenchanted with psychoanalysis because, in his view, it failed to satisfy the most fundamental requirement of a science, that being the generation of reliable data: "Reports of clinical findings are mixtures of facts, fabulations, and fictives so intermingled that one cannot tell where one begins and the other leaves off. …we never know how the reports are connected to the events that actually happened in the treatment sessions, and so they fail to qualify as acceptable scientific data." In 1961 he spent a year as a Fellow at the Center for Advanced Study in the Behavioral Sciences, where he developed several of the ideas that were to inform the rest of his career. Among these was the conviction that computer models of the mind promised a more scientific approach to the study of cognitive processes and their aberrations. Following this conviction, he joined the Department of Computer Science at Stanford University in the early sixties, and soon became a pioneer in the emerging field of artificial intelligence. In 1967 the National Institute of Mental Health recognized his research potential when he was awarded a Career Research Scientist Award. At the Stanford Artificial Intelligence Laboratory, Colby created a natural language program called "Parry" that simulated the thinking of a paranoid individual. This thinking entails the consistent misinterpretation of others motives – others must be up to no good, they must have concealed motives that are dangerous, and their inquiries into certain areas must be deflected - which Parry achieved via a complex system of assumptions, attributions, and "emotional responses" triggered by shifting weights assigned to verbal inputs. This program was the first to pass the "Turing Test" (named for the British mathematician Alan Turing, who defined as "intelligent" any computer that could successfully impersonate a human in a typed "conversation"). Parry did so in the early seventies, when human interrogators, interacting with the program via remote keyboard, were unable with more than random accuracy to distinguish Parry from an actual paranoid individual.

Professor Colby came to UCLA as a professor of psychiatry in 1974, at the invitation of Jolly West, M.D., then chair of the Department of Psychiatry and director of the Neuropsychiatric Institute. He was jointly appointed professor in the Department of Computer Science a few years later, and continued to work on the theory and application of artificial intelligence in neuropsychiatry. One project entailed combining a Cromemco computer with a Votrax voice synthesizer into Intelligent Speech Prosthesis. This system, which ultimately utilized an extremely early "notebook computer"(built at UCLA), allowed individuals suffering from aphasia to "speak" by helping them search for and articulate words using whatever phonemic or semantic clues they were able to generate. During his tenure at UCLA Colby also published important theoretical works on the unreliability of diagnosis in psychiatry (Colby & Spar, 1983) and on cognitive science and psychoanalysis (Colby & Stoller, 1988). He was one of the first to appreciate the possibilities of computer-assisted psychotherapy, and with his son Peter created a program called "Overcoming Depression," which included a natural language component that administered a version of "cognitive-behavioral" therapy for depression. He and Peter formed Malibu Artificial Intelligence Works in 1989, soon after Professor Colby retired from full-time academic life, and they continued to develop and market "Overcoming Depression" until Professor Colby's death at age 81, on April 20, 2001.

Colby was a rigorous scientist and a creative and original thinker, but one who always recognized his debt to his predecessors, "We are always aided and burdened by our predecessors' knowledge. Thinking is furthering the thinking of others." He also was an excellent chess player, and in 1979 published a well-received book titled Secrets of a Grandpatzer, which was recommended by candidate master Daniel Waite for "pattern recognition and having fun" (The Chess Journal, February, 2001).

Besides his son, Peter, of Malibu, he is survived by his wife of 43 years, Maxine Hansbold Colby, a daughter, Erin Johnson of Santa Maria, California, and two grandsons.

James E. Spar
Michael T. McGuire

About The Author

Kenneth Mark Colby, M.D. is a Professor of Psychiatry, Biobehavioral Sciences and Computer Science at the University of California at Los Angeles. He has written 10 books and over 100 papers in the fields of psychiatry, psychology and artificial intelligence. He is a USCF Class A chessplayer and a Class A tennis player living in Malibu, California where he heads the Malibu Chess Press.

Contents

Explanation of Symbols and Notation

! = Good move
!! = Great move
? = Bad move
?? = Blunder
\+ = Check

The algebraic notation used in this book follows the convention that the files are lettered from a-h and the ranks from 1–8 as shown in the diagram.

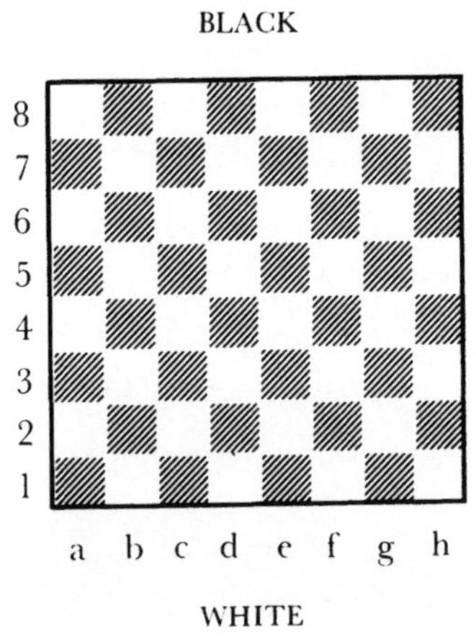

Introduction

This book is written for chessplayers who cannot beat most people and computers. Computers are becoming very strong chessplayers, beating even grandmasters at 5-minute chess. If you can learn to play like these computers, you will become a strong chessplayer also. You can now buy small chessplaying computers (Chess Challenger, Boris etc) for $200–$300. You can play endlessly against them at home without any embarrassment at losing. If you cannot beat one of these every game, then you are a patzer who needs this book. If you cannot beat one of the larger chessplaying computers once in a while, then you must become a grandpatzer.

A patzer (German: Verpatzen = to make a mess) is a chessplayer looked-down on by stronger players. He is a duffer, fish, woodpusher or rabbit of Class E, D, C, or weak B with a USCF rating of between 1200 (or less) and 1700. Evans, a grandmaster, calls a 1700 player 'average'. According to Elo's statistical survey, in 1973, out of 61,000 USCF members, the average rating was 1362. A rating above 1700 would put a player in about the top 14%. For my expository purposes I will term a player rated between 1700 and 2200 a grandpatzer, a strong chessplayer. Ken Smith says anyone under age 50 should strive to become a master, i.e. a player rated 2200 or above. As your Grandpatzer mentor (Dr. G), I propose that a patzer of any age strive to become a grandpatzer and the greatest grandpatzer of them all is a computer which can be emulated. (Nature copies art).

Why should a patzer seek to become a grandpatzer? Because of the aristos (Greek: Aristos = best). Life is more than ham sandwiches and beer. Humans strive, not just to survive, but to enhance the *quality*, the excellence, of survival. Striving for excellence of endeavor, developing yourself to become *your* best at what you do, is rewarding and fulfilling to aspirations higher than happiness. Merely happy people, without aristic goals, vegetate in incomplete, hobbled and impoverished lives. To reach a commendable and worthwhile life, one transcends material determinants of happiness and aspires to become better, to become one's best. A patzer of any age who studies the teachings of this book, who strives for excellence by implementing them in his games, who emulates chess-playing computer programs, can become a grandpatzer within a short year or two. He may or may not elect to go further but, on becoming a grandpatzer, he will be able to take justifiable pride in the self-realization of at least this level of excellence. A grandpatzer is a strong chessplayer, a threat to anyone (including himself) in a given game.

Thus, this book is intended to help patzers towards the aristic goal of becoming grandpatzers. Much master and grandmaster advice is of little use to them. Sometimes it is banal ('watch out for checks'), misleading ('learn the Knight and Bishop mate') or even fatuous ('don't select too few candidate moves and don't select too many'). Masters may understand chess but they do not necessarily understand chess players. Masters have better chess memories then the rest of us, possess a very large bag of tricks and know many things we do not know. They are not about to disclose secrets while they are trying to scratch out a living as a chess professional. As Dr. G. will show you, becoming a grandpatzer involves understanding the ego-game in addition to knowing lots of patterns, themes and tricks.

I am indebted to my daughter Erin for courageously undertaking the deciphering and typing of an encryptically handwritten manuscript and to International Master Imre König for his corrections and emendations.

I
Your Basic Background

1.1 *Patzers*

After floundering around as a 1600 patzer for 3–4 years, I decided to do something about it. In these doings, I developed, and utilized the herein described heuristics to raise my USCF rating to 1800+ in a year of weekly rating tournaments. When I was a patzer, I spoke as a patzer, I understood as a patzer, I thought as a patzer: but when I became a grandpatzer, I (mostly) put away patzerish things. Being of generous disposition, I am now passing these secrets on to you so you too can become a grandpatzer. Why should I reveal all these secrets? Because now that I have become a grandpatzer I don't need them anymore. (I need new ones.)

Patzers endlessly read books and chess journals containing master games annotated by masters. Most of this activity is a waste of time. (Chess itself is a great waste of time (as compared to what?) but that is another matter). The reason typical patzer study is a waste of time is that the games played by patzers bear little resemblance to those played by masters. These are two different levels of play with different principles governing each. For example, a master doesn't ask himself on each move whether what he has selected is a blunder. But a grandpatzer must. Maybe the master should. Here are a couple of my favorites. In this position:

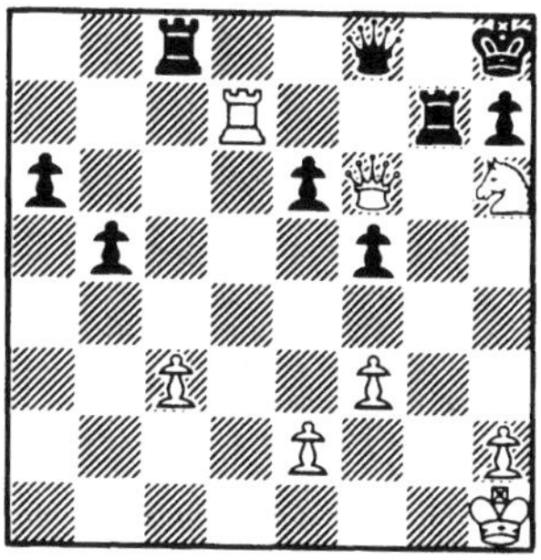

DIAGRAM 1. TSCHIGORIN–RUBINSTEIN, 1906

White played ♖f7 which wins. But in the same position with the colors reversed, (Smyslov–Lundin, Groningen 1946) Smyslov could find only ♘f7+ and took the perpetual check. Another jewel is Szabo–Reshevsky, Zurich 1953 (Diagram 2), where White overlooks a mate in 2. If you think such things just happened in the old days, consider Polugaevski–Eising, Solingen 1974 (Diagram 3), where White, a 2600 grandmaster, didn't see that Black mates in 3. Or take Tarjan–Gheorghiu, Orense, 1975 (Diagram 4).

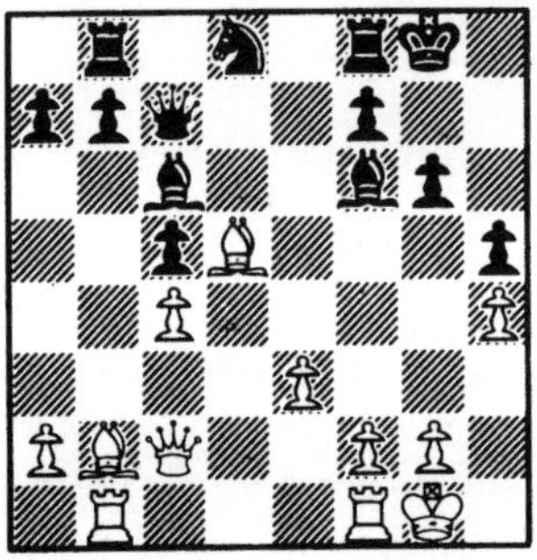

DIAGRAM 2. SZABO–RESHEVSKY, 1953

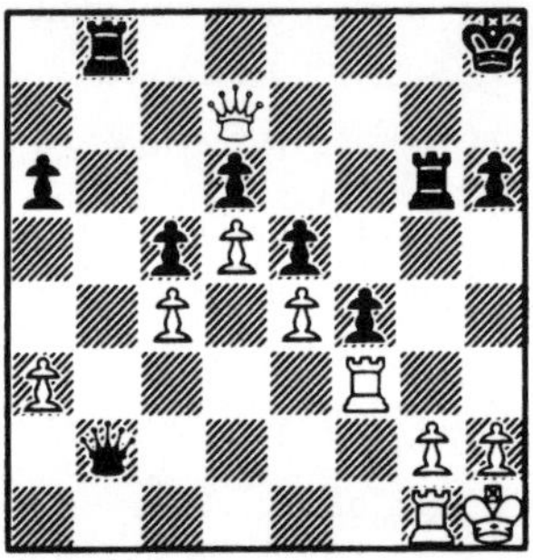

DIAGRAM 3. POLUGAEVSKY–EISING, 197

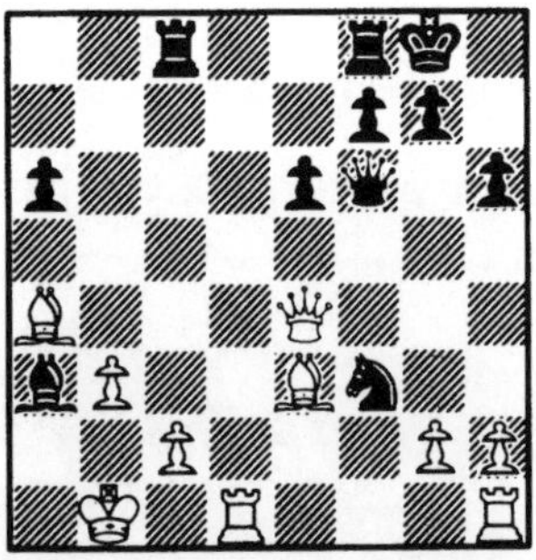

DIAGRAM 4. TARJAN–GHEORGHIU, 1975

White played 26. ♗c1? ♗×c1 27 ♖×c1 ♘d2+ overlooking the simplest King and Queen fork known to every patzer and grandpatzer.

These examples remind us only of the painful platitude that everyone can blunder. Few grandmaster games are won this way but a large majority of patzer games are won or lost through such simple blunders and oversights. *A grandpatzer does not blunder.* He makes mistakes, but he does not blunder. Much of my advice will concern blunders but before we get to them, let us consider the traditional classification of patterns or themes.

1.2 Patterns

Before you can aspire to the rank of grandpatzer, there are at least 132 basic key patterns you must know. By 'know' I mean you must be able to set up examples of them on the board. They are absolutely essential. If you do not know them, you will remain a patzer forever. They are listed here alphabetically, which inadvertently makes them look like an index to a chess text.

1. Advantages

A. Exchange of one for another:

In Diagram 5 White is a Pawn up. He offers to exchange this advantage to get his King into the Black Pawn structure to win the Pawn ending.

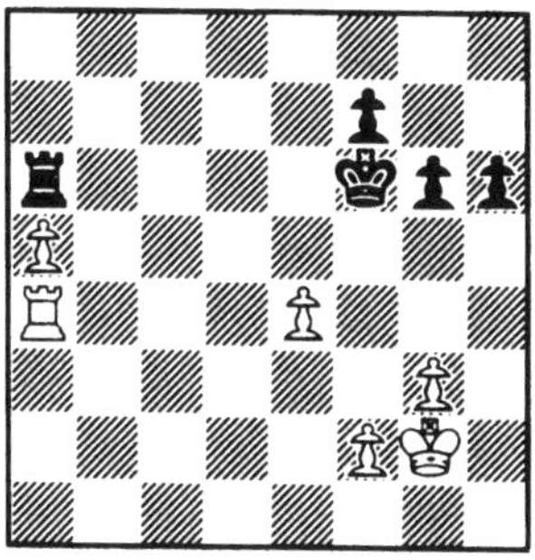

DIAGRAM 5.

1	♔f3	♔e5
2	♔e3	h5
3	♔d3	♔d6
4	♔c3	♔c5
5	♖a2	♔b5
6	♔d4	

If 6 . . . ♖×a, White exchanges Rooks and invades the King side. If 5

. . . ♚d6 6 ♚b4 ♚c6 7 ♚c4 ♚d6 8 ♚b5 pushes the Rook back and advances the Pawn.

B. Material versus mobility

In Diagram 6, White gives up two Pawns to gain great King mobility.

1 ♔g3!!	♖×c+
2 ♔h4	♖f3
3 g6!	♖×f+
4 ♔g5	♖e4
5 ♔f6!	♚g8
6 ♖g7+	♚h8
7 ♖×c7	♖e8
8 ♔×f	

and Black is lost because of White's dominance of the 7th rank.

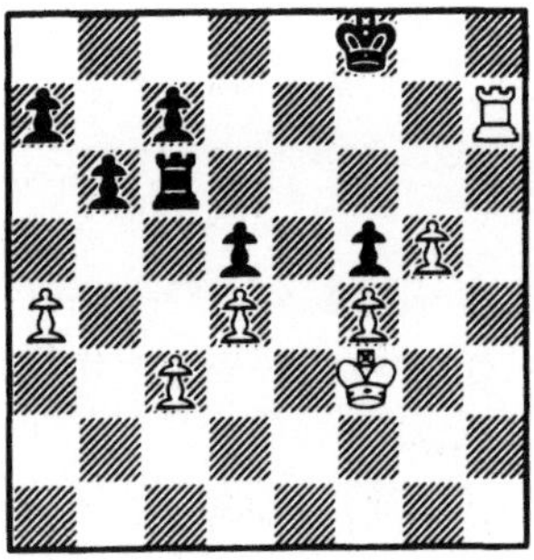

DIAGRAM 6. CAPABLANCA-TARTAKOWER, NEW YORK, 1924

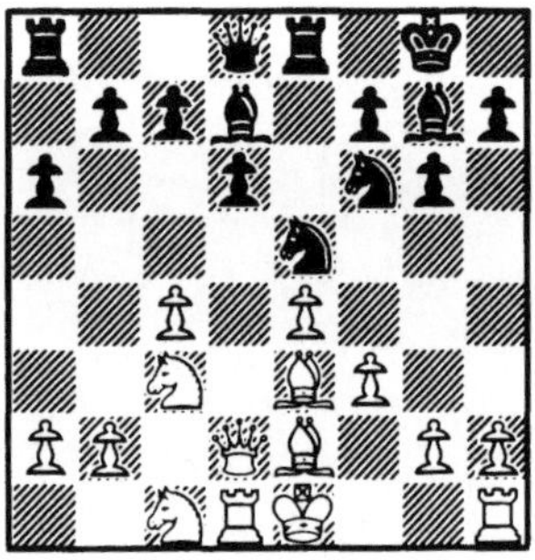

DIAGRAM 7.

C. Of Preventing Castling

In Diagram 7, Black prevents White from castling by a Pawn sacrifice. Although there are lots of pieces in-between, the Black Rook on e8 threatens the White King.

12 . . .	b5!
13 c×b5	a×b5
14 ♗×b5	♘×e4!
15 f×e4	♗×b5
16 ♘×b5	♘×c4

If

14 ♘×b5	♘×f3+!
15 g×f3	♘×e4
16 f×e4	♕h4+
17 ♗f2	♕×e4

D. Positional:

In Diagram 8, White has a simple positional advantage because his King gets to the center, he has a potential passed King Pawn, and Black has 4 isolated Pawns, three of which are on the same color as his Bishop and the same color as White's Bishop.

1	♔d4!	♔b6
2	♗c4	♗g4
3	e5	f×e
4	f×e	h6
5	h4	♗h5
6	e6	♗e8
7	e7	♗h5
8	♔e5	c5
9	b×c+	♔×c
10	♗×a	

and the King Pawn will cost Black his Bishop.

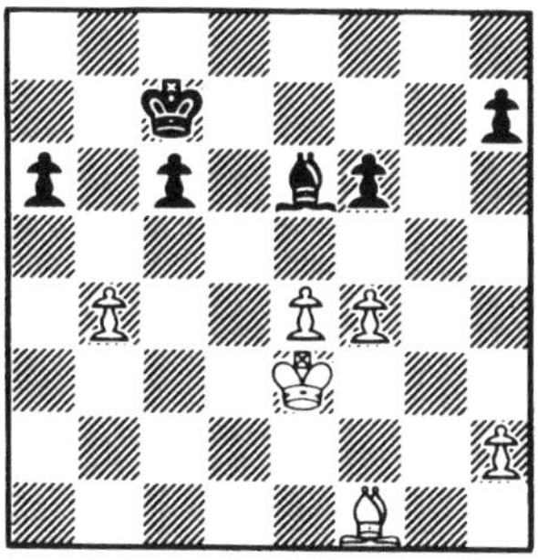

DIAGRAM 8. ELISKASES-CAPABLANCA, SEMMERING-BADEN, 1937

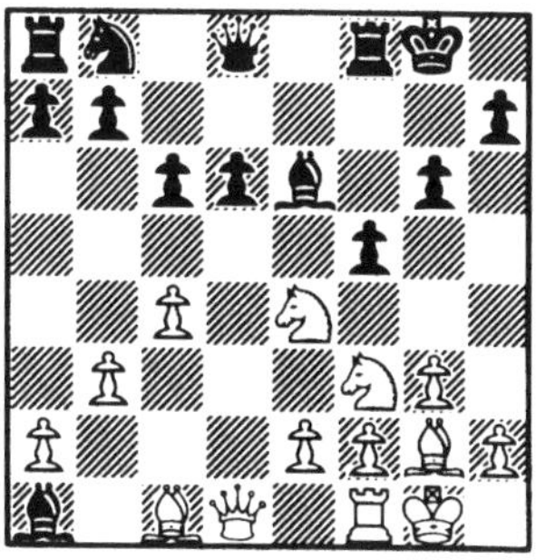

DIAGRAM 9. SYRE-PAHTZ, GERMANY, 1975

E. Space versus Material:

Although the Exchange down in Diagram 9, White has a great spatial advantage.

12	♕×d6!	♕×d6
13	♘×d6	♗c8

and Black is tied up. If

13	. . .	b6
14	♗g5	♗f6
15	♖×f6	♖×f6
16	♘e8	♖f7
17	♘g5!	

and White wins because of the Knight fork on the Rooks.

F. Space Versus Time:

In Diagram 10 White controls more squares but Black, being more developed, is ahead in time and can sacrifice against the uncastled King.

12 . . .	♖×c3
13 b×c3	♕c7
14 ♗d2	b5
15 h5	♘c4
16 ♗×c4	b×c4
17 h×g6	f×g6
18 ♕h2	♕b6!
19 ♗h6	♕b2
20 ♔d2	♘×e4+!
21 f×e4	♗×d4!!
22 Resigns	

because of forthcoming mate.

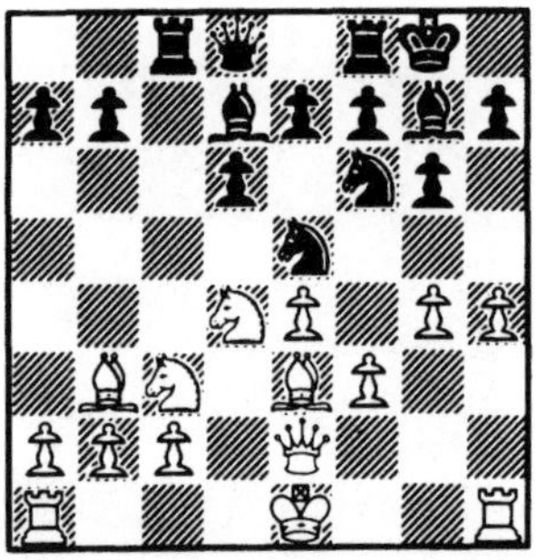

DIAGRAM 10. FILIPOWICZ–SKROBEK, POLAND, 1975

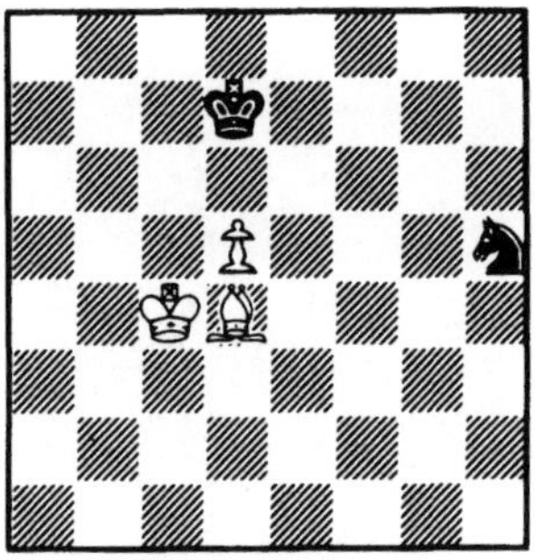

DIAGRAM 11.

2. Bishops

A. Advantage Over Knight:

There are two advantages of a Bishop over a Knight. First, when the Knight is on the edge of the board, it can be trapped. In Diagram 11 White moves 1 ♗e5 and the Knight is trapped.

1 ♗e5!	♔e7
2 ♔c5	♔d7
3 d6	♔e6
4 ♔c6 and wins	

Second, when there is play on both wings, the Bishop can swoop around to pick up Pawns whereas the Knight is limited to short-range hops. In Diagram 12, the Bishop attacks a6 which ties down the Knight.

1 ♔e4	♔e6

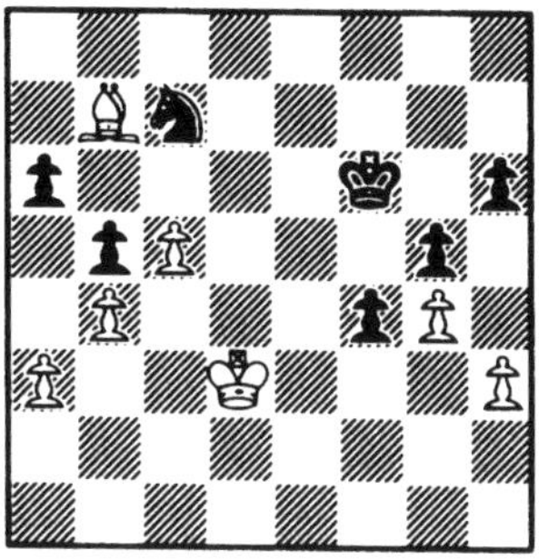

DIAGRAM 12. GILG-SZEKELY, STUBNANCE-TEPLICE, 1930

2	♔d4	♔f6
3	♗c8	♘e6+
4	♔d3	♘c7
5	♔e4	♔e7
6	♔e5	♔d8
7	♗b7	♔e7
8	♗c6!	♘e6
9	♗d5!	

White must win a tempo to drive the King back.

9	. . .	♘c7
10	♗b7!	♔d7
11	♔f5	♘e6
12	♗×a	♔c6
13	♔×♘!	Resigns

Black resigns because 13 . . . f3 14 ♔e5 f2 15 a4! b×a 16 ♔d4 and White can catch both Pawns.

B. The Bad Bishop

A bad Bishop is one whose Pawns are fixed on the same color. The disadvantage is not only that the Bishop is thereby constricted but that the squares of the other color are so weak and the opposing King can penetrate on them. Diagram 13 illustrates both these points. The scope of the Black Bishop is limited and Black is weak on the Black-colored squares.

1	♗e2	♗g6
2	♗d3	♗h7
3	♗c2	♗g6
4	♗b1!	♗h7
5	♗d3	♗g6
6	♗c2	♗h7
7	♗b3	♗g8

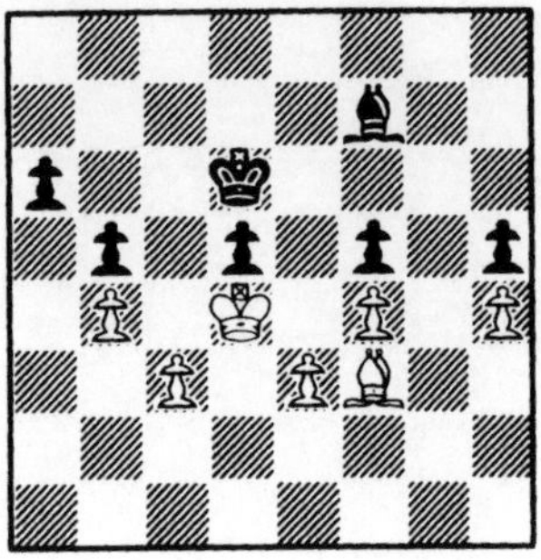

DIAGRAM 13.

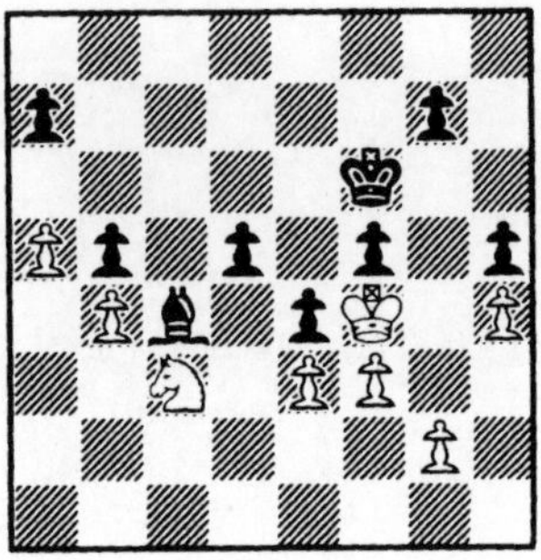

DIAGRAM 14. SMYSLOV-DERKACH, KIEV, 1937

8	♗d1!	♗f7
9	♗f3	

and Black is in Zugzwang. He is forced to move and loses a Pawn.

C. Disadvantage versus the Knight:

In blocked positions when the Bishop is restricted by its own Pawns, the Knight is superior. A Bishop can control only squares of its color whereas the Knight can press on both colors. In Diagram 14, the White King threatens to penetrate on the weak black-colored squares.

1	a6	g6
2	f×e	f×e
3	g3	

playing for Zugzwang.

3	. . .	♔e6
4	♔g5	♔f7
5	♘d1	♗f1
6	♘f2	♔g7
7	g4	h×g
8	♘×g	♗h3
9	♘f6	♗e6
10	♘e8+ and wins.	

D. Exchange of Bad Bishop For Good Bishop:

In Diagram 15, Black's central Pawns locked on black squares makes his KB the bad one. Hence he is happy to exchange it for White's QB which is good because his center Pawns are on white squares.

1	. . .	♗h6!
2	♘b3	♗×c

3 ♖×c

Now Black's QB is the good one and White's KB the bad one.

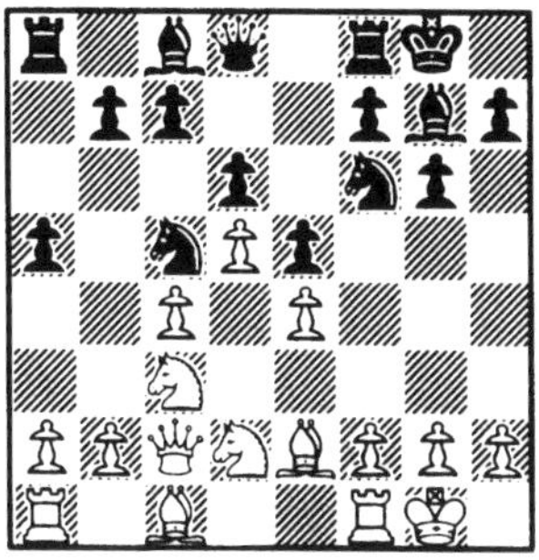

DIAGRAM 15.

E. The Good Bishop:

A bad Bishop is one whose Pawns are *fixed* on the same color as the Bishop. If the Pawns are *transient*, the Bishop may be a good one. In Diagram 16, White's Queen-side Pawns are on white squares but they are not immobilized. Black's King-side Pawn is fixed on a white square. Hence the White Bishop is the good one.

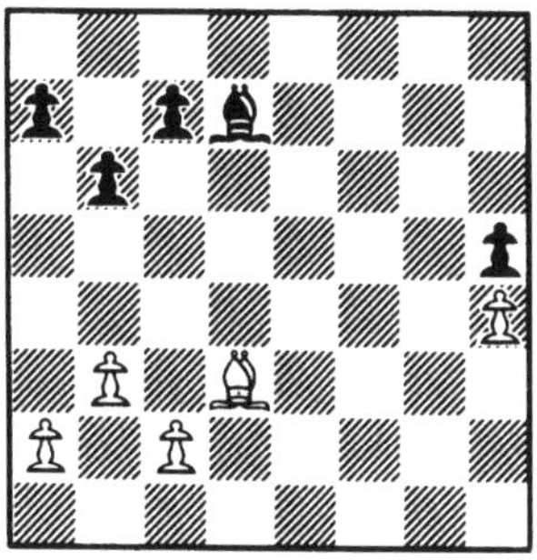

DIAGRAM 16.

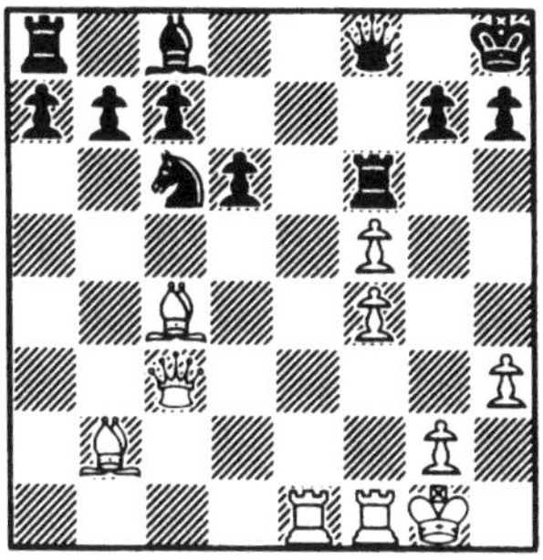

DIAGRAM 17.

F. The Two Bishops:

The two Bishops are stronger than Bishop and Knight because they control squares of both colors on both sides of the board. When they press against the castled King as in Diagram 17, watch out!

1	♖e8!	♕×e
2	♕×f6!	♕e7
3	♕×g+!!	♕×g

4	f6	♕f8
5	f7+	♕g7?
6	f8=♖ mate	

Can you recognize the lion by his paw? White was Morphy. Black's 5th move was weak. But even after 5 . . . ♘e5:

6	f×♘	h5
7	e6+	♔h7
8	♗d3+	♔h6
9	♖f6+	♔g5
10	♖g6+	♔f4
11	♔f2	

and White mates, as shown by Morphy.

3. Blockade

A. With a Piece:

A blockade consists of stopping a Pawn by placing a piece up front of it. In Diagram 18, the White Knight blockades Black's passed QP. It is better to blockade with a Knight than with a Queen, Bishop or Rook because these long-range pieces should have scope to move around. One removes the blockade by exchanging off the blockading piece. But then its place may be taken by the King which is an ideal blockader in most endings. (A little secret: in Knight and Pawn endings it is often better to blockade with the Knight and let the King move around freely.)

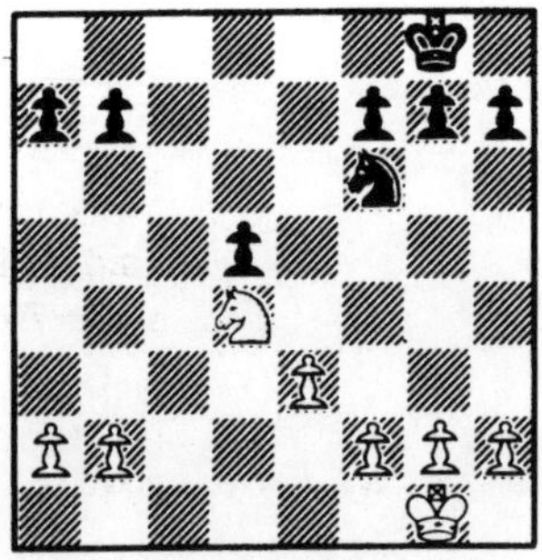

DIAGRAM 18.

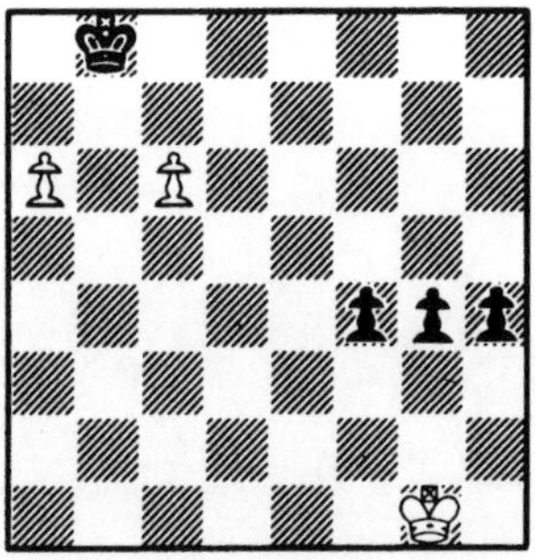

DIAGRAM 19.

B. With the King:

The King can even win against three pawns, as illustrated in Diagram 19. If 1 . . . f3 then 2 ♔f2 or 1 . . . h3 2 ♔h2 getting in amongst the Pawns and winning them. But if White must move first, 1 ♔ any, then the Pawns win in all variations. Some magic by Reti is worth illustration here. In Diagram 20, White certainly looks lost.

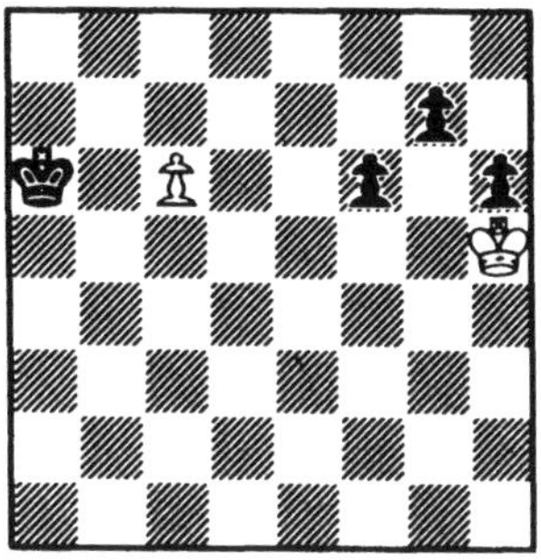

DIAGRAM 20.

1 ♔g6	♔b6
2 ♔×g	h5
3 ♔×f	draw

because by threatening to support his own Pawn, White catches the Black RP. If

2 . . .	f5
3 ♔f6	f4
4 ♔e5	f3
5 ♔d6	draw

White draws all variations with the trick of simultaneously supporting his own Pawn and entering the square of the passed Black Pawn.

4. Center

A. Control:

Everybody knows the center consists of the four squares d4, e4, d5, e5. Pawns in the center prevent opposing pieces from moving freely. Pieces in the center press on many more squares than they do on the sides of the board. Besides occupying it with Pawns, one can control the center from a distance by pressure on it from fianchettoed Bishops. In classical openings beginning with 1 d4, the idea is to eventually get e4 in and in 1 e4 openings to eventually play d4. Modern openings attempt to press on the center from afar as for example in Diagram 21. White's Pawn on c4 presses on the central square d5. The Knight on c3 presses on d5 and e4. The Bishop on g2 presses on e4 and d5. The position is symmetrical in that Black presses in a similar manner on the squares d4 and e5. Neither side is occupying central squares directly but each is exerting pressure on them.

B. Destroying:

When the center is occupied by Pawns, they provide an object of attack in an attempt to reduce their center effectiveness. Modern openings allow the opponent to occupy the center squares with Pawns in order to attack the

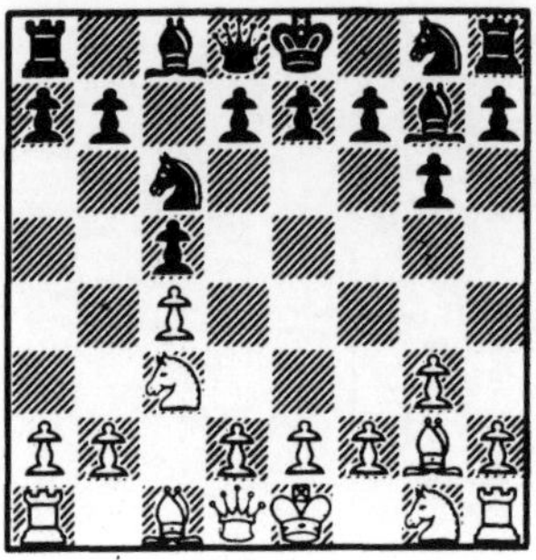

DIAGRAM 21.

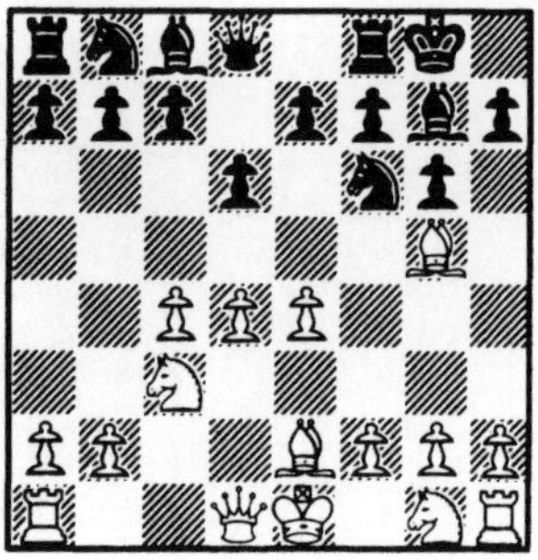

DIAGRAM 22.

Pawn structure. This is well-exemplified by the King's Indian Defense, as in Diagram 22. Black attacks the central Pawns.

1	. . .	c5
2	d5	h6
3	♗e3	e6

Again Black hits at the central advance Pawn structure.

4	♘f3	e×d
5	e×d	

Now Black has an open file and he can further attack the Pawn structure by an eventual b5.

In Diagram 23 White should strive to hit at e5 with f4 and Black should hit at e4 with an eventual d5.

C. Giving Up The Center

In Diagram 24, if Black plays d×c, he gives up the center. He eventually will attack White's center by c5.

D. Locked Center

In Diagram 25, the center is locked since both White and Black central

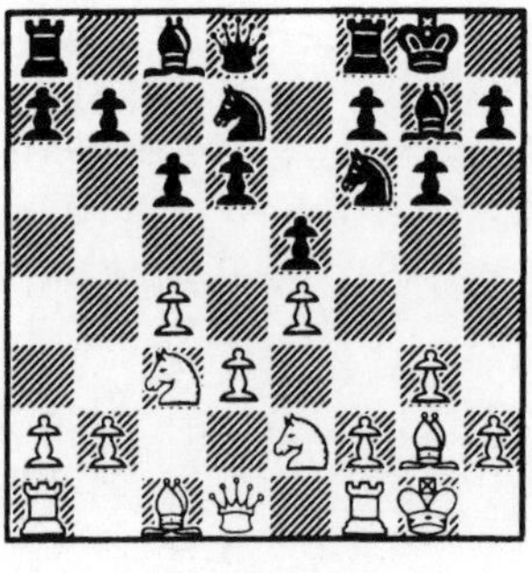

DIAGRAM 23.

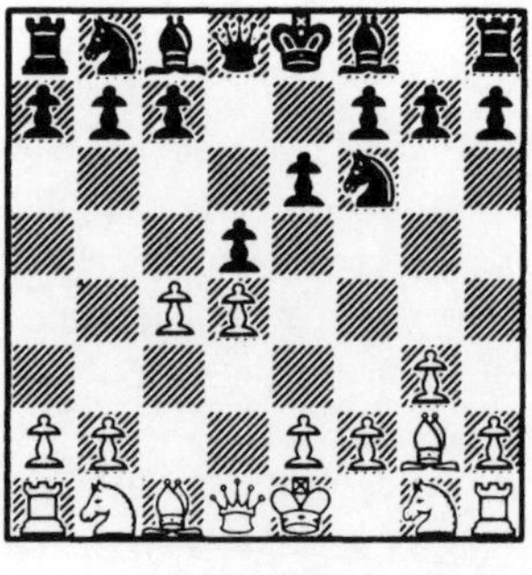

DIAGRAM 24.

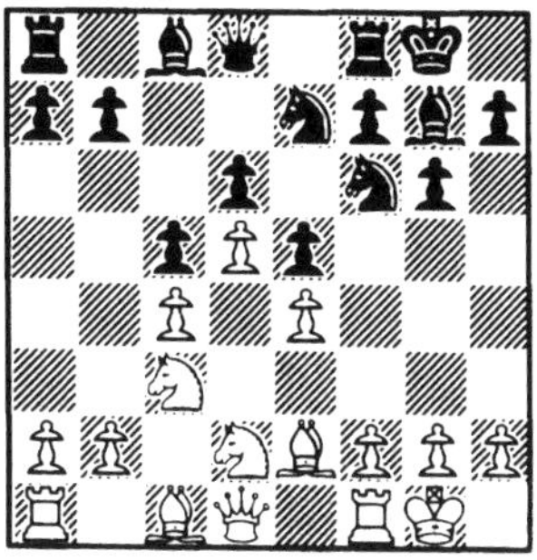

DIAGRAM 25.

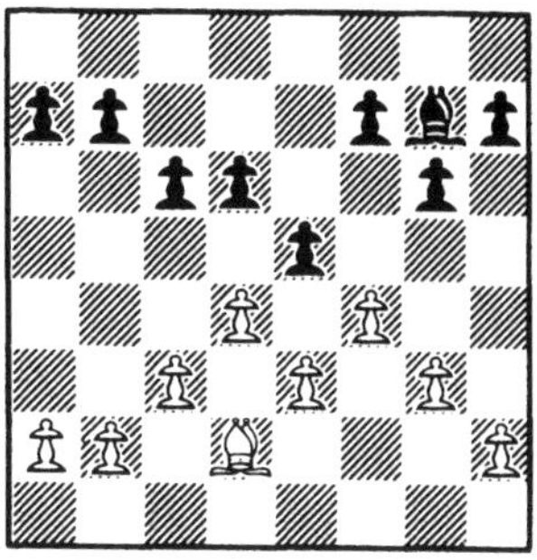

DIAGRAM 26.

Pawns are immobilized. White will try to hit against c5 with b4 and Black will eventually strike against e4 with f5.

5. Strong and Weak Colors

We have already seen an example of weak color squares in Diagram 24. When the Pawns are all on one color, the opposite color is weak, allowing the opposing pieces and the King to occupy them. When the Pawns are on one color and the opposite color Bishop has been exchanged, the squares are weak for one side and strong for the opposing side. In Diagram 26, White's White squares are weak, Black is strong on both colors. If Black exchanges the KB, he will be weak on the Black squares of f6 and h6.

6. Combinations

Patzers are not beginners. Hence I will assume the reader knows what comprises a pin, a fork, a double attack, etc. Also he knows the standard sacrifices on the RP, NP, and BP squares. If not, Fine's *The Middle Game of Chess* gives a good account of them.

7. Development

The main idea of the opening is to get the pieces out in an inter-connected way, castle, connect the Rooks and away we go. Being three tempi ahead in development can be worth a Pawn. Consider Diagram 27 which stems from a Reversed Dragon variation of the English opening. White is a Pawn down but ahead in development. Black's Queen will be chased around as White develops further and gains tempi. For example:

1 . . .	♝c5
2 e3	♕c4

If 2 . . . ♕d3 or 2 . . . ♕d5 3 ♕a4+

3 ♗b2	0–0
4 ♖c1	♕b5
5 ♕c2	

White regains the Pawn and has all the initiative.

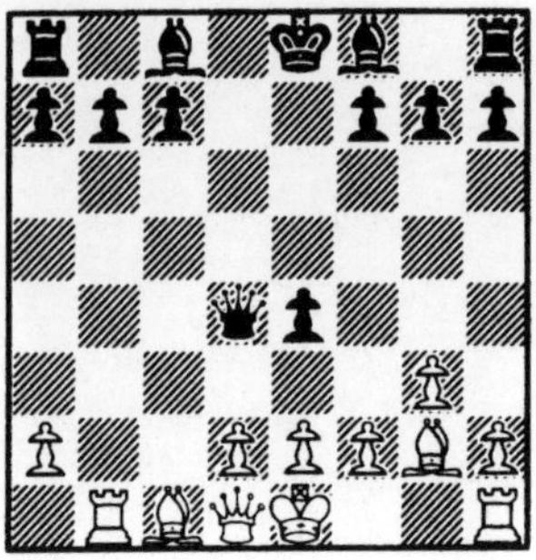

DIAGRAM 27.

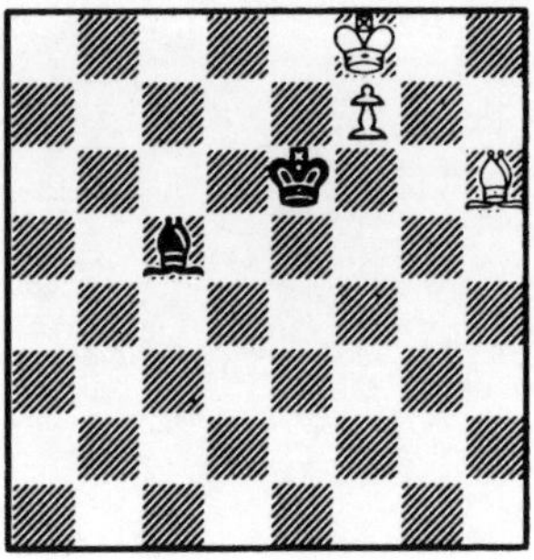

DIAGRAM 28.

8. Diagonals

Controlling the long diagonals usually means that a Bishop or Queen or Queen plus Bishop dominate the a1–h8 or h1–a8 diagonals. But in general, a long diagonal has more squares open than a short diagonal. (How long is a piece of string?). The long and short of it in an ending is illustrated in the following two positions, Diagram 28 and Diagram 29. To sacrifice the Bishop for the White BP Black must operate on the long diagonal a3–f8 which has six open squares or the short diagonal h6–f8 which has three open squares. White's King moves over towards the short diagonal, making it even shorter, by reducing the occupiable squares, and thereby wins.

1 ♔g8 ♔f5

White threatens 2 ♗f8 ♗e3 3 ♗a3 ♗h6 4 ♗b2 and 5 ♗g7.

2 ♗f8 ♗e3

3 ♗b4 ♗h6

4 ♗d2!

The BP queens.

To defend this type of position, Black must have four squares on the short diagonal as in Diagram 29. The four-squared h5–e8 diagonal is just long enough to draw.

1 ... ♗e8

2 ♗c2 ♔g5

which prevents 3 ♗g6 and the Black Bishop cannot be caught by the White King.

9. Eighth Rank

Also known as the back-rank weakness, the eight-rank mate with the Rook is indeed the crudest of all mates. In Diagram 30:

1 ♖d8+

leads to mate. But White should not be overconfident in Diagram 31. With

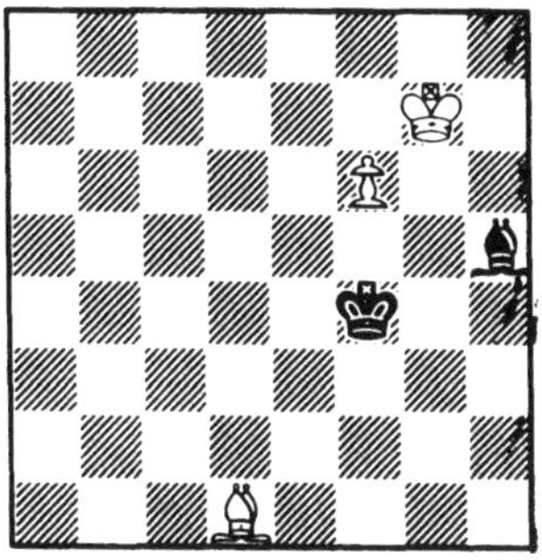

DIAGRAM 29.

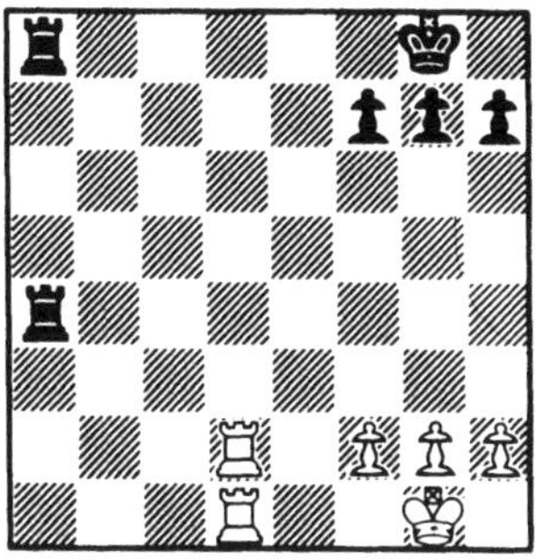

DIAGRAM 30.

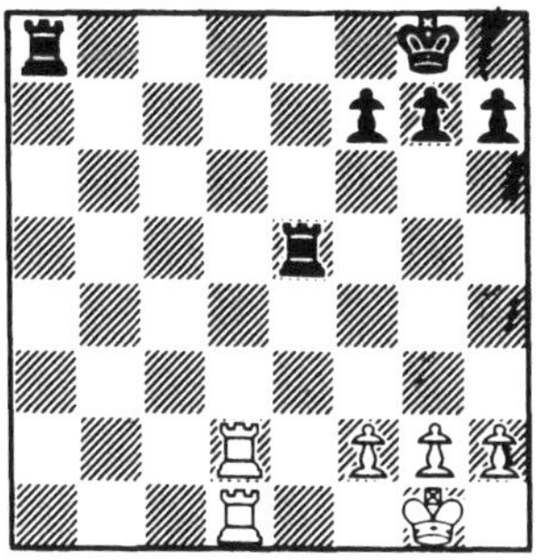

DIAGRAM 31.

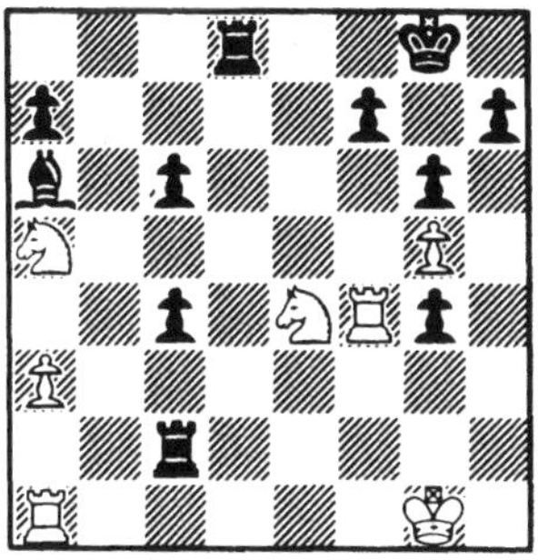

DIAGRAM 32. A PLAYER– DR. G, 1977

a slightly different position of the Black Rook on e5, 1 ♖d8+ does *not* lead to mate because Black plays Rook to e8 and holds everything.

Here is a practical example from a Rating Tournament game against a fellow Grandpatzer. It looks like White has various threats after ♘×c6 but the eighth-rank weakness forces White to give back the piece.

1 . . .	c3!
2 ♘×c6	♖dd2!
3 ♖f2	g3
4 ♖×d	c×d
5 ♘×d	♖×d

and White resigned shortly because his remaining weak Pawns were picked off by the active Black Rook.

10. Exchanging

Everybody knows that when you are ahead in material, you keep exchanging down to a simpler win because it prevents the opponent from generating counter-chances. It is also well known that in defending against an attack it is wise to exchange off the attacking active pieces and to reduce the pressure. A grandpatzer secret is to keep exchanging against a much stronger player because when threatened with a draw, he may over-extend himself and make mistakes in an effort to win.

In a tournament game against a ferocious combinational player rated 300 points ahead of me, I kept swapping down, striving for the draw. In this position chances are about even.

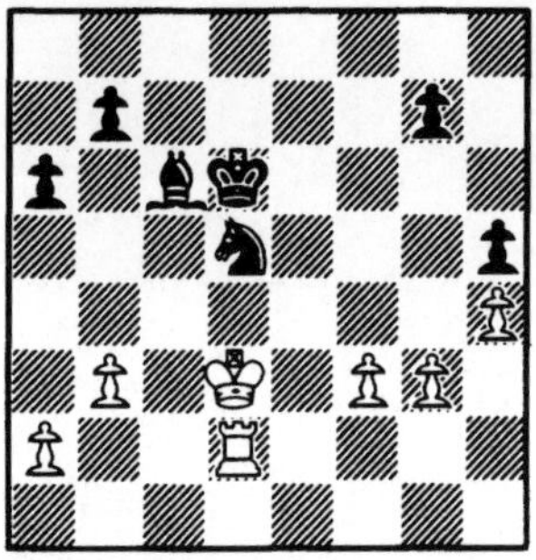

DIAGRAM 33. DR. G–A PLAYER, 1977

He (Black) has two pieces against the Rook but I have 3 vs. 2 Pawns on the King side. Threatened with a draw against a much weaker player, he becomes over-aggressive.

1 . . .	♔c5
2 ♖c2+	♔b4
3 ♔d4	♔a3
4 ♖f2	

Since he is going to clean up my Queen-side Pawns using his King, I might as well go for some passed Pawns on the side of the absent King.

4 . . .	♘b4
5 g4	h×g
6 f×g	♘×a
7 ♖f7	♔×b
8 ♖×g	♘c3
9 h5	a5
10 h6	a4
11 h7	a3
12 h8 = ♕	a2

But now Black is lost because White's King and Queen are too much for the exposed King (Diagram 34).

13 ♕a8	♘b5+
14 ♔c5	♘a3

15 ♖×b+ ♗×b
16 ♕×b+ ♔c2
17 ♕g2+ ♔b3
18 ♕d5+ ♔b2
19 ♕d4+ ♔b1
20 ♕b4+ Resigns

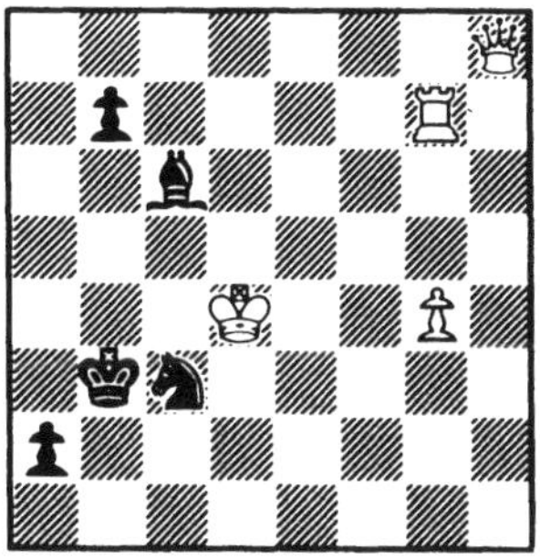

DIAGRAM 34. DR. G-A PLAYER, 1977

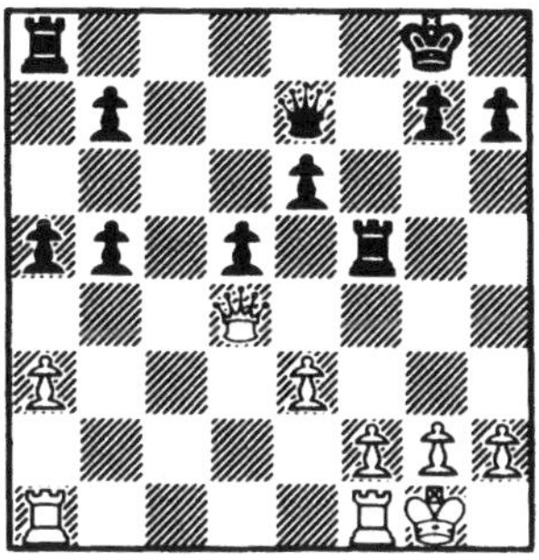

DIAGRAM 35.

11. Files

The reason one likes to control an open file with a Rook is not so much to command the space but to get the Rook to the seventh rank where it attacks Pawns on both sides and threatens the King. Consider the play in Diagram 35.

1 . . . ♖c8

White cannot oppose a Rook because he loses his QRP.

2 ♕b6 ♖c2!
3 ♕×a ♕f6
4 ♕a8+ ♔f7
5 ♕×b+ ♔g6
6 f4 . . .

This holds the Pawn but now Black increases the pressure along the seventh rank against g2 and h2.

6 . . . ♕b2
7 ♔h1 ♖×g2
8 ♖g1 ♖fg5!!

which forces mate.

12 Pawns

Probably the hardest piece for a patzer to manage is the Pawn. When in doubt as to what to do, he usually moves a Pawn. (Is this because there are so many of them?). Lasker said to mistrust every Pawn move you make. This is because one cannot bring the piece back like one can with all the others. The aspiring grandpatzer must know the common Pawn configurations: isolated Pawns, doubled Pawns, hanging Pawns, passed Pawns, protected passed Pawns, Pawn majorities, and Pawn chains. Pawn chains are especially important in modern openings such as the King's Indian, which I advise all grandpatzers to play.

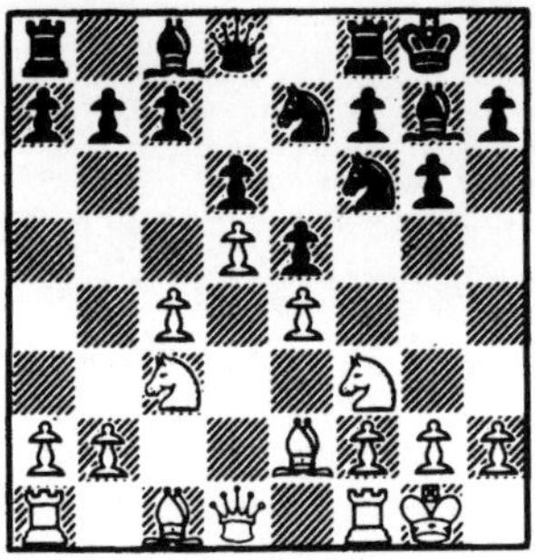

DIAGRAM 36.

Diagram 36 represents a characteristic Pawn chain position in the King's Indian Defense. White's chain is represented by the Pawns on e4 and d5, Black's by the Pawns on e5 and d6. The *head* of White's chain is on d5, Black's on e5. The *base* of White's chain is on e4 and Blacks on d6, *not* the Pawn on c7 as many patzers mistakenly believe. A good rule of thumb is that the base of a Pawn chain is the Pawn which cannot move. Since the Pawn on c7 can move, it does not represent the base.

The idea for each player is to attack the base of the opponent's chain. White strives for c5, attacking d6. If Black plays d×c5, he deprives the head of his chain on e5 of support. If Black allows White to play c×d6, Black keeps a base for his chain but now the c-file is open and White tries to get a Rook to c7. Black should play the Knight on f6 back to e8 or d7 and advance the f-Pawn to f5, attacking the base of White's chain. White usually should not play f4 because this attacks only the head of the chain, not the base.

If White plays his Knight back to e1, and follows it with moving the Pawn to f3, then the base of his chain becomes f3 rather than e4. Black will now try for g5 and g4 to attack the base and open the g-file against the White King.

The best book on Pawn configurations is *Pawn Structure Chess* by Soltis. This book is a boon to every patzer and grandpatzer for whom the management of all those buttons can be quite perplexing.

13. Pressing and Releasing

Several times I have referred to the concept of pressure. Each piece presses on certain squares. When the opponent moves you ask yourself “‘What is he now pressing on?’” (I represent inner self-talk by three quote marks). But a true Grandpatzer secret lies in asking yourself “‘What is he now *not* pressing on that he was pressing on before?’” My friend, Robert Abelson, a top postal player, calls this a new-move generator, because answering the second question may suggest a move not previously considered.

For example, in some variations of the Sicilian Defense, White plays his KB to e2 and then to f3. On e2 the Bishop presses against f1, d1, d3, c4, b5, a6 and f3, g4, and h5. When the Bishop moves to f3 it now presses on d1, e2, g4, h5, h1, g2, e4, d5, c6, b7, and a8. But by moving to f3, it has *released* pressure on f1, d3, c4, b5 and a6. Therefore Black can think of doing something on these squares which hitherto he could not. Every move creates pressure and releases pressure. When pressure is released, it allows you to consider a new plausible move which was rejected as implausible prior to the pressure release.

14. The two Zs

Zugzwang and Zwischenzug are two German terms you can throw around to indicate the intimate knowledge of cognoscenti. But you had better know what the concepts mean also.

When it is your turn to move and you are forced (Zwang) to make a move that leads to a loss, you are in Zugzwang. This fate is most commonly found in the end game but here is a beautiful example in the middle game.

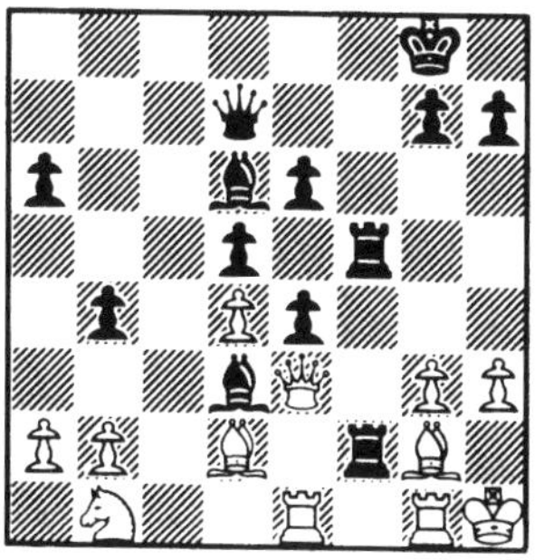

DIAGRAM 37. SAEMISCH–NIMZOVICH, COPENHAGEN, 1923

1 . . .	h6!!
2 Resigns	

If 1 ♖f1, ♗×f or if 1 ♖d1 ♖e2 wins the Queen. If 1 g4 ♖5f3 2 ♗×f, ♖h2 mate. If 1 b3 a5 and the Zwang state still holds.

Zwischenzug means an in-between, interposed move which disrupts an expected sequence of moves. For example, here is Dr. G (Black) against a fellow grandpatzer in a tournament game.

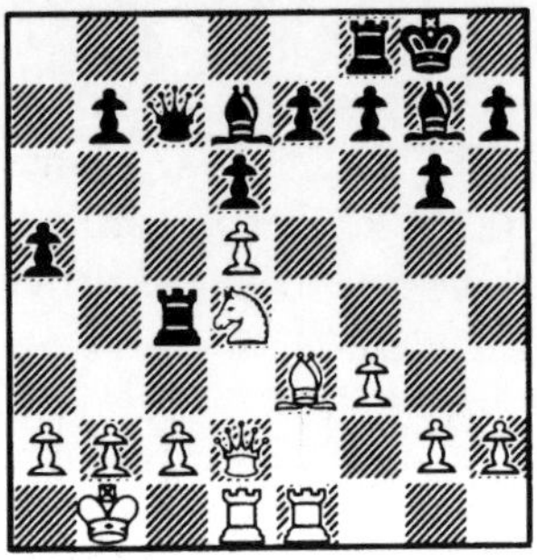

DIAGRAM 38. A PLAYER–DR. G, 1977

1	b3	♖c3
2	♘e2	

It looks like Black loses something but he interposes:

2	. . .	♖×c!
3	♕×c	♗f5
4	♖d3	

And now another Zwischenzug by Black.

4	. . .	♖c8
5	♕×c	♗×d+
6	♔c1	♖×c+
7	♔d2	♗f5

Black has won a Pawn and the White King is exposed.

Naturally this has not been an exhaustive treatment of all the themes, patterns and motifs and tactics of chess. There are thousands and perhaps hundreds of thousands of patterns and tricks known by grandmasters. Still these are the common but crucial everyday patterns. You *must know* them as routine elementary knowledge if you are to become a strong chess player. Chess-playing computer programs know them and if you are to emulate (or perhaps surpass) these computers, you must know them also. There is absolutely no way of becoming a grandpatzer without this knowledge. If you do not understand these key themes, go over them time and again until they become an automatic computer-like part of you.

Just knowing what these themes and patterns are is the first step but of course it is not enough. One must next know what to do about them. The weak square hole on g6 in Diagram 39 should make you, as White, think of

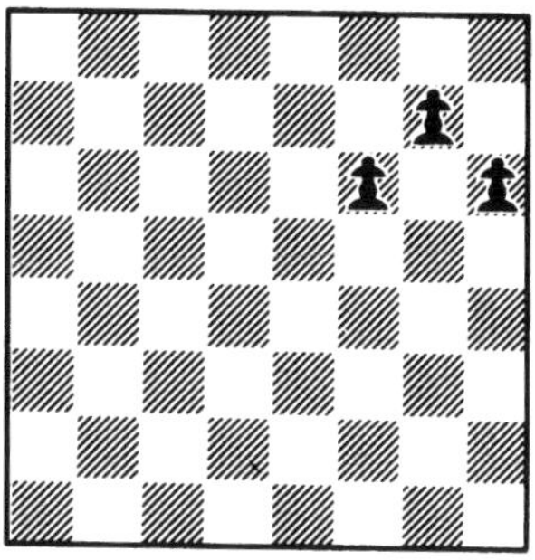

DIAGRAM 39.

plonking an outpost piece in there. (That Knight will be strong as a horse). Certain patterns trigger certain actions. Pattern recognition forms the basis of what to think about in a position. A grandpatzer also learns how these patterns interplay with one another and which ones are more relevant than others in a given position. Many serviceable examples of this interplay are given in Euwe and Meiden's *The Road to Chess Mastery*, if you want to practice them.

II

How to Study

2.1 *Openings*

It is a great waste of time to study all the openings, especially those no longer used much in tournament play. I still see young players and beginners worrying about how to play some weird thing like the Latvian Gambit or the Inverted Hanham. They wonder, 'how can I learn all this?' A big secret is, you don't have to. The major area where an aspiring grandpatzer can profit from master practice is in the opening, regardless what masters say about memorizing. Play only opening systems which current masters repeatedly use because they are constantly being improved for you through tournament play. (What chess calls opening 'theory' is really practice from the court of experience). By studying these systems and your pet critical variations of them, you simply memorize, as far as you can, what the best current continuations are as given in *Chess Informant* and *Chess Player*. As Ken Smith says, 'You must buy each issue of these two books as they come out and study the openings you use, trying to remember the continuations further and further into the middle game.' For example, I now know several critical variations of the Sicilian Dragon for Black 15 moves deep. This is simply a matter of memory. I know them not because I have a superb memory (I do have a pretty good memory—it's just that it's rather short) but because I go over and over these lines many times during a six month period. Constant repetition and rehearsal is the key to remembering. Masters tell you not to memorize openings but to understand them. You need both. To paraphrase what Mark Twain said about thunder and lightning: understanding is good, understanding is impressive, but it is memory that does the work.

The middle game is dividable into the positional and combinational middle game. In the positional middle game, stemming from the opening, your knowledge of the exact moves has become exhausted and you are on your own. In the later combinational middle game when the pieces have come into contact, sacrifices and combinations become possibilities to be examined. Naturally it is advantageous to be playing a memorized opening while your opponent finds himself sweating over his own choices in what is, for him, still a positional middle game.

Ken Smith and your Dr. Grandpatzer recommend that you pick one opening for White and two for Black, one against e4 and one against d4. Don't handicap yourself with old-fashioned openings like the Stonewall, as recommended by Horowitz, or the Colle, as recommended by Koltanowski. Not only are they passive and easily defended against by the King's Indian, but not enough current tournament practice is conducted on them to help you extend your memory of the variations further into the positional middle game. Evans and Dr. G suggest that as Black, you use the King's Indian System because masters will constantly do your work in exercising the various possibilities. Your task is to memorize their results as far into the game as you can.

One of the worst pieces of advice repeatedly offered to patzers is 'Don't memorize'. Ridiculous! You must memorize certain things. Masters themselves don't figure out the opening during play. They know it by heart for 1–10 moves and you must do likewise to become a grandpatzer. If you know the opening by heart for ten moves, you have a great jump in time and energy over your opponent. You will still be comfortable in what for you is an opening whereas your opponent may be struggling on his own resources in his positional middle game. For example, if you are Black in the following opening:

1	d4	♘f6
2	c4	g6
3	♘c3	♗g7
4	e4	d6
5	♘f3	0–0
6	♗e2	

DIAGRAM 40. POSITION AFTER 6 ♗e2

Don't sit there with the clock ticking away and wondering what to do. You should know from simple memory the move is 6 . . . e5, so just go ahead and make it without wasting time worrying about what will happen next. The move 6 . . ., e5 is the book move, the correct move and you must simply know it. It has been played millions of times, and you must have memorized it by now, otherwise you will forever remain a patzer trying to play the King's Indian.

When memorizing your opening variations in home study, try to remember them a move or two further each time. In fact, try to look a move or two beyond the printed variation. If you do, you will find amusing perplexities like this (from Boleslavsky's book on the Gruenfeld, p. 246):

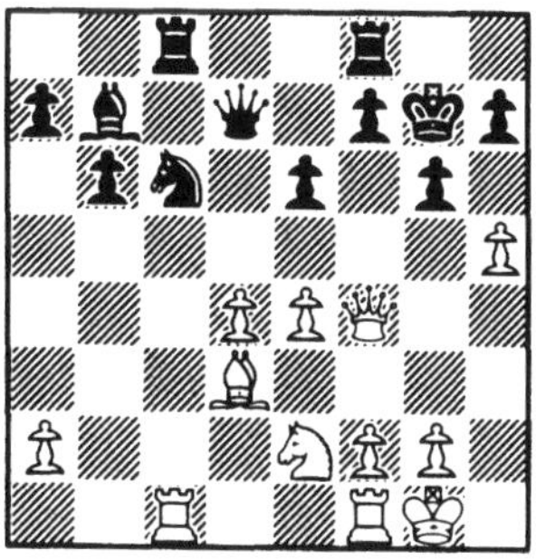

DIAGRAM 41.

The recommendation is:

19 . . .	e5??

'with good counterplay' overlooking that it is mate with 20 h6+, King any 21 ♕f6 forces mate. Obviously this is a typo. The Black Queen should be on e7.

You must own and study books on traps, memorizing those which arise in your opening system. In wandering around the room during a tournament (it's good practice to observe what openings your future opponents use) I have seen this old trap worked many times.

1 e4	c5
2 ♘f3	♘c6
3 d4	c×d
4 ♘×d	♘f6
5 ♘c3	d6
6 ♗c4	g6?
7 ♘×c6	b×c6
8 e5!	. . .

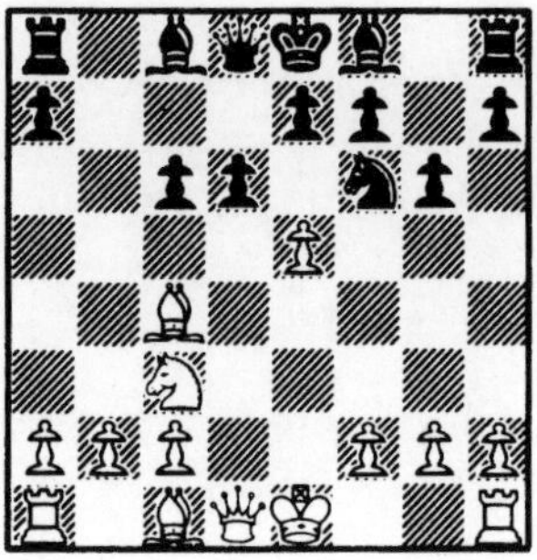

DIAGRAM 42. POSITION AFTER 8 e5!

The Dragon is gasping because of 8 . . . d×e 9 ♗×f+ wins the Queen. If 8 . . . ♘d7 9 e×d e×d 10 0–0 and Black cannot fianchetto the Bishop. If 8 . . . ♘g4 9 ♗f4 ♕b6 10 ♕f3 ♗f5 11 e×d e×d 12 0–0–0 d5 13 ♖he1+ is overwhelming. If you are going to play the Dragon, you must know this trap. Incidentally, the Dragon is so-called because the Pawn formation looks like the star constellation Draco, which is Greek for 'dragon'. This is useful to know only because ordinary people may ask why we call it the Dragon.

In a club Rating Tournament, as Black, I played the first 13 moves in a minute or two as follows:

1	d4	♘f6
2	c4	g6
3	♘c3	♗g7
4	e4	d6
5	♘f3	0–0
6	♗d3	♗g4
7	h3	♗×f3
8	♕×f3	♘c6
9	♗e3	♘d7
10	♘e2?	♘de5! (Diagram 43)
11	d×e	♘×e
12	♕g3	♘×d+
13	♔d2	♘×b2

and my opponent resigned! When this was being considered for the best game award, I naturally had to reveal that none of this was original on my part. I simply remembered this sequence of moves from Chernev's *Winning Chess Traps*, where it is noted that two masters have fallen into this trap, and even Alekhine overlooked it in his annotations.

Patzers study and try to play all the openings, seeking breadth but

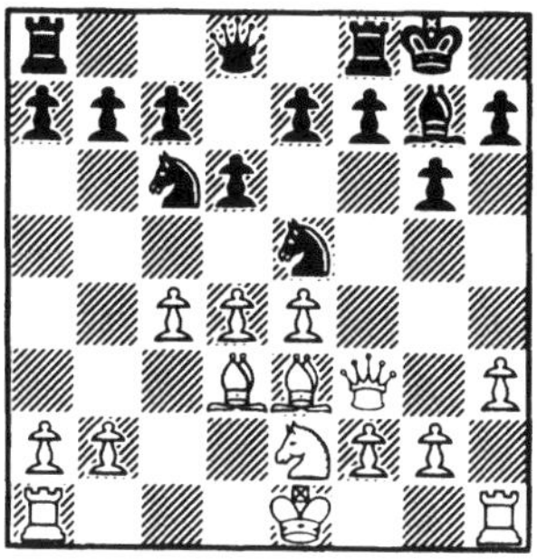

DIAGRAM 43. POSITION AFTER 10 . . . ♘de5!

sacrificing depth. What good does it do to know 30 openings 4 moves deep? Portisch studies the openings 8 hours a day and knows far more openings than Fischer. But what Fischer knows, he knows deeply. Aspiring grandpatzers must study only a few opening systems but learn them deeply by studying master games in those openings *all the way through to the end* of the game. In doing so, they will gradually absorb what the major ideas are, what kind of *both* positional and combinational middle games develop, what end game positions are likely to eventuate. This adds to one's library of 'tricks'. (There are thousands of 'tricks' in chess. I'll bet you don't know what the Fischer trick is in the King's Indian with ♘h5 for Black). I recommend that you utilize fianchetto openings as much as possible such as English–Reti, King's Indian, Sicilian Dragon. (As White, you must decide *now* what to do about the Dutch Defense and, as Black, about the Smith–Morra Gambit). Fianchetto openings tend to keep the position closed for a long time, and they transpose into one another both for Black and White. All these openings allow a continuous and harmonious development. One can be very busy with controlling the long diagonal, hitting his center Pawn-structure, conducting flank attacks after locking the center, etc. The positional middle-game plan is ready-made for you. By keeping the position closed, nothing bad is going to happen to you for a long time. Nobody wants to go home after 10–12 moves. You cannot force your opponent to blunder but you can wait for it. As a disgruntled loser said to Gligoric—'you're not a grandmaster, you just wait for the blunder', which of course is exactly the way to play against a patzer. To become a grandpatzer you have to learn to beat patzers regularly. Masters and other grandpatzers provide additional problems, but even against them it is best to wait cautiously and not make over-aggressive moves. Everybody would like to be fierce and full of fireworks like Alekhine, Tal or Fischer, but for most of us, it's best to play steadily and pragmatically like Korchnoi and Karpov.

Let me illustrate with an actual game how wonderfully busy, both positionally and combinationally, one can be on the Black side of a King's Indian system. Some accompanying grandpatzer thoughts for the Black side provide shallow but pragmatic annotations.

1 d4	♘f6

Here we go again with a King's Indian. The idea is to fianchetto, play d6, castle, wait and see what he does.

2 c4	g6
3 ♘c3	♗g7
4 e4	d6
5 ♘f3	0–0
6 ♗e2	e5

Remember what Dr. G said on p. 37?

7 0–0	♘c6
8 d5	♘e7
9 ♗d2	. . .

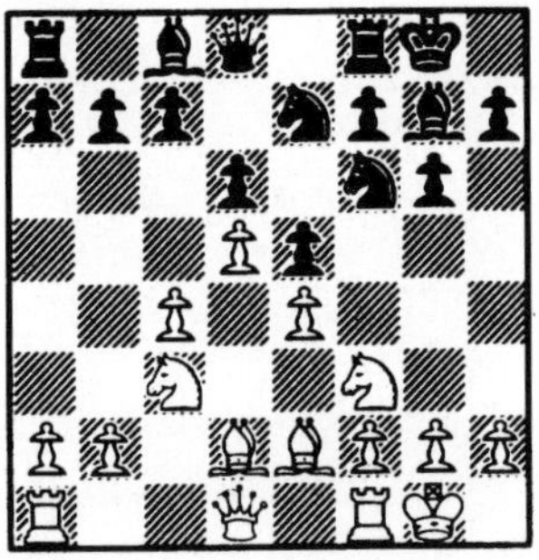

DIAGRAM 44. POSITION AFTER 9 ♗d2

This is as far as I can recall the exact moves, but I know the general positional idea is to play the Knight on f6 back to e8 or d7, or forward to h5 in order to get in f5 for a king-side attack.

9 . . .	♘e8
10 ♘e1	f5

With the center locked, Black wants to play f4 and then let the king-side Pawn mass and pieces surge forward towards the White king. (Nimzovich wrote like this). Notice how much there is to do without deep thinking.

11 ♘d3	♘f6
12 f3	f4
13 c5	. . .

White is not just going to sit there. Black must expect a Queen-side attack and especially look out for the square c7.

13 . . .	g5
14 c×d6	c×d6
15 ♖c1	. . .

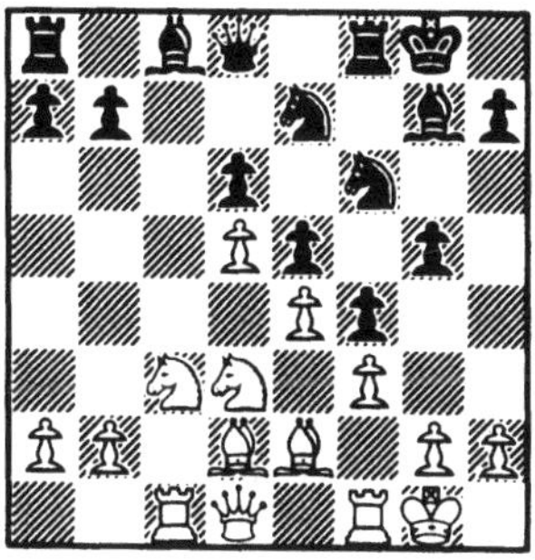

DIAGRAM 45. POSITION AFTER 15 ♖c1

White is obviously heading for c7. A good defensive trick here for Black is to put his Rook on f7 and bring the Bishop back to f8 to hold d6. Busy, busy! Note how far into the positional middle game we are with very little mental work, just utilizing a few ideas and themes.

15 . . .	♘g6
16 ♘f2	♖f7
17 ♘b5	♘e8
18 ♕b3	♗f8
19 ♖c3	. . .

He wants to pile up on c7 but Black can hold it for a while.

19 . . .	a6
20 ♘a3	♗d7
21 ♘c2	h5

Back to work with the long-range plan of expanding on the King-side.

22 a4	♘f6
23 h3	. . . (Diagram 46)

He is getting nervous over there and weakens himself in front to the King. Look at that hole on g3! Another trick characteristic of the King's Indian combinational middle game is to take the Pawn on h3 with the Queen's Bishop to shatter the defenses in front of the White King. (See next game).

23 . . .	♘h4
24 ♖c1	♖g7
25 ♗e1	g4

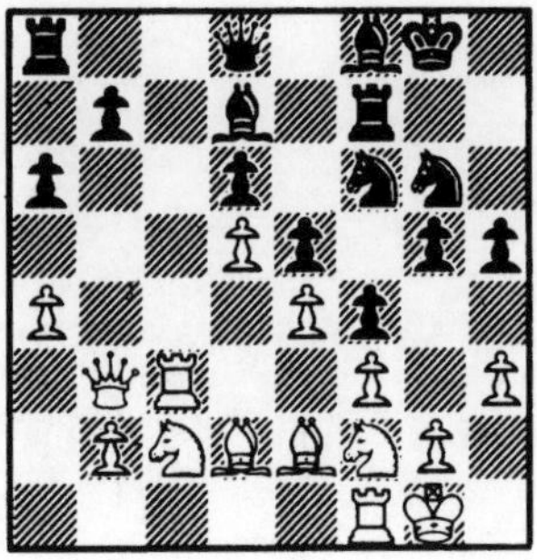

DIAGRAM 46. POSITION AFTER 23 h3

Crash in on the King. Now is the time to explode open the position.

26	f×g4	h×g4
27	♘×g4	♘×g4
28	♗×g4	♗×g4
29	h×g4	. . .

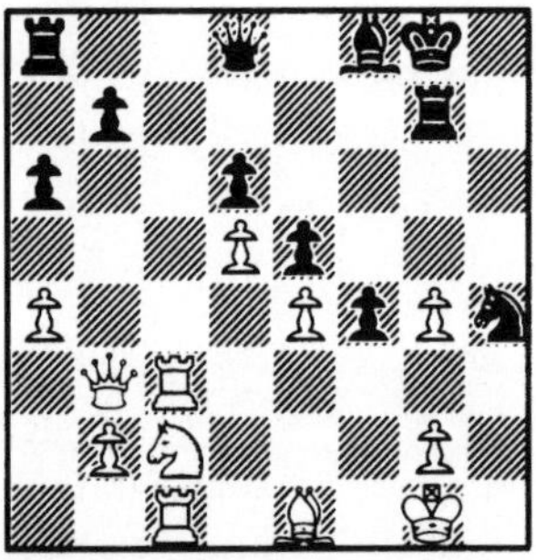

DIAGRAM 47. POSITION AFTER 29 h×g4

Here comes the big moment. If White takes off the Knight on h4, Black doesn't have much left to attack with. So now we have a deep thought for a change.

29	. . .	♘×g2!
30	♔×g2	♕g5

Nice and slow. When the check comes, it will come with a bang behind it.

31	♖f3	♕×g4+
32	♗g3	♖c8!

Another slow power accumulation.

33	♖h1	♗e7

The target is the g3 square and its contents.

34	♕d3	♗h4
35	♖h3	♗×g3
36	♘e3	♕g5
37	♖h×g3	f×g3

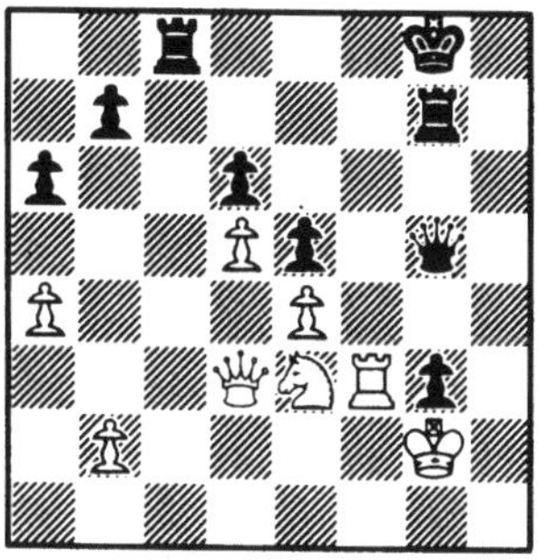

DIAGRAM 48. POSITION AFTER 37 . . . f×g3

38	♘f5	♕c1!
39	♘×g7	♖c2+
40	♔×g3	. . .

The position is widely opened up with the White King exposed to all sorts of checks and mates.

40	. . .	♕g5+
41	♔h3	♕h6+
42	♘h5	. . .

Most annotaters would say 'desperation' here but let it pass, let it pass.

42	. . .	♕×h5+
43	♔g3	♕g5+
44	♔h3	♕h6+
45	♔g3	♖h2
46	Resigns. (Diagram 49)	

I would like to claim this as a Dr. G game but it is actually Didisko–Juferov, USSR 1974. The moral of this fine play should be apparent to the aspiring grandpatzer. And if you think this is a one-shot fluke, just whip through the following (Larsen–Torre, Bauang 1973).

1	c4	g6
2	♘c3	♗g7
3	d4	♘f6
4	e4	d6
5	♗e2	0–0

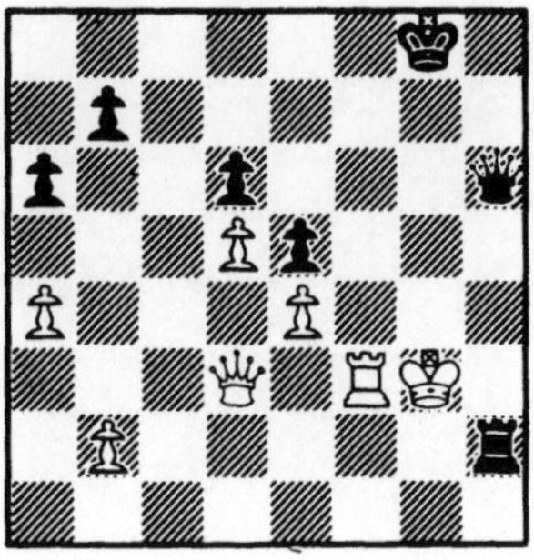

DIAGRAM 49. FINAL POSITION

6	♘f3	e5

Are you getting tired of seeing this move?

7	0–0	♘c6
8	d5	♘e7
9	♘e1	♘d7
10	♗e3	f5
11	f3	f4

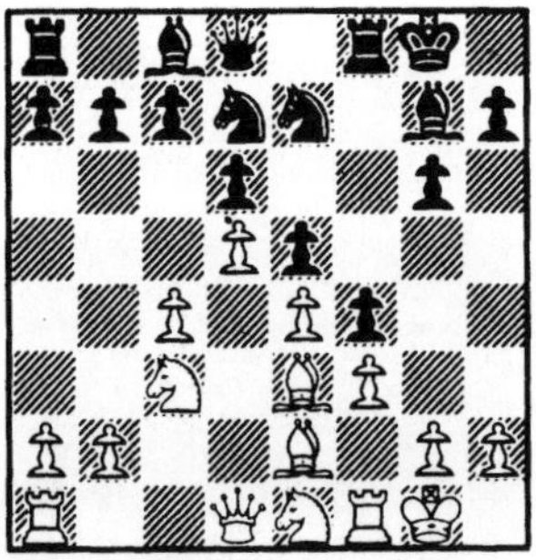

DIAGRAM 50. POSITION AFTER 11 . . . f4

Play old f4 and push the Pawns.

12	♗f2	g5
13	♘d3	♘f6
14	c5	♘g6
15	a4	h5

Any of this look familiar?

16	c×d6	c×d6
17	a5	g4
18	♘b5	g3!

19 ♗×a7	♘h7
20 h3	♕h4
21 ♗b6	♗×h3

Here is that combinational trick at h3 I told you about in the previous game.

22 g×h3	♕×h3
23 ♖f2	♘h4
24 ♕f1	g×f2+
25 ♘×f2	♕g3+

Again the f3 square is the one to ponder over.

26 ♔h1

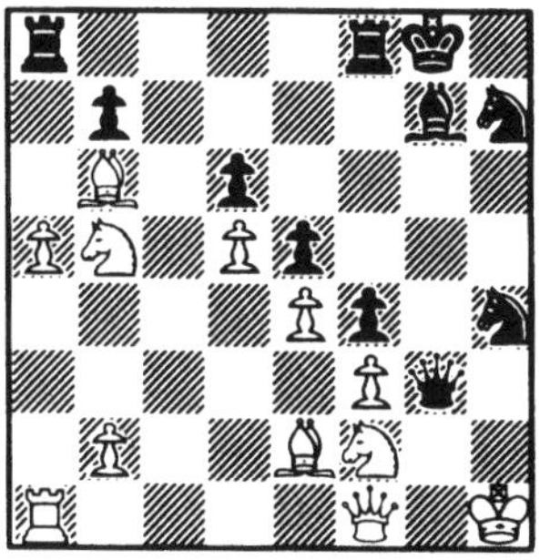

DIAGRAM 51. POSITION AFTER 26 ♔h1

26 . . .	♖f6??

And here with 26 . . . ♘×f3 Black could have won against a world-class player. Even Larsen, who eventually won, commented that this game required very little energy (for White) to play because he was busted but lucked out. (For British readers this means that Larsen was lost and lucky to win. For American readers the common British annotation 'Black is very much in the game' means that with perfect defense, Black can perhaps draw).

You don't have to think hard on every move. Memorize key variations of opening lines, trying to get to the 6th–10th move relying on memory alone. Follow the major ideas of the opening and remind yourself of the themes and tricks associated with this particular opening system. You think hard only at certain points. One of Fischer's secrets is how little energy he uses much of the time but at crucial points, he burns it with awesome intensity.

For example, let us suppose you have decided that your defense against 1 e4 will be the Sicilian Dragon. The major ideas of this defense are: (1) play d6; (2) when he plays d4, take c×d; (3) fianchetto the King's Bishop and castle King-side; (4) play the Queen's Knight to c6; (5) strive for d5, work on the half-open c-file, put pressure on the square c4; (6) if he castles Queen-side, play b5 and /or a5, sacrificing a Pawn to open up on the King; (7) in the meantime White will be attacking on the King-side; (8) watch out for the Marco hop by White (♘d5). These ideas constitute the basis for crude plans to get you into the combinational middle game. You do not need elaborate positional plans to be a grandpatzer. As we shall see when considering the Grandpatzer Machine (p. 115), you hardly need a big plan at all to be a strong chessplayer.

Each time your opponent moves, you must ask yourself '"what is *good* about that move?"' To control thinking you must ultimately control feeling, especially the emotion of contempt (see p. 70). Before you can win the game, you first have not to lose it. Train yourself to search for the *merits* of your opponents position. CAUTION is the main characteristic of the grandpatzer.

2.2 *Middle Game*

Well-meaning master annotations can be infelicitous for the non-master player. It does little good to mechanically play through master games move by move while reading off the annotations. It does not rub off on you. Often the most puzzling parts of the game are not commented on at all or the statement 'White has an advantage' is superfluous, White being a piece up. Grandmasters even disagree in their evaluation of positions.

Consider Game #6 in the Piatigorsky Tournament of 1966 between Spassky and Unzicker. This tournament book is most interesting because it gives the comments of both players. In this position:

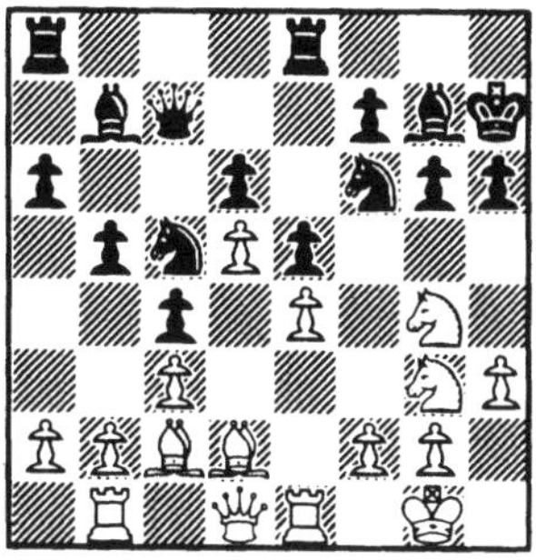

DIAGRAM 52. SPASSKY-UNZICKER, 1966

Spassky says: 'Also possible was 24 ♗×h6 ♘×g4 25 ♗×g7 ♘×f2 26 ♔×f2 ♔×g7 27 ♔g1 and the semi-open KB-file gives White chances for an attack'. Unzicker says: 'Not recommended was 24 ♗×h6 ♘×g4 25 ♗×g7 because of ♘×f2! 26 ♔×f2 ♔×g7 with very good prospects for Black'. So what are we to believe? Easy—forget it. Chess is a game full of uncertainties, mistakes, contradictions, conflicts, pressures, luck, give-an-take, disagreements, unpredictables, opinions, and so on. One does not learn much from an uncritical reading of master and grandmaster gospel.

But one must play through master games because your own games are too few in number to generate the required experience. And there is a way to profit from the study of master games. It is repeatedly beamed to us by Ken Smith in *Chess Digest.* Take a master game from *Chess Informant* or *Chess Player* in one of your opening systems. Look at the first move but not at the reply to it. (At first you may have to notch a card across an edge and slide it across the page so that you can see only one ply (half-move) at a time. But, with practice, you can discipline yourself simply not to look at the next move.) Now guess at the reply and then look at what the actual move was. If it's the same as yours, fine. If not, try to see why the master selected the move he did. Don't spend more than a few seconds over it, don't spend much time on the first few opening moves and don't spend more than 10–15 minutes on the whole game. Don't agonize over the fact that your selections do not match those of the masters. Sometimes your move might even be better but take it for granted the master's move is best. Study this way with current games from *Chess Informant* and *Chess Player*. What you are doing here is training your unconscious chess mind to conduct dynamic pattern-recognition, otherwise known as chess intuition. As you do this for hundreds and thousands of games, even going over the same games 10–20 times, your mind will *automatically* begin to grasp characteristic patterns which chess positions fall into. 'Fischer knows many positions' say the Soviets. Fischer himself says he knows many *types* of positions (I wonder what his secret classification is.) He obviously studied thousands of master games. Dynamic pattern recognition means that once a pattern is recognized, you know what sort of pattern it should be changed to in the next few moves. Guess-the-next move for both sides with every game you come across involving your particular opening system. Chess intuition will in time rub off on you. This has been the way masters have studied for years; they just never bothered to tell us about it until Ken Smith came along.

2.3 End Game

The most difficult part of the game to study is endings because you cannot imagine how one of your own games could ever arrive at such 'unusual' positions. Patzers complain 'What good is it to study Rook endings? Two weeks later I have forgotten it all'. This is absolutely true. You can experience the same openings over and over but play a Rook and Pawn ending maybe once in six months. But if you are going to become a grandpatzer, you must make yourself study endings over and over because this is where patzers are weakest. (To become a grandpatzer, one must learn how to beat patzers.) And remember, constant repetition is the key to remembering. I have studied Rook and Pawn endings in Keres' book so many times that the page-edges of that section are black from repeated thumbing. The endings are stable. No new discoveries in them have been made (or at least reported—masters have their own secrets) in the past 30–40 years.

If you uncritically follow master advice about studying endings, you are equally doomed to great wastes of time. Masters will have you studying the Bishop and Knight mate or some other monstrosity which never comes up. *TIME*—you have only so much *TIME* to devote to chess. The problem is how to use *TIME* effectively. You must be pragmatic and realistic. Don't waste your *TIME* studying endings where each side has two Queens and several Pawns. Study Rook and Pawn against Rook.

At first I used *Basic Chess Endings* by Fine to look up endings which occurred, or could have occurred, in my own games. The work was written in 1941 and has not been corrected since. It is charming, comprehensive, fascinating but *full of errors*. Many is the time I was driven to exasperation and frustration. I thought there was something wrong with me when Fine said the position was a draw, and I could see a win. For example, the position in Diagram 53 drove me bats.

Fine says this position is, in effect, the same as Diagram 54:

DIAGRAM 53.

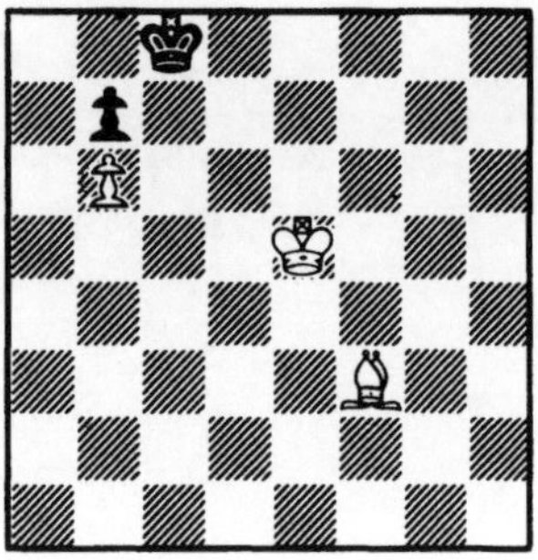

DIAGRAM 54.

This is a stalemate draw because the King cannot be driven out of the corner. But in Diagram 53, why doesn't Black simply play as follows?

1 ♔d1 ♗g3

(Fine says: '3 . . . ♔f2 stalemate')

2 ♔c1 ♔e2

3 ♔b1 ♔d1

4 ♔a1 ♔×c

I have wasted many hours agonizing over positions like this, being unnecessarily gullible about the authority of published opinions. Fortunately for all aspiring grandpatzers, Larry Evans has come along with a great column in *Chess Life and Review* in which a flood of corrections to BCE (including the above) have appeared. Buy a paperback copy of BCE and add the corrections as they appear.

Najdorf boasts 'I don't play endings.' That seems true of his style. For example, in Najdorf–Liberzon, Netanya 1975 in this position

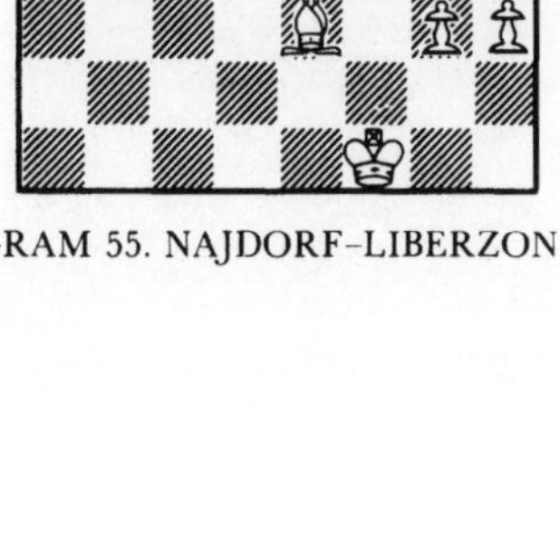

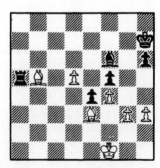

DIAGRAM 55. NAJDORF–LIBERZON, 1975

Najdorf played

42 ♗c4?	. . .

Where ♗c6 was a simple draw. White then went down as follows:

42 . . .	♗e7
43 g4	♔g6
44 d6	♗×d6
45 ♗e6	f×g4
46 h×g4	♗c5
47 ♔e2	♔f6
48 ♗g8	♗×e3
49 ♔×e3	♖a3+
50 ♔×e4	♖g3
51 g5+	♔g7
52 ♗d5	h5

And he even had a win as Black against Spassky, no less (Spassky–Najdorf, second Piatigorsky Tournament, 1966).

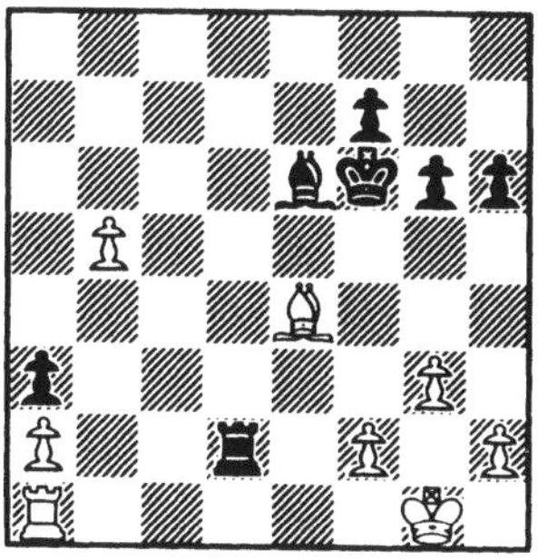

DIAGRAM 56. SPASSKY-NAJDORF, 1966

Najdorf played 31 . . . ♖×a2? and the game was drawn. The win is:

31 . . .	♖b2
32 ♖b1	♗×a2
33 ♖×b2	a×b2
34 b6	♗d5!
35 ♗b1	♔e5

I am not picking on Najdorf; *somebody* has to be an example. To appease his fans (grandmasters will scorn this book) here is an example to show he *can* play endings, Diagram 57.

1 ♖d3	

He wants the c-file.

1 . . .	♔e6
2 ♔f3	♖c8

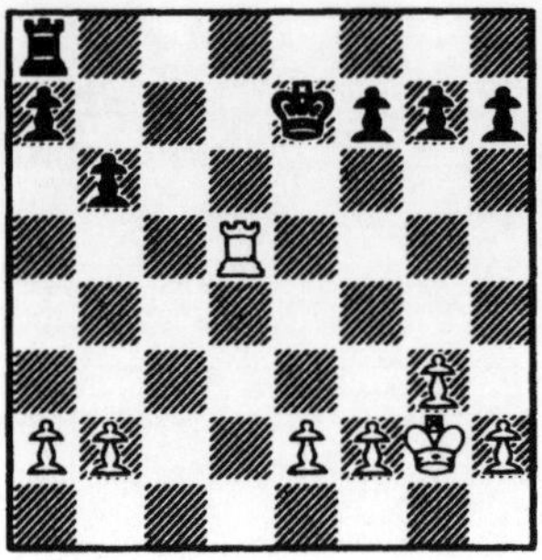

DIAGRAM 57. NAJDORF–KOTTNAUER, AMSTERDAM, 1950

3 ♖c3 ♖d8
4 ♖e3+ . . .

A beauty of a move. If the King goes to f5, White wins another Pawn.

4 . . . ♚f6
5 ♖d3 ♖c8
6 ♖c3 ♖d8
7 ♖c6+ . . .

And Black resigns because of the threat 8 ♖c7.

Patzers do not play endings much because somebody has won a piece or so in the middle game and it is all over before the ending is arrived at. But grandpatzers play endings. In fact, the safest (if unimaginative) way not to lose against patzers is to continuously swap everything off to get to an ending, a stage which patzers seldom get to, never study and hence are quite at sea. But the simplifications involved carry with them the danger of forcing the patzer into a draw since he has few options to make bad decisions about.

It took me a long time as a patzer to realize the real object of the game was *not* to win a piece or force a brilliant mate but to arrive at the following position (Diagram 58). This simple but overpowering truth is a grandpatzer secret to be treasured.

Knowing this secret will tell you how to win this frequently occurring position (Diagram 59) as White and draw it as Black. White on the move must play b5 to block the pawn, bring up the King and capture on b6. If he plays the King to e4, Black plays b5, takes the opposition and draws. If it is Black's move, he draws with b5.

Chessbooks are known to be generous with the contradictory advice, as in Bishop and Pawn endings—'Never put your Pawns on the same color as your own Bishop because this makes it a bad Bishop and do not put your Pawns on squares that can be attacked by his Bishop'. That is, if his Bishop

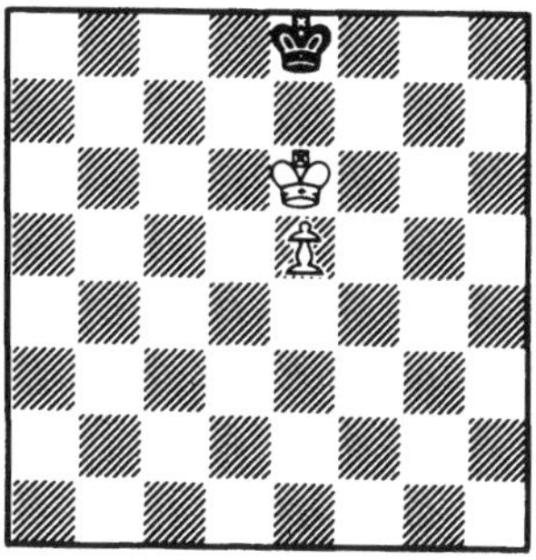

DIAGRAM 58.
THE OBJECT OF THE GAME

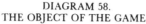

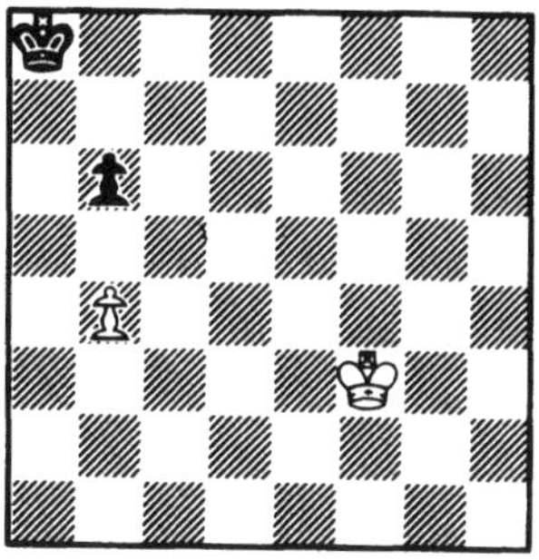

DIAGRAM 59.

is black, put your Pawns on safe white Squares, but that makes your white colored Bishop bad. The real secret here is to keep your Pawns off the squares of the same color as your Bishop and not worry about his Bishop picking off your Pawns. You want to control squares of both colors as much as possible. Mobility and two-color control are everything in these endings because freedom of action and occupation of both colored squares provides a greater variety of lines to choose from.

It always irritated the patzer in me when annotators dismissed the remainder of a game with 'the rest is a matter of technique', implying it's a simple win although I could see all kinds of play and counterplay in the position. Mednis in *Chess Life and Review* has now given us a clear explanation of what this otherwise obscure phrase means and I pass it on to you in gratitude.

(1) Don't allow counterplay.
(2) Deep material advantage.
(3) Establish a clear plan and stick to it.
(4) Be careful—CAUTION!
(5) Hurry not.
(6) Avoid complications.
(7) Simplify to a known theoretical win.
(8) Keep working, the game will not play itself.

Here is how I, as White, was able to follow this good advice against another grandpatzer last year (Diagram 60): White is a Pawn up, has a better King position, and the Bishops are not of opposite colors. The only danger is that Black might draw using the old Bishop-of-the-wrong-color trick (See p. 79). Otherwise it's a matter of following the rules outlined by Mednis:

Rule (7) 'Simplify to a known theoretical win'

1	♗f4	♗e1
2	♔d5	a5

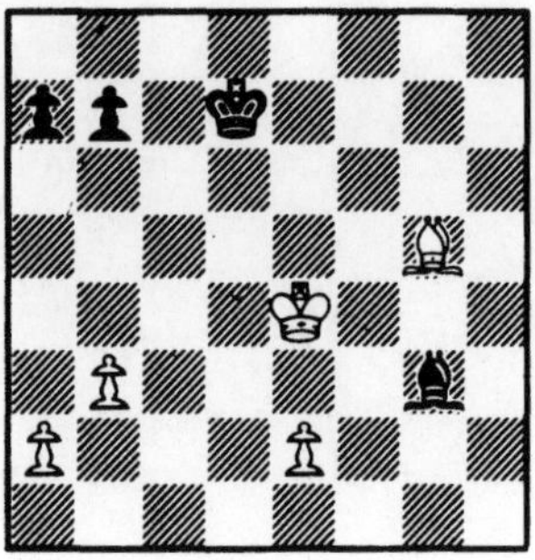

DIAGRAM 60.

Rule (1) 'Don't allow counterplay' and Rule (6) 'Avoid complications'

3	a4	♗b4
4	♗g5	♔c7

Rule (3) 'Establish a clear plan and stick to it'. White is going to push the passed Pawn until something goes.

5	e4	♔d7
6	e5	♗e1
7	e6+	♔e8

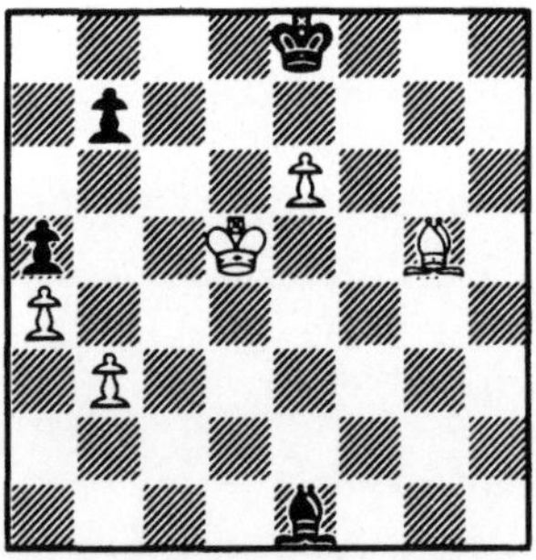

DIAGRAM 61.

Rule (8) 'Keep working'

8	♗f4	♗f2
9	♗d6	♔d8
10	♔c4	♗e3

Rule (4) 'Be careful' and Rule (2) 'Keep material advantage'. White doesn't want Black to pick up the passed Pawn for nothing.

11	♔b5	♗d2
12	♔b6	♔c8

13 ♗c5	♗e1
14 e7	♔d7
15 ♔×b	♗h4
16 ♔b6	♗e1
17 ♔b5	♗d2

Rule (7) 'Simplify to a known theoretical win'

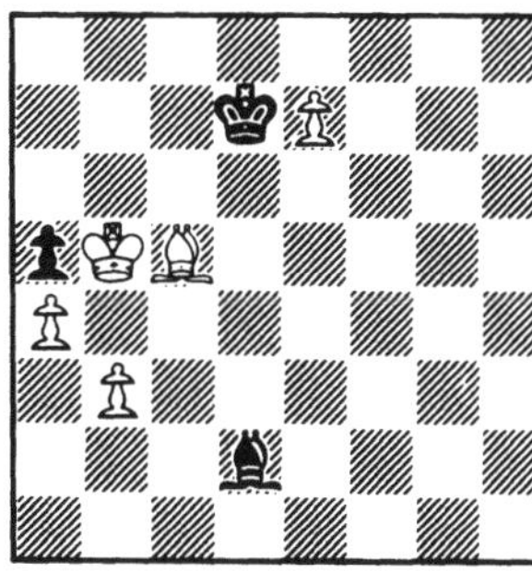

DIAGRAM 62. POSITION AFTER 17 . . . ♗d2

18 ♗b6	♔×e
19 ♗×a	♗f4

Rule (6) 'Avoid complications'. White keeps the Black King from a8 to avoid any drawing tricks.

20 ♔c6	♗g3
21 ♗b6	♗b8
22 a5	Resigns

This is how 'with technique' you inexorably grind out the win, surely, safely, solidly.

Watch out for myths like '*Always* put the Rook behind a passed Pawn', and '*Always* take the opposition'. For example, in this position:

DIAGRAM 63.

If White places the Rook behind the Pawn, Black draws:

1	♖c7	♔d5
2	♔g7	♔d4
3	♔f6	c3
4	♔f5	♔d3
5	♔f4	c2
6	♔f3	♔d2

.e should win as follows:

1	♖h5	♔d6
2	♔g7	c3
3	♖h3	c2
4	♖c3	. . .

A blind following of immediately taking the opposition can throw the win away and even lose. For example (Diagram 64): If White takes the opposition with ♔e1, it is a draw. ♔g2!, threatening to bypass and invade via h5, is the right move so that if 1 . . . ♔f6 or ♔f8 2 ♔f2! gains the opposition. In Diagram 65 when White moves ♔f3, if Black takes the opposition with ♔f7?, he loses to ♔g3.

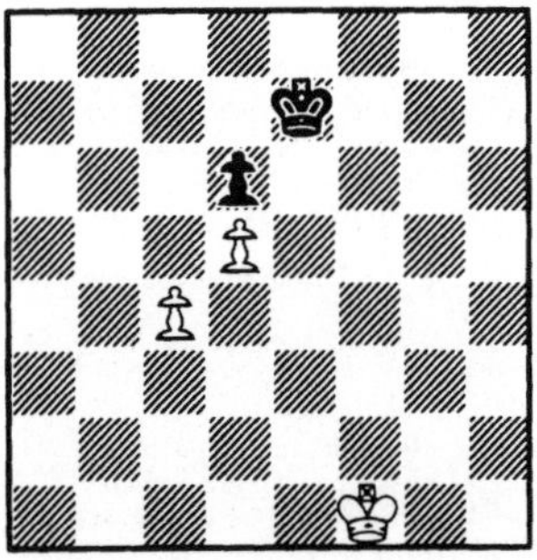

DIAGRAM 64.

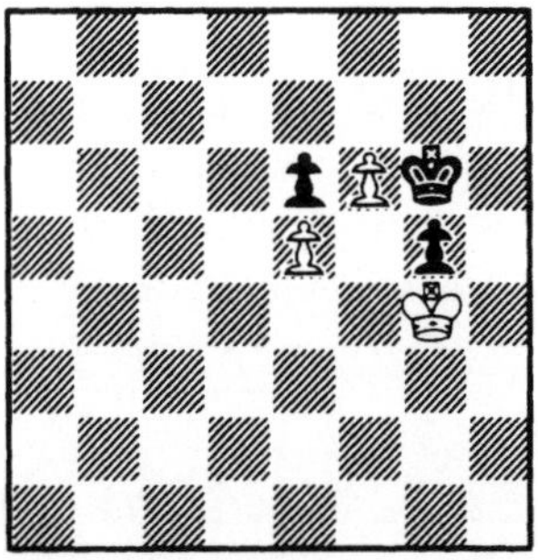

DIAGRAM 65.

Another endgame myth to be wary of is that 'Bishops of opposite colors draw, even when one side is a Pawn up'. I sat back and lost several games this way before I realized this is by no means a routine draw and must be played *very carefully*. Consider this beautiful win by Botvinnik (Kotov–Botvinnik, Moscow 1955) (Diagram 66).

1	. . .	g5!!
2	f×g	. . .

White loses after 2 h×g h4 3 ♗d6 ♗f5 4 g6 ♗×g 5 f5 ♗×f6 ♔×b3 ♔g2 because he must give up the Bishop for the h-Pawn.

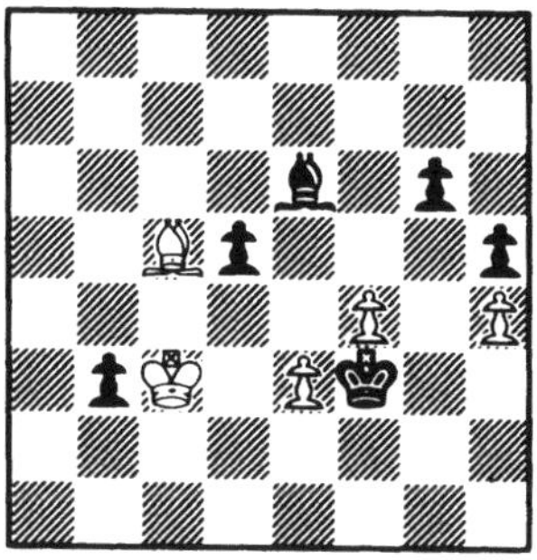

DIAGRAM 66. KOTOV–BOTVINNIK, 1955

2 . . .	d4+
3 e×d	♔g3
4 ♗a3	. . .

If 4 ♗e7 ♔×h4 5 g6+ ♔g4 wins.

4 . . .	♔×h4
5 ♔d3	♔×g5
6 ♔e4	h4
7 ♔f3	♗d5+

and White resigned.

These 'rules', 'principles', 'maxims', or whatever they may be called, should be used only as mnemonics, reminders of what to think about. *Think* about taking the open file or putting the Rook behind the passed Pawn but don't *automatically* do it. 'Rules' have many exceptions (some have more exceptions than instances) and blindly following them will throw away wins into draws and even lose you a lot of games.

Add the corrections to Fine, study the endgame books by Hooper, Keres, Averbach, Euwe and Hooper, going through them time and again.

In the back of each issue of *Chess Informant* are end-games from current play. Use the guess-the-next-move method. As mentioned, it is difficult to make oneself study these endings because one cannot foresee how one would ever find oneself in such weird positions. But you must know the endings well because (1) this is where you will beat patzers, and (2) as you get stronger against grandpatzers, the games will last longer and longer into the endings. A win against a 2100 player or a draw against a master constitutes a rating victory for a grandpatzer.

2.4 Combinations

Hans Müller studied 8000 master games played between 1900 and 1950. A staggering 82% were won by tactical combinations. An even higher percentage at the patzer and grandpatzer level are won by means of combinations. Hence I will recommend study of this aspect of the game above all others. One beats patzers through (1) combinations, and (2) end-game play with combinations reigning supreme. It is the combinational powers of computers which makes them so strong. They can calculate the combinations accurately and so must you.

What is a combination? It is extremely difficult to define in words. To Botvinnik a combination is a forced variation with sound (advantageous) sacrifice. He contrasts it with a forced maneuver which is a forced variation without sacrifice. Botvinnik assumes the advantage gained by a combination is clear. Bronstein amended this with the idea that the resultant advantage may be unclear or incalculable. So let us define a combination as a forced variation with sacrifice that yields a material or positional advantage which may or may not be clear. Most of the time let us hope it is clear or the combination would not be undertaken. A small percentage of the time the advantage of the sacrifice may not be entirely calculable and an intuition or feeling of advantage may be all that we can go on.

Books and articles giving positions where combinations win must be gone over repeatedly but don't spend too much time on each position—there may be an error in the published diagram. If you do not solve a given position, put a check mark alongside it along with the date. Next time through the book or article see if you can do the ones that were missed before. If not, put another check mark and the date. Over time you will notice that you accumulate check marks for certain kinds of positions and that as late as a few months ago, you missed a particular combination. This tells you what sort of chess blindspots or myopia you have. In my copy of Reinfeld's book *1001 Brilliant Chess Sacrifices and Combinations*, I have as many as eight check-marks alongside some diagrams and one as late as 9/13/76. Here is the position which has so often baffled me:

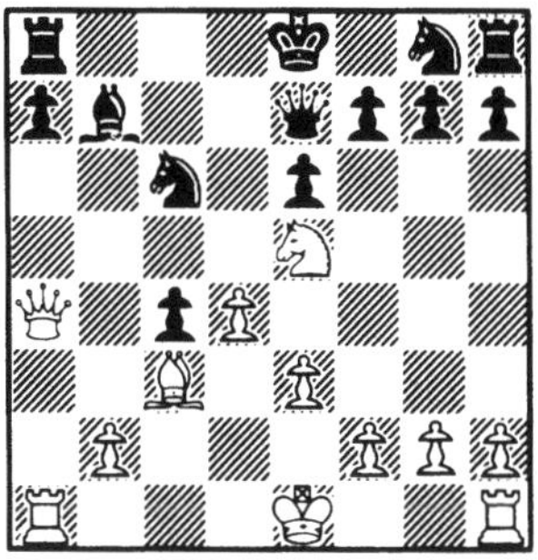

DIAGRAM 67.

White moves and wins. If you see it, you are a better man (in this position) than I am.

Here is another position I have repeatedly missed but this one has only seven check-marks beside it and I haven't missed it for the past two years:

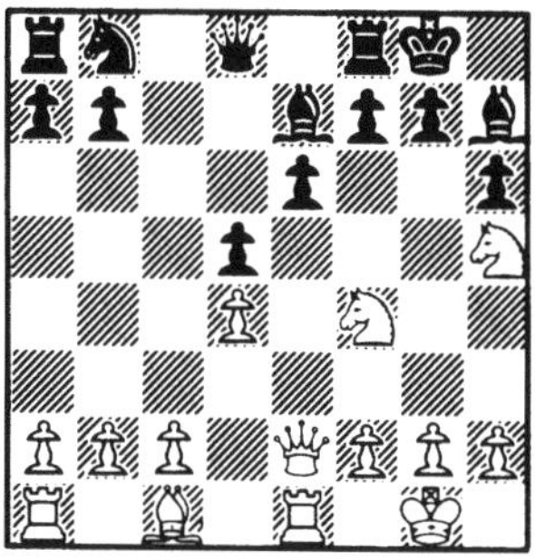

DIAGRAM 68.

This one is trickier than the first, but it should not be beyond the powers of a true grandpatzer. If you don't see it, don't write me.

In studying positions known to contain a beneficial combination, you should be striving for *accuracy* of calculation. Finding the first move is not enough; you must analyze the sequence of moves accurately—no holes allowed. As we shall see, it is this accurate combinational ability which makes the Great Grandpatzer Machine so formidable. Of course it is of great advantage to know that a combination exists on a position. During actual play, many combinational opportunities are simply missed. It would help us all if chess periodicals published positions in which there may or may not be a combination and the problem is to decide which situation is the case.

In the *Chess Informant* and *Chess Player* a diagram is given at the crucial point in the game in which a decisive move was (or could be) made. One must try to solve these for every diagram, not just the ones within your opening systems. *Chess Informant* also has combinations from current play collected in the back. Some of these are far too deep to be solved in a few minutes so skip them. I have found the combinations in the front of *Chess Life and Review* to contain too many misprints and errors, making them too exasperating to deal with. The ones in *Chess·Digest*, however, are usually accurate. The *Chess Player* diagrams tend to have amusing errors such as these below where in Diagram 69 a third Black Rook takes on c7 and gives White an advantage. And where c5 is an excellent move in Diagram 70 because White has three Bishops. My belief is that it is impossible to publish an error-free chess book, which the reader can easily verify from his experiences with this one.

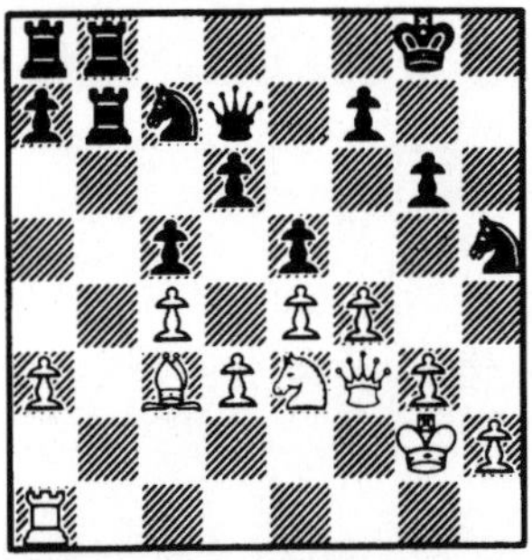

DIAGRAM 69. PRIBYL–FINN, 1975 (CHESSPLAYER #9)

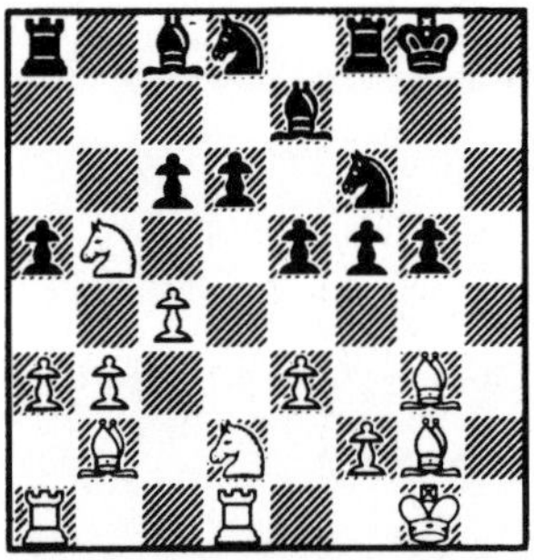

DIAGRAM 70. POLUGAEVSKY–CLEMENS, 1974 (CHESSPLAYER #7)

The great problem with all study is *TIME*. You have a job, family, friends, dogs, plants, other pastimes. You are lucky if you can study 3–4 hours a week. The trick is to concentrate and use the *TIME* efficiently. I know my own weakness is combinations. I have a bad case of chess myopia in that I just don't see many of the potentials in a position. Hence I spend much of my *TIME* trying to overcome this chess blindness by studying diagrams in which a winning combination lurks. I study current variations of my pet openings as they appear in the literature. I now study only those endings that my own games lead to. Everyone has to find his own way to distribute study-time. Playing time is distributed for you.

III
How to Play

3.1 How to Think

Thinking over-the-board involves inner speech acts, talking to oneself. Fischer advises us 'Look ahead' and 'Concentrate'. But look ahead at *what* and concentrate on *what?* Beginners look at everything because they have not yet developed 'chunking' abilities (lumping the information into units larger than the positions of individual men). Patzers lack good rejective mechanisms which tell them what is irrelevant. Intensity of attention is fine, but it is important to know what *not* to think about. Patzers waste time by analyzing specific variations when it is the opponent's turn to move. In his book, *Think Like a Grandmaster*, Kotov finally gives us the masters' secret: when it is your turn to move, analyze specific variations; when it is your opponent's turn to move, ponder about more general considerations. What does this mean in practice?

The greatest mistake patzers make when it is their turn to move is immediately to talk to themselves about what their next move is going to be. Obsessed with their own intentions, they charge ahead as if the opponent had no intentions of his own and often act as if the opponent did not even exist. Your first inner speech act should be:

'''STOP—WHAT IS HIS THREAT?'''

(Remember I place talking-to-oneself, inner speech expressions, in triple quotes.) That is, you must suppose *it is not your turn to move, it's his and what can he now do?* Make believe it is his turn to move, not yours. '''What bad thing can he now do to me?''' ('Mistrust is the most necessary characteristic of the chessplayer'—Tarrasch'). '''Stop, there is a *danger* here; what is it?''' It took me a long apprenticeship as a patzer to realize this first step of '''STOP—THREAT''' in analyzing the position. Kotov doesn't even mention it. He says just go ahead and select the candidates for the next move. Evans does make a point of it in his chapter in *How To Open A Chess Game*. (Ken Smith and Evans are the best advisors for patzers and grandpatzers.)

Finding the threat takes a simple form of intelligent inner speech questions which you ask yourself while *making believe it is your opponent's turn to move*:

"'"Can he check?"'"
"'"Can he capture something?"'"
"'"Is there a pin?"'"
"'"Is there a fork?"'"
"'"Is there a double attack"'"
"'"Is there a weak Pawn?"'"
"'"Is there a weak square?"'"
"'"Is there a Pawn push?"'"

Once you see what the threat is, you can decide what steps to take to thwart it, since it is, in reality, your turn to move. Or you can decide to ignore the threat. The latter course is dangerous. (CAUTION characterizes the grandpatzer. Having been burned so many times, whenever I see my King and Queen lined up on the same file, I immediately get nervous no matter how many pieces and Pawns are in front of them.) If you see no threat, only then begin to consider your next move which does not have to take into account any immediate disaster.

The threats are mainly tactical in nature in patzer and grandpatzer chess. Tactics means doing something; strategy means planning when there is nothing to do. While it was your opponent's turn to move, you have already been thinking about general positional considerations involving the major ideas of this particular opening, that radiant center, (keep your eye on the flank but your mind on the center), King safety, Pawn structure, diagonals, lines, the connectivity of the pieces and "'"What is he trying to do in general?"'" Naturally there is overlap and interplay between tactical and positional considerations. (These vaporous statements abound in chess books.)

Fischer advises us 'Look ahead'. When it is my opponents turn to move, and I have examined the rough positional aspects, and there is no other game I want to check for the opening being used, and I don't need a little stroll for my circulation, I am inclined to look at each piece, each Pawn, and each square. I wonder about what each piece may want (anthropomorphically) to do and what is going to happen on each square in the future. This is TIME-consuming and should only be done on your opponent's time when there is nothing else to do. Such browsings usually take place late in the opening or early positional middle game. Later on, things get too hectic for the luxury of these elaboratenesses. The position opens up, combinations become possible, fatigue becomes a factor, the clock runs faster, and TIME begins running out.

Let's assume it is your turn to move, you have passed the 6–10 moves memory stage of the opening, you are in the positional middle game, and there is no serious threat. Kotov says to select a set of candidate moves with the vague advice to select 'as many as seem necessary in the given circumstances'. I find this hard to do. (That's only one reason why I am not a master.) I select a move and analyze it a few moves, then select another and try it out, and so on. In this process, the greatest TIME-waste consists of returning several times to a move previously analyzed. C. H. O'D. Alexander, a British master, described the situation perfectly:

'I analyze line A, don't greatly like it, leave it in the middle and look at B, leave that in the middle, have another quick glance at A, then look at C and D, take another look at A, B, C, and D more or less simultaneously, look at the clock and find I have taken about twenty minutes, think I must move, play line E (not previously examined) after about 30 seconds thought and spend the rest of the game regretting it.'

Does this remind you of anyone? Such unsystematic floundering around is very hard to control. This is what distinguishes great players from the rest of us lesser lights; they discipline themselves to conduct systematic analysis.

Depth of analysis counts for little among patzers and grandpatzers. It is *accuracy* of calculation which counts. Unless the moves are forced, there is no point in looking deeper than 6–8 ply (half-moves) because there are too many possibilities for flaws in the analysis. ('Long analysis is wrong analysis'—Lasker.) An accurate 5–6 ply usually suffices. For example: '"(1) I go there, (2) He goes there, (3) I go there, (4) He goes there, (5) I go there and that looks good for me."' It is that final judgement of the preferred position at the end of the analysis ('"that looks good for me"') which matters and which is so difficult for the patzer to evaluate. He may look at the same moves as a master but judge that the position which eventuates is 'bad' whereas the master sees without further calculation that it is 'good' or at least 'not bad'. The master knows what matters.

The final move selected cannot always be the 'best' move. A patzer thinks he has to be perpetually doing something fierce, forceful, fiery, or scintillating. In many positions, there is no best move and a modest one suffices, especially if it restrains or frustrates your opponent's intentions. But the move selected should be the result of a concentrated intelligent effort, a treasure. 'Every move is a treasure to be spent only in the most useful way'—Gligorich. Intelligent means selecting what is best in a situation. In chess, it is what is good enough *given the TIME limitations*.

Evans teaches us: 'Make the best move each time and let the chips fall where they may. You can't force your opponent to blunder, so relax and try to avoid making one yourself. Accumulate small advantages and keep piling on the pressure.'

We are all cognitively lazy. Mechanical, automatic, and superficial selections have cost me many a game. This usually happens in the latter stages of the game when I am too tired for self-admonitions. (Danger, Danger, Caution, Caution!)

How to avoid the blunder? With what I shall call (seeking eponymic fame) the Grandpatzer 3-Step. Step 1 = "'Stop—what is his threat?'" Step 2 = Thwart it if necessary, otherwise pick a move. Step 3 = Imagine in your mind's-eye that you have made the move and cycle back to the Step 1 rule, "'Stop—threat.'" That is, if I make my selected move, "'*Now* what is his threat?'" But suppose when you return to Step 1, you see another threat. You must now analyze how to deal with *it*. It looks like you can get into an infinite loop here because of endless threats in which every time you get to Step 3 you must return to Step 1 and to go through the cycle again. But there are no endless threats unless the position is totally lost. Here is a helpful secret used in fact by large chess-playing computers. You analyze until the position becomes quiet or dead; that is, a stable position in which no material can be further exchanged and no immediate threat exists (that you can see, which is, of course, a trouble). Quiescence or stability does not mean the position is not *positionally* alive, only that it is dead from the standpoint of material exchanges by the opponent and he has no direct threat at his disposal.

Kotov in *Think Like A Grandmaster* reminds us of 'Blumenfeld's Rule'. He suggests you write down your move, without making it, and then look at the position again 'through the eyes of a patzer'. This is, check the position for elementary one-move threats. My only emendation of this 'rule' is that you do it both before and after writing down the move. The interruption of writing takes your attention away from the board momentarily so that when you look back at the position it will be with a somewhat fresh view and you can check against those simple oversights which characterize the losing of most patzer games. If you now see your selection is a mistake, you can cross out the move on the score sheet and replace it with a (hopefully) better one. Careful here, distrust your subsequent choices even more so. One blunder often leads to another because a 'blundering' mood seems to take on a momentum of its own. A patzer will often select a blunder, and then select a move which constitutes an even worse blunder.

The above maxims apply to the entire game beyond the point where your memory of the opening ceases and the positional middle game begins. If you know your opening lines by heart for 6–12 moves, you are saving not only time but a great amount of energy you will need later in the game. You do not have to conduct the Grandpatzer 3-Step each time on these first memorized moves if your opponent is following the expected lines.

You will not be spending energy fighting uphill on your own resources and you can be emotionally relaxed *knowing* nothing bad will happen because masters and grandmasters have already seen to that by doing all the work for you. On the slightest deviation, naturally, you must shift into the Grandpatzer 3-Step and no longer reel things off by rote. But the position will still contain something of the original line which may turn out to be useful.

All the books advise you to construct plans, short-range and long-range. But as experience with the Great Grandpatzer Machine is teaching us (See Chapter V), it is not necessary to have an elaborate plan to play strong grandpatzer chess. To be a master or grandmaster perhaps one must understand the planning of sophisticated positional play. But the Great Grandpatzer Machine beats almost everybody except a master and it has hardly any plans at all. It just waits for combinational opportunities. Should nature copy art? In this case, yes. Your initial plan stems from the nature of the opening system and its major ideas which guide you into the positional middle game. For example, if it is the English Opening, your plan is to try to get something like Diagram 71 or 72 in which all the pieces are harmoniously (connectedly) developed and the center is strongly held. This is what you are striving for and your opponent, in the meantime, may have a say or two about it.

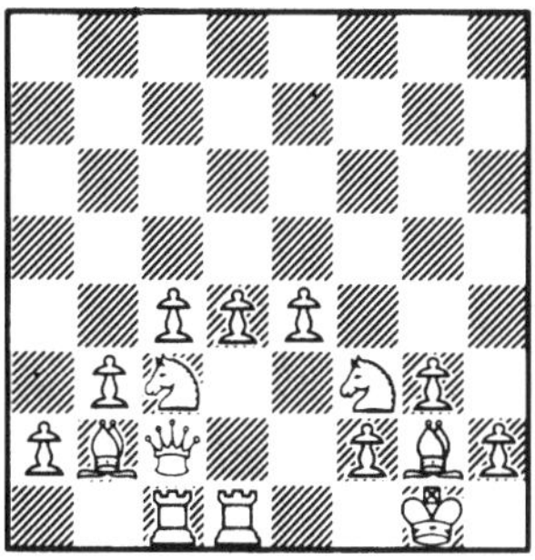

DIAGRAM 71.

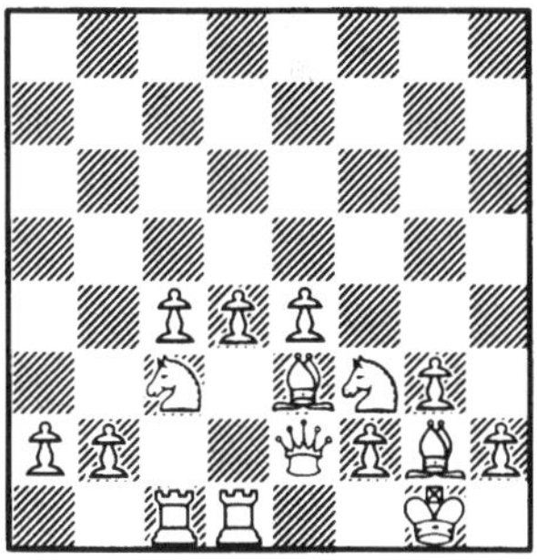

DIAGRAM 72.

Once into the positional middle game and your are on you own, the plan 'derives from the characteristics of the position', as Pachman says (*Modern Chess Strategy*). Your guess-the-next-move study will pay off here if you have not made the mistake of studying your preferred opening variations for only 15 moves or so. 'You must play through the complete game'—Ken Smith. When you study through the complete game by guessing the next move, you are building middlegame plans into the action part of your dynamic pattern-recognizer. You want to get to the combinational middle game intact. If you have done your homework as prescribed, something will automatically tell you when to combine, or if no combinations exist, to go into the ending.

The hardest thing to do is to keep up the recommended Grandpatzer 3-Step move after move, all the way through the game, especially when the heated hurly-burly of it all gets exciting. I tend to get slovenly, lazy, and reckless as *TIME* and energy run out. It's so easy for me to fall into the following inner monologue: "'The hell with it—that move is good enough—if it isn't, let's pack it in and go home—I'm tired of all this—there's more to life than chess—you can't work all day and play good chess hour after hour at night.'" The lack of sustained will-power and the making of 'what-the-hell' moves is another reason one does not become a master.

3.2 *Nerves*

At the start of a tournament game, everybody is a little nervous. It's amazing how often the board is set up incorrectly, with a Black, instead of a White square in the lower right corner. (Incidentally, for some reason the board is almost always set up incorrectly in this manner in advertisements and on TV). Twice, I have even played several moves before either of us noticed this error. Once against a 1900 player noted for his contempt of others, I, a bit drunkenly (but not intentionally), set up the board incorrectly. This raised his disgust and lowered his caution so much that I was able to swindle him in a combinatorial middle game, to which he paid little attention because I was an obvious patzer dimmed by alcohol.

Speaking of being nervous and being drunk, I have found it useful to be slightly swacked at the start of a game. Holmov, a Soviet grandmaster, was suspended from tournaments for a year for drinking too much. He went a bit too far with it but he sure could make some great moves. In this position:

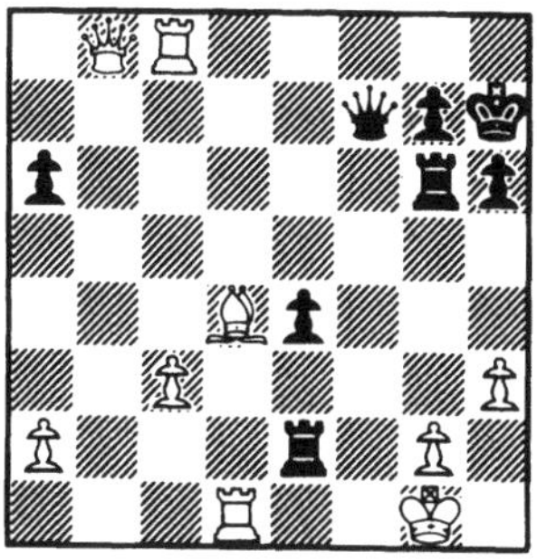

DIAGRAM 73. SAKHAROV-HOLMOV, KIEV, 1965

It would take somebody who is very loose to see that the faraway capture on a2 will be decisive, so he does not start with the prosaic 1 . . . ♖g×g+. Instead:

1 . . .	♖e×g+!
2 ♔h1	♖h2+!!
3 ♔×h	♕×a2+

which leads to mate. If 3 ♕×h ♕f3+ also mates.

I know this is heresy (my daughter typed this as 'heresay', which is probably an improvement) but I advise a few drinks before a serious game. This is hard to do when the game begins in the morning but afternoon and evening games are ideal for this opportunity. Some players drink coffee, but, if sober, that can make you all the more jittery. Younger players smoke drugs or take amphetamines and I once played a young 2300 player who was zonked on LSD. He made some very exotic moves and beat me in a most bewildering game. He is now a senior master, but I'll bet he doesn't play under LSD any more. It's too devastating to the continuity of thought; it tends to sizzle the mind.

Anything to calm down your nerves is good. Chew gum. Fischer eats and drinks enormous quantities. I used to smoke large cigars until smoking was banned in my club. It is not good to drink more booze during the game because you get more drunk. Even Alekhine couldn't handle it. Speed (methamphetamine) is too heavy.

First you get the board set up, ready the clock and score sheet, shake hands with your opponent, etc. Then begin to size him up as a person. Computers do not evaluate people from their appearances and you should not either. It is a very dangerous thing to do for reasons I will now spell out. The greatest psychological danger for an aspiring grandpatzer lies in playing the ego-game. In physical sports, playing the ego-game is expressed by the formula 'I am better than you are', the 'better' referring to strength, speed, skill, etc. In chess, this formula unfortunately becomes, 'I am smarter than you are'; that is, it takes on an intelligence dimension. Since chess is a struggle of ideas, the winner is smarter, right? This belief leads to the downfall of many a patzer who sees the game as a test of intelligence. He associates intelligence with personal self-worth. Now victory means pride and loss means shame and humiliation. The outer game of chess becomes an inner game of esteem with the ever-hovering threat of personal humiliation. The Greeks called aversion *phobos*, and it had two forms, aversion to harm which produced fear, and aversion to disgrace, which produced shame. One unlucky way to minimize and prevent shame-induced distress is to adopt the paranoid mode of thought in which the cause of distress is mislocated in the evil intentions of others instead of in one's own imperfections. Witness how paranoid the Soviets became as Fischer began to beat Spassky; they even had the playing chairs taken apart to find hidden malevolent influences that must have been affecting their losing player. How else were they to explain this humiliating defeat?

John Dewey said the deepest human urge is to feel important. Nobody wants to be a nobody. It is precarious to use chess as a way to defeat a sense of nobodiness. (If a Martian came here, he would be astounded to hear of the powers of our 'Nobody'. 'Nobody' is perfect; 'Nobody' can give birth to himself'; 'Nobody' can be in two places at once.)

Alekhine felt chess was a matter of vanity. Capablanca, in 1913, had the mayor of Havana clear the playing room so no one would see him resign to Marshall. If you size up your opponent as 'dumb', you ('the great me') are in great danger from your most dangerous opponent, yourself. 'Vanity rather than wisdom determines how the world is run'—Vonnegut.

Shame and humiliation originate in childhood from being ridiculed and treated with contempt by others. Of all the various types of game-players and athletes I have known, chess players suffer most, both as subjects and objects, from the emotion of contempt. When Alekhine referred to appealing to your opponent's 'vanity', I think he had something like this in mind. Chess players, from patzer to grandmaster, tend to look down on the opponent; they try, and usually manage, to find something imperfect or inadequate about him. Most masters I know have absolute contempt for chess-playing computers but of course there is a growing threat to them here. I remember vividly a tournament opponent of mine who was a 75 year old, trembly-handed janitor for a grammar school in a back-country California town. He opened the game atrociously, moving the same Knight four times. I couldn't believe he would want to enter a tournament. He won the game. Nimzovich protested allowing a 'stupid idiot' of a player to enter a tournament and then lost to him!

I have never seen a 'noble gesture' in chess. Have you? Why is this? Is it because of some characteristic of *chess* players? (Since we are not noblemen, why should we be expected to be noble?) It is obvious that compassion can hurt your own chances in any sport. Here is a good example of unnecessary largesse. My opponent was a young unrated Chicano with little English and new to a country where life is not easy for him. I felt sorry for him. In this position (Diagram 74), after a Smith–Morra gambit (he knew it quite well, which should have been a tip-off), White touched the Rook on c3, released it, and played ♕×d4. I said nothing but should have made him move the Rook (♖g3 is the only move) whereupon I trade Queens, win the Pawn on a2 and am two Pawns up in the ending. The game dragged on for another 22 moves because my domination of the Queen-file was not enough for a quick decision. Black won, but this sort of generosity can be

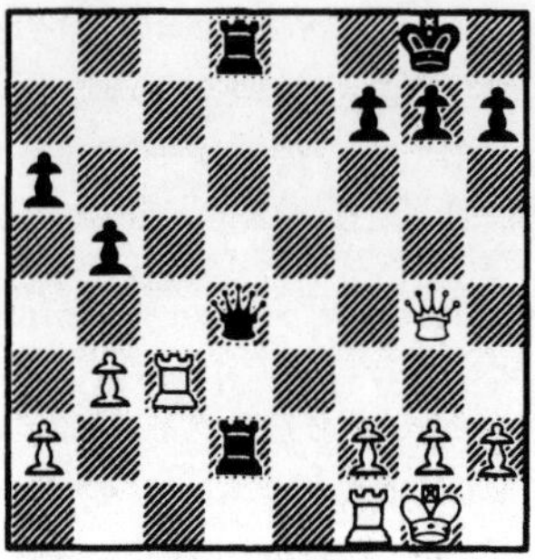

DIAGRAM 74.

dangerous. Especially in cases like this when it turned out that the unrated White player achieved a rating of 1835 in the tournament!

A grandmaster said, 'I have never had the satisfaction of beating a perfectly healthy opponent'. If you realize this excessive pride of chess players, it may be worth a Pawn or more. Some booked-up teen-agers are the best examples of contempt-in-action. They have three or four chessbooks at their side (one in Russian) along with a math text or something by Sartre. They can play blitz chess at blinding speed, talking and joking about the crazy Polugaevsky variation in the Najdorf. They treat you as vermin, view your moves with disgust, slam the pieces around with curled upper lip, read while you are analyzing, take 5 minutes to your 50, sneeringly try to blow you off the board and slaughter you if you don't look out. The way to get an edge on them is to increase their conceit and disdain for you by acting as bumbling as possible. Of course, being a bit drunk helps this role immensely.

Alcohol is an inhibitor, not a stimulant, but the brain involves inhibitory as well as excitory processes. You want to inhibit the inhibitory processes and depress the excitatory ones. I am told that some champion Olympic pistol shooters perform best when quite drunk. You've got to be very relaxed to have a steady hand. The more you try to control it, the tighter you get, and the more the hand shakes. Advanced intoxication is not good for chess because you can't concentrate and tend to want to drop the whole scene and adjourn to the nearest bar for a couple more belts. (There are eight bars within one block of my chess club).

In chess, and in all sports, it is not just concentration but *relaxed* concentration which must be achieved. Some chess players are so tight, they jiggle their legs constantly. This can be unnerving to an opponent who can feel the table shaking. The leg-jiggler and the constant-cougher are opponents to be feared because they can upset your own relaxed concentration. I tend to get annoyed at the cougher (why doesn't he take a cough pill to stop the cough?) so I know I have to find ways to distance myself from it. Being swacked helps. Not too swacked. If you feel too good, then you can't take the game seriously, losing determination and tenacity.

Moving the pieces can be a problem of nerves against opponents who don't quite get them in the middle of the squares and repeated 'J'adoube'-ing is required. Some opponents 'j'adoube' the piece you have moved after every move. I used to think there was a rule that you could only adjust your own pieces, not the opponents, but I was wrong. You can adjust pieces only when it is your turn to move. A well-known, high-ranking woman player adjusts several pieces after each move, even ones that have been sitting there for 10 moves and which she has adjusted several times before. It's hard, but you can't let such annoyances rattle you.

3.3 *Pressures*

All sorts of pressures besiege the player over the board. A general inventory of them is of little use. Each grandpatzer must find, know., and attempt to control his own. One man's meat is another man's poisson. I know players who became so extremely tense and excited when they have a winning position that it is unbearable to watch them because they are so vulnerable to making a quick blunder in this state. Other players look so cool and nonchalant, only careful study of the board reveals they are absolutely lost.

To be a master one needs good physical and mental stamina. But health, mental or physical, is not necessary for the grandpatzer. If you look at a group of us in a chess club tournament, you will observe what wrecks we are. We play in rating tournaments at night after working all day. I, and my opponents, are tired, coughing, aching, aging, etc. Two guys are in wheelchairs, one has severe crippling arthritis, I have hypertrophic pulmonary osteoarthropathy, a bad back, and so on. Having problems is not the problem; it's what you do in spite of them that counts. To rise above physical illness and pain, to strive for your best in spite of these distressful states, represents a challenge for the aspiring grandpatzer with aristic goals.

Discouragement and despair come early to the patzer. He even becomes contemptuous of himself for blundering. Capablanca said you have to lose a thousand games before you become any good. And you will always lose them. The patzer tends to give up both during and after a game. During the game, when he gets a piece or even a couple of Pawns down, he becomes demoralized, resigned and even actually resigns. For example, here is a game of mine against a 1600-rated patzer (White).

1 d4	♘f6
2 c4	g6
3 ♘c3	♗g7
4 e4	d6

5 ♗e2 0–0
6 ♘f3 e5
7 0–0 ♘c6
8 d5 ♘e7
9 ♗d2 ♘e8
10 ♘e1 f5

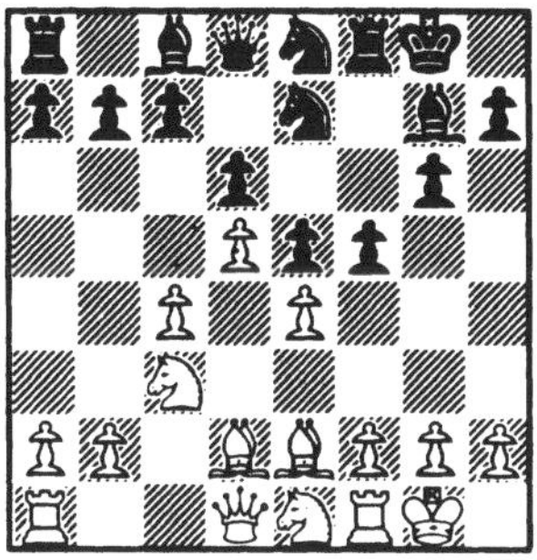

DIAGRAM 75. POSITION AFTER 10 . . . f5

All book and very straightforward. This patzer may not be a patzer for long.

11 ♘d3 f4
12 f3 g5
13 ♖c1 h5
14 c5 ♘g6
15 c×d c×d

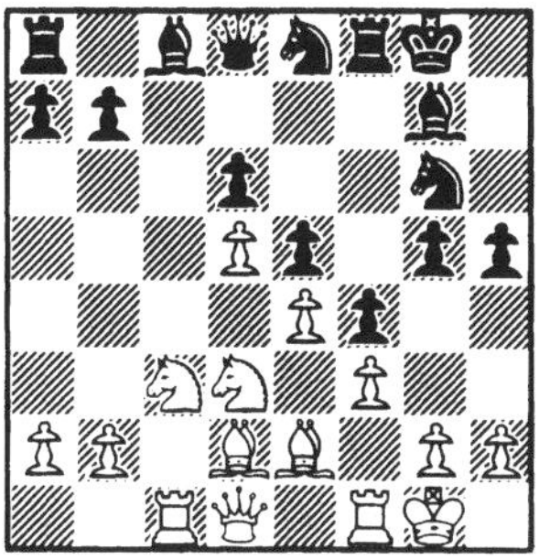

DIAGRAM 76. POSITION AFTER 15 . . . c×d

White knows what he is doing. Careful, careful, *caution*.

16 ♘f2 ♖f7

17	♘b5	a6
18	♕a4??	♗d7
19	Resigns	

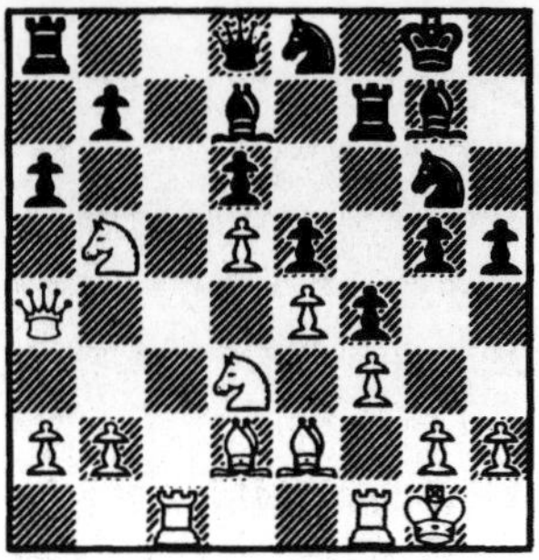

DIAGRAM 77. POSITION AFTER 18 . . . ♗d7

'Patzer games are won and lost by oversights.' A piece is lost and White looked crestfallen. If White were a grandpatzer, he would have played on, knowing that Black might blunder back.

Paradoxically, losing a piece sometimes gives you an advantage in mobility, one less thing to worry about, and provokes overconfidence in the opponent. For example, here is how initially to lose but eventually win against a 1400-rated patzer (White).

1	d4	♘f6
2	c4	g6
3	♘c3	♗g7
4	♗g5	h6
5	♗h4	0–0
6	e4	d6
7	♗e2	c5
8	d5	e6
9	♘f3	e×d
10	♘×d	. . . (Diagram 78)

Not a book move, so now I am on my own and, as you will soon see, questionable resources.

10	. . .	♕a5+
11	♕d2	♕×d+
12	♘×d	♘×d
13	e×d	♖e8
14	h3	♘d7

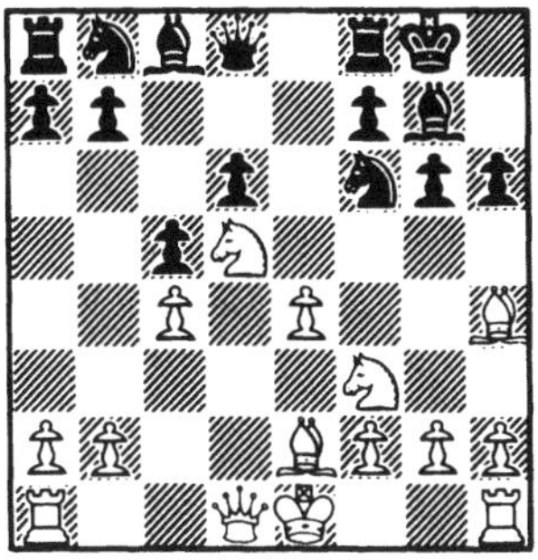

DIAGRAM 78. POSITION AFTER 10 ♘×d

Why doesn't Black just take the Pawn on b2? He has a much worse plan in mind.

15 f3	♘b6
16 ♘e4	♘×c
17 ♗×c	♗f5??

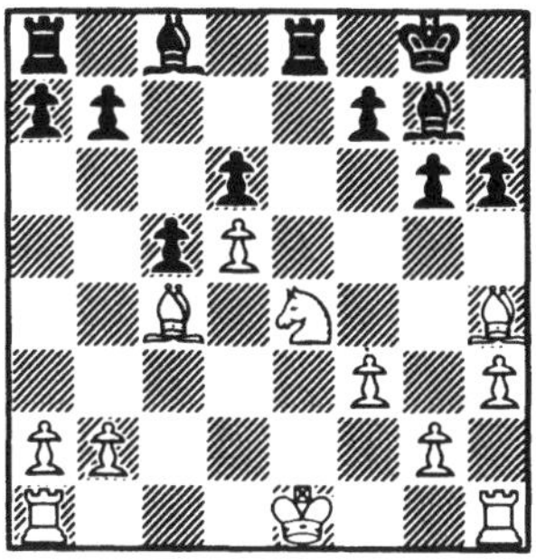

DIAGRAM 79. POSITION AFTER 17 . . . ♗f5??

Because of the pin on the White King, Black thinks he wins the piece back. But he does not and now he is just a piece down. Grandpatzers do not give up when they are only a piece down. When patzers think 'I can't lose this one—I'm a piece up' they are in trouble, because the term 'lose' has come to the mind's focus. It's like *not* thinking about a hippopotamus.

18 ♗d3	♗×e
19 f×e	f5
20 0–0	f×e
21 ♗c2	♗×b

Chomping away and coming back. That e-Pawn can cause trouble.

22 ♖b1	♗d4+

23 ♔h1	b6
24 ♖be1	e3

DIAGRAM 80. POSITION AFTER 24 . . . e3

25 ♗×g	e2
26 ♖f2	♖f8
27 ♖×f+	♖×f
28 ♖×e	♗e5
29 g4	b5

Black is dogged. Now he is pushing another passed Pawn.

30 ♗d3?	♖f3
31 ♖×e?	d×e
32 Resigns	

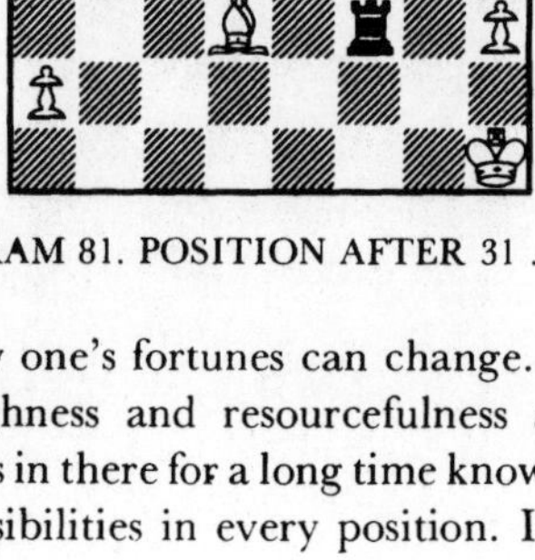

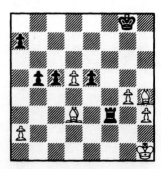

DIAGRAM 81. POSITION AFTER 31 . . . d×e

It is staggering how one's fortunes can change.

Tenacity and toughness and resourcefulness are the marks of the grandpatzer. He hangs in there for a long time knowing there exists a great variety of hidden possibilities in every position. If you beat him in the opening, you must beat him in the middle game as well. And if it gets into the ending, you may have a hell of a time putting him away because he knows a lot of drawing tricks, like this one which shocks every patzer sooner or later. Although a piece and a Pawn up, White cannot win because the King, being in a corner whose color is opposite to that of the Bishop, cannot be driven out to promote the Pawn (Diagram 82).

DIAGRAM 82.

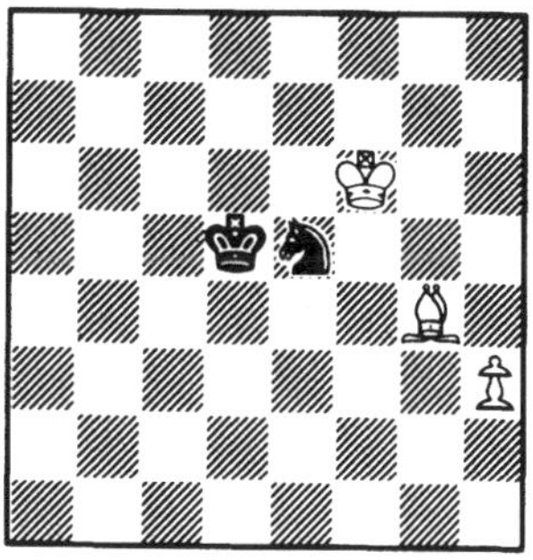

DIAGRAM 83. FISCHER–TAIMANOV 1971

I have seen this drawing trick applied, and failed to be applied, countless times. It is probably the most common drawing-trick of all. I couldn't believe my eyes in the Fischer–Taimanov match, 2nd game, 1971, in Diagram 83. All Black has to do to draw is give up the Knight and get the King to h8 by:

81 . . .	♘d3
82 h4	♘f4
83 ♔f5	♔d6!!
84 ♔×f	♔e7 Draw

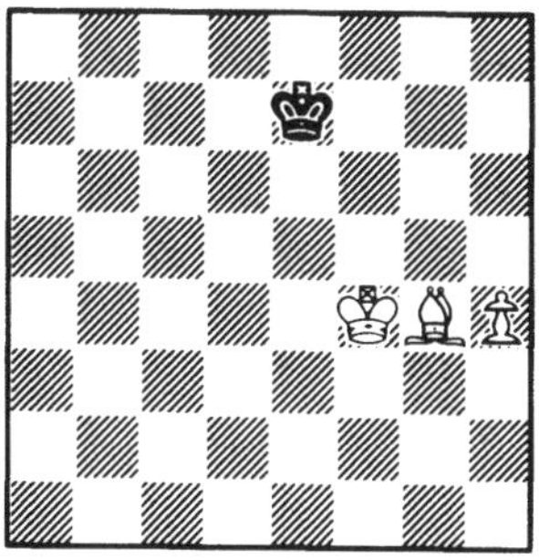

DIAGRAM 84. POSITION AFTER 84 . . . ♔e7

Instead Black played:

81	. . .	♔e4?
82	♗c8	♔f4
83	h4	♘f3
84	h5	♘g5
85	♗f5	♘f3
86	h6	♘g5
87	♔g6	♘f3
88	h7	♘h4+
89	♔f6	Resigns

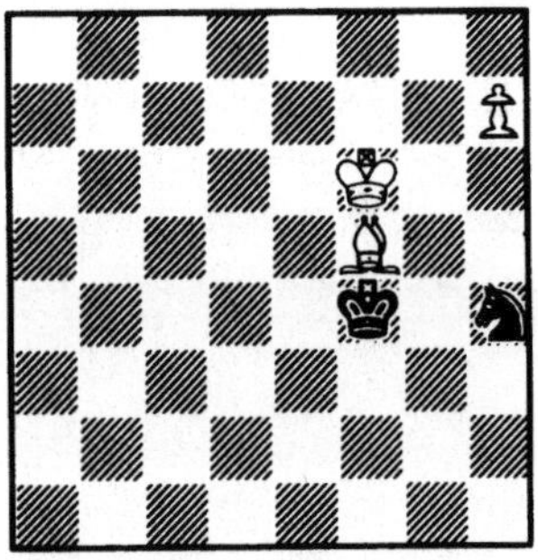

DIAGRAM 85. POSITION AFTER 89 ♔f6

What happened? What could Black be possibly thinking about in overlooking this simple draw? Was he tired, sick? Grandmasters have great pride and dignity. They are silent on these matters and we should not trouble them further.

And here is another such drawing trick you must know because not even the Knight's Pawn can win.

DIAGRAM 86.

The lost grandpatzer is determined, he waits, is patient, he plays on doggedly, he does not yield. This may annoy you, you get impatient, you overplay the position, you start swimming, you even forget there is such a thing as stalemate. The classic master example in our times is Evans–Reshevsky, U.S. Championship, 1964

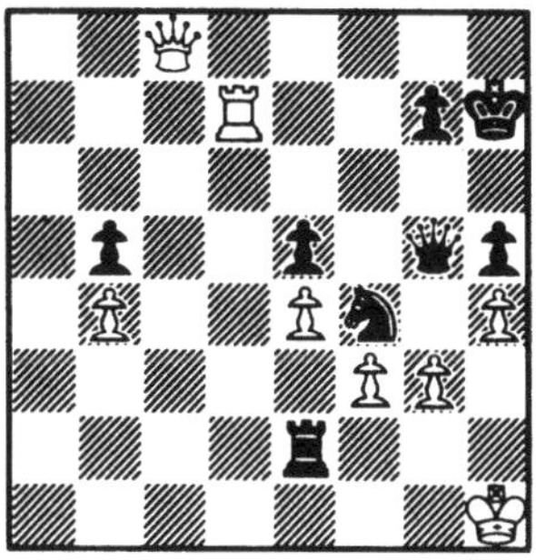

DIAGRAM 87. EVANS–RESHEVSKY, 1964

where Black, a full Knight ahead played:

48 . . .	♕×g3??
49 ♕g8+!	♔×g8
50 ♖×g+!	. . .

and White drew because of the stalemate or perpetual check. Oi!—that hoits!

3.4 *Clocks*

Everybody tells you not to get into time-trouble. This is sound advice, which few except Fischer seem to follow. Also, we are taught not to move quickly when the opponent is in time-trouble. But as your grandpatzer mentor, I advise the opposite. I have won (and never lost) many a game by moving promptly (but not recklessly) when opponents have less than a minute to make 5 or 10 moves. It creates an atmosphere of raw panic because no one wants to lose just because the flag falls. When he starts bending way over to look at the clock, or angles it towards himself to get a straight-on view, or bangs his button to make sure it is down—he is becoming nerve-wracked and will blunder. So will you under similar conditions.

There are a few things about the clock which most patzers do not realize and you should, as a coming grandpatzer. For example, at the start of a game, the rule is that Black starts White's clock by pressing its plunger. (Article 14.3, Laws of Chess of the World Chess Federation (FIDE)). Therefore, if you are White and your opponent is not present, you may start his clock, *but you do not have to make your first move.* When Black arrives at the board 30 minutes late, he may claim that the clock be started from scratch because you have not made a move, but he is wrong. The advantage of not advertising your first move is small but obvious to experienced tournament players who know everyone has friends (and scouts).

Nor do you have to make a move and then write it down, as Fischer once maintained. In fact, as you have been taught herein, it is not only legal but prudent to write down the move first. Another mistaken idea is that you must punch the clock with the same hand you use to move a piece. *There is no rule to this effect.* You can use both hands as long as they are synchronized properly.

In time scrambles some players try to make your flag fall by banging on the clock or picking it up to look at it (to tilt it). There is no rule about this, but it is certainly worth some strongly expressed objections.

A player may offer a draw only when it is his turn to move, but nobody pays much attention to this rule, not even grandmasters.

Once during a tournament, an old guy fell over backwards in his chair. As I was trying to get his pulse (he was dead), a true chessplayer rushed up to the board shouting 'Stop his clock, stop his clock!' (Article 14.6). The ending to this funny-not-so funny story is that a few years later this same chessplayer died of a coronary during a tournament game.

3.5 Conduct

Lots of things happen during a game besides chess. There is more to chess than moving the pieces. Fischer says one should not talk to the opponent at all but lesser humans tend to. Talking, eating, staring, belching, drinking, glowering, nose-picking, (are you squeamish about taking off his pieces?) joking, smoking, finger-drumming, reading, and writing all go on. When I played the boy Fischer some 5 minute games, he did not talk; he studied Cheron's book on the ending (in German). I did not win a game (a couple of generous draws). Fischer never had more than two minutes expired on his clock.

Chess is play, a game having its own reality. We can obliterate one everyday reality, not by dimming awareness, but by intensity of concentration in another. It is serious play since it is a struggle, but there are no ill-feelings about it as in other types of fights. It lacks social usefulness and is a waste of time (according to Puritans) because is does not make money. It contrasts with our work-life in that it lacks manipulation of personal relations for economic, political or reputational gain. One of its funniest lines comes from Eliot Hearst: 'A amateur chess player is one who plays for money; a professional chess player is one who cannot make a living at it.'

You are supposed to be *enjoying* the game in spite of what H. G. Wells says. 'No chessplayer sleeps well. There is no remorse like the remorse of chess. It is a curse upon man. There is no happiness in chess.' These are the laments of someone who views chess as a battle of egos and whose personal worth gets bruised as a consequence. I find it enjoyable just to be lost and absorbed in chess thought, creating emphemeral patterns and trying to fathom the problems of deliberately created complications. If there is no pleasure in it for you, you will retire from serious play because the inevitable losses are not counterbalanced by compensatory joys. I hope your aristic goal in studying the preachings and teachings of this book is to improve your play *in an enjoyable way.* It is simple hypocrisy to deny enjoyment in winning. But wins do not prove personal superiority over others because the other's mistakes contribute to the outcome as much as one's own powers. 'Victory has very narrow meanings . . . and can become a destructive force. The taste of defeat has a richness of experience all its own'—Bill Bradley, a professional *basketball* player!

It is hard for me not to look at the games on either side of me (Concentrate! says Fischer). Also, I walk around the room occasionally and glance at the positions of even the lowliest patzer. They may be a mess of clogs and scattered pieces, but they are human creations with intentions behind them, and it's interesting to look at them and wonder how you would handle the position. ('To become a grandpatzer you must learn how to beat patzers'—*Secrets of a Grandpatzer*. (Why can't a book refer to itself?)).

It is worth the grandpatzer's notice that the section on Conduct of the Players (Article 19 of the Official Rules of Chess) occupies only 1½ pages. (Obviously, we are gentlemen who need no one to instruct us as to proper conduct.) Article 19.1 (c) is a true gem of ambiguity—'It is forbidden to distract or annoy the opponent in any manner whatsoever'. There is no telling what a chessplayer might find distracting or annoying. Nimzovich was bothered by his opponent holding an unlit cigar because it was well known, even in those days, that in chess the threat is often greater than the execution. The great Lasker was first invited to play in the New York Tournament of 1927. He angrily refused, charging unfairness in the 1924 New York Tournament. He was then disinvited for unsportsmanlike conduct. Among other things, he was accused of cheating because over-the-board, he smoked cheap five-cent cigars, but away from the board, he smoked only expensive Havana cigars.

It is very impolite to ask your opponent to resign. I tried it once with another grandpatzer to avoid driving 30 miles the next day for resumption of an adjourned game. But my impoliteness roused his hackles and, within his rights, he made me make the journey although he was dead lost in the 'matter of technique' ending described on page 53.

IV
How to Miscellaneous

4.1 *Young Guys*

Playing young guys provides two sorts of problems for the grandpatzer, (1) opening knowledge and, (2) coffee-house style. Young players, being still students and scholars, like to study books and hence tend to know their openings well. (Playing creates the illusion of doing intellectual work but studying actually is.) You must know openings well against young guys. Some are masters of the future. One heuristic method to use against them involves a deceptive speed of reply. Suppose you are playing a line which you know cold for, say 24 ply (12 moves). Your young opponent also seems to know it because as soon as you move, he quickly makes the next move right out of the current book. Keep moving quickly with him for about 6 or 7 moves, then abruptly slow down and on the 8th–12th moves take some time, not because you don't know them but because you want to appear as if you don't know them. You pose as if you don't know this line as well as you really do. Then, as you study the position, seemingly on your own resources in the positional middle game, and come up with the best move for several moves, the young player tends to become angry and unstrung. '"How lucky can the guy get?"' he says to himself as you repeatedly stumble along the correct line, move after move. He may in fact know the line deeper than you do, but this prescribed pseudo-naievete causes many a young player to overestimate himself and underestimate you. If it doesn't, and he knows the line further than you do, and he doesn't get contemptuous, then, in all justice, he deserves to have the better position in the middle game.

By no means try to take the young guy 'out of the book'. Over and over I have heard this as a strategy to be adopted. To improvise an opening over the board is conducive to disaster. So many millions of chess games have been played that the good lines are well worked out for you. To deviate from them on your own over the board, is patently to handicap yourself with an inferior position. If you win games by adopting unique opening moves, it is only because you are a good middle and end game player.

The second problem with young guys is that they tend to have a high-spirited, ebullient style. They have not yet lost the youthful exuberance of play to prudence and calculation. They want to get it over with fast. They try to blow you off the board in a short time. Beginners move Pawns because there are more of them in sight than anything else, but young guys are always shoving 4 or 5 Pawns at you to overwhelm you, regardless of development and the weaknesses created behind the Pawns. Consider this example (White = Young guy, Black = Dr. G):

1	d4	♘f6
2	c4	g6
3	♘c3	♗g7
4	e4	d6
5	f3	0–0
6	♗e3	♘c6
7	♕d2	♖e8

Both players evidently know the Saemisch variation of the King's Indian. White wants to swap off Black's fianchettoed Bishop whereas Black plans to hang on to it by playing ♗h8 when White plays ♗h6.

8	g4	. . .

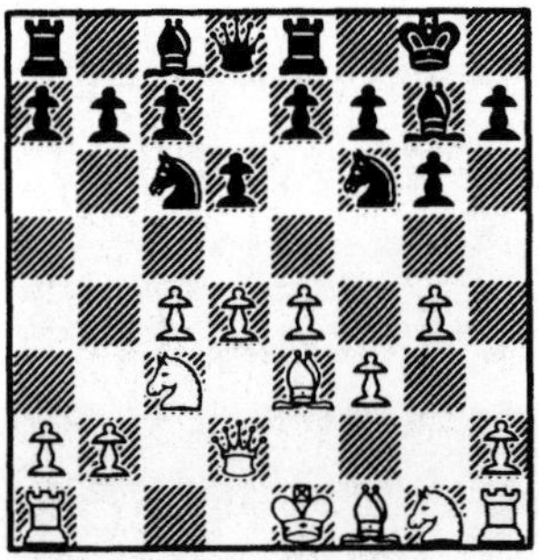

DIAGRAM 88. A PLAYER–DR. G
POSITION AFTER 8 g4

Here comes the Pawn storm! He has 4 Pawns coming at me, but he is undeveloped. Haven't we been instructed several thousands of times by masters that one answers a flank attack by hitting the center. Enough of those laments about trite advice. Bombast against authority has its limits. Let's adopt a master suggestion for a change.

8	. . .	e5
9	d5	♘d4
10	♗×d4	. . .

He wants to win a Pawn but gives up his good Bishop.

10 . . .	e×d
11 ♘b5	. . .

DIAGRAM 89. POSITION AFTER 11 ♘b5

11 ...	♘×e4!

It is time for combinations and the sacrifice in the center should be of obvious value. It opens up on his exposed King and brings out the Black pieces rapidly:

12 f×e	♖×e+
13 ♔d1	♗×g+
14 ♗e2	♕h4
15 ♘f3	♕h5
16 ♘b×d	♖ae8
17 ♖e1	♗h6!

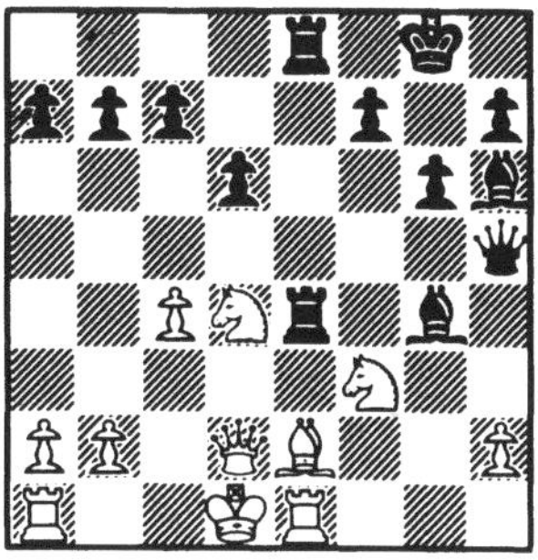

DIAGRAM 90. POSITION AFTER 17 . . . ♗h6

and wins. White is tied up in knots, a piece will soon go and the coffee-house attack has suffered a demolition job.

4.2 *Old Guys*

Old guys who still play tournaments are apt to be very tough, resilient and unflappable. They have won and lost so many games that one more doesn't make that much difference. They may make horrible moves at times but over time they seem to keep stumbling into good positions. Their hands tremble as they reach for a piece, they seem confused about things, they are a bit deaf, they wear hats and eyeshades, their eyes water. All this is not intended to put you off guard but it tends to anyway. You must be objective and not play the ego-game with old guys. Remember that all young guys look down on old guys and that there is always somebody older and somebody younger. When you are 20 playing somebody 21, you are the young guy and when you are 40 playing somebody 25, you are the old guy.

The way to play old guys is to remain objective, searching for what is good about their position, playing the board rather than the ego game, and trying to keep as many pieces around for as long as possible to retain complications for the eventual combinational opportunity. It is tiring to analyze complicated positions move after move. Knowing the opening lines, playing closed positions and not simplifying will give you an advantage. If you simplify, you may be steering your opponent into only one or two variations to be analyzed. If there are only a very few things to consider, a veteran's long experience will automatically guide him, and he is patient. If you get into too simple an ending, he will draw or even win if you try to force things. Case in point (Diagram 91). My opponent, White is a 1600 rated patzer in his 70's. At the start of the game, the clocks, the rules for adjournment, everything seemed to confuse him a bit. Here I should play the bishop to c5, increasing the pressure and keeping the pieces on the board. But I lazily break my own rules and follow an ill-conceived plan of simplification. (36 . . . ♘e5 might even win).

36 . . .	♘c5
37 ♘×d	♘×d

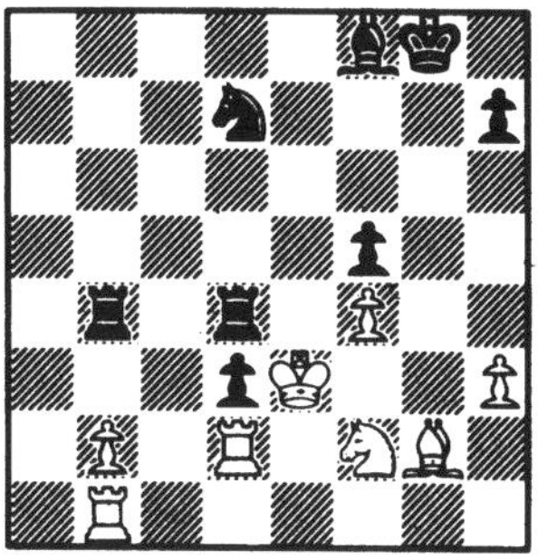

DIAGRAM 91. A PLAYER–DR. G, 1977

38	♖×d	♖×d+
39	♔×d	♖×f
40	♔e3	♖b4

Unfortunately, I may have steered him into a drawnish ending. It's Bishops of opposite colors, but there are still Rooks on the board, and my passed f-Pawn may cause trouble.

41	b3	♔g7
42	♔d3	♔f6
43	♔e3	♗h6+
44	♔f3	♔e5
45	♗f1	♗g5
46	♗c4	♖b6
47	♖e1+	♔f6
48	♖d1	♔g6
49	♖d7	♖f6

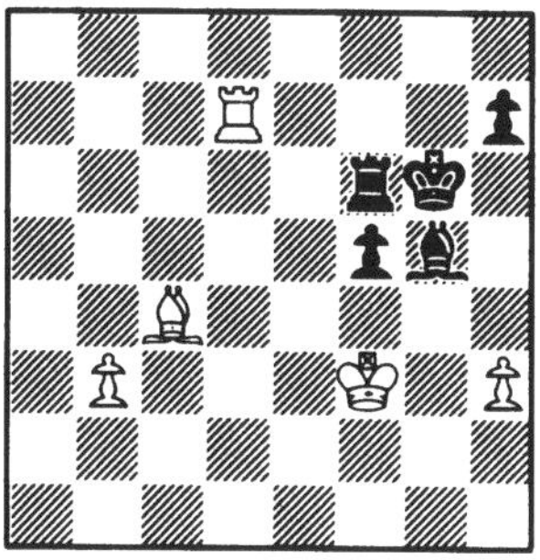

DIAGRAM 92. POSITION AFTER 49 . . ., ♖f6

See how stubborn he is? He fights back by obtaining good mobility for his pieces in contrast to mine.

50	♗g8	h6
51	♗c4	f4
52	♖d4	♔h5

I am heading over to win the Pawn on h3, except for a slight case of mate if I take it—which I did not see at this point.

53	♖d1	♔h4
54	b4	♖c6
55	♗d3	♖e6
56	♗e4	♖b6
57	♖b1	. . .

Now he is playing backwards again and all this is pretty boring to the reader but watch what happens to the overconfident grandpatzer.

57	. . .	♖a6
58	♖d1	♖a2
59	b5	♖b2
60	♗d3	♖b4
61	♗e2	♗f6
62	♖d6	♖b3+?
63	♔×f	. . .

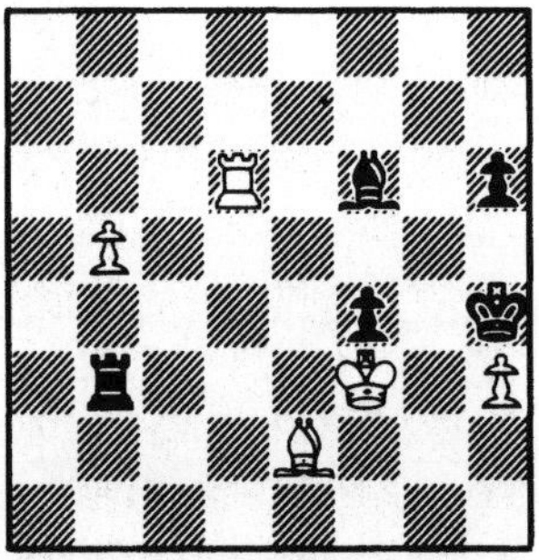

DIAGRAM 93. POSITION AFTER 62 . . . ♖b3+?

Just like that I lose my main man on f4. I thought he had to go back when checked. It is now 11:30 PM. We adjourn at the 65th move. A few nights later we are at it again and, believe it or not, I am still alive at the 90th move with the same pieces and Pawns. We adjourned at 11.30 PM again! The next day we agreed to a draw over the phone, neither of us wanting to see anymore of this mess again. How did I manage to hold the draw from the 63rd move? That's another grandpatzer secret. (Oh, all right—just keep the Rooks on the board when down like this. A draw counts more than a loss.)

4.3 *Women*

Playing women forebodes danger for the patzer with a big male ego. Fischer said—'They're all weak, all women. They're stupid compared to men. They lose every single game against a man. There isn't a woman player in the world I can't give Knight-odds to and still beat'. Our greatest player is here playing the 'I am better than a woman' game. Every one of these statements is obviously mistaken. The world's woman champion, Nona Gaprindashvili, would murder Fischer at Knight-odds. She tied for 1st at Lone Pine (March 1977) beating Shamkovich, Lein, and Tarjan!

Look at this position from Ferrer-Savereide, Haifa, 1976, with Black (Diane Savereide) to move:

How many of you would dare play as follows:

DIAGRAM 94. FERRER-SAVEREIDE, HAIFA, 1976

25	. . .	♕×c3
26	♖×c	♖b1+
27	♗d1	♘e4!
28	♖c2	♖d8
29	g3	♗b7!

and White resigned.

A 1600-rated woman player should immediately invoke the greatest caution in a male patzer who realizes his main adversary is always himself. The problem of pride and vanity can become acute and egos can be severely damaged when the opponents are of opposite sexes. (This goes for life also). Women who are aspiring grandpatzers should realize where their advantage lies with male opponents who cannot be objective and who play the ego game 'I am better than a woman'. Appeal to his vanity, bumble a bit, forget to push your clock a couple of times. If he is away from the board when you move, signal him to let him know it's his turn to move. The ego-gamester will inflate with all this, and a bloated ego's position can be easily perforated with a resounding el collapso. Knowing this is worth at least half a Pawn or more right at the start.

Women players will find that men do not resign at the point they would against other men. They play on hoping for the blunder. And if a man asks you for a draw, examine the position very carefully, because there is a high probability that you have a win.

How should a woman play another woman? I haven't the foggiest idea. Of that which one cannot speak, one must remain silent.

4.4 Masters

There is only one way to play a master, and that is to play super-soundly knowing what the inevitable will be, the only question being when it will happen. As the game goes on, the strong player gets stronger and when the position becomes combinational and opens up, the grandpatzer has little chance against a master. The master might make a big mistake or simplify so much that you can hold the draw, but it's rare. That's why he is a master—he possesses a mastery of the game. Not entire mastery, of course. There are many chess masters, but no one has mastered chess.

I have won and drawn only a few games against masters and have never beaten a grandmaster. (That's because I have played only three).

The best struggle I have ever put up against a grandmaster in a tournament was against Donald Byrne, a former U.S. Champion, here playing White against my pet Yugoslav variation of the King's Indian.

1 d4	♘f6
2 c4	g6
3 g3	♗g7
4 ♗g2	0–0
5 ♘c3	d6
6 ♘f3	c5
7 0–0	♘c6
8 d5	♘a5
9 ♘d2	♖b8
10 a3	♘g4 (Diagram 95)

My first original move. It holds White back for a while.

11 ♕c2	♘e5
12 ♘d1	b5

I'm moving ahead, gaining space, and he's playing backward to regroup.

13 c×b	♖×b
14 h3	♘d7

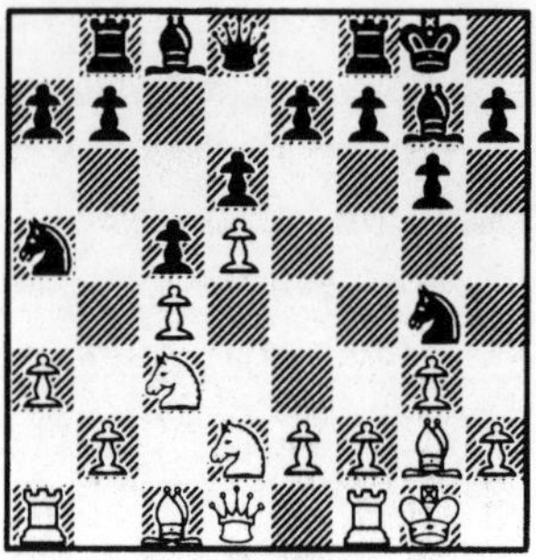

DIAGRAM 95. D. BYRNE–DR. G POSITION AFTER 10 . . . ♘g4

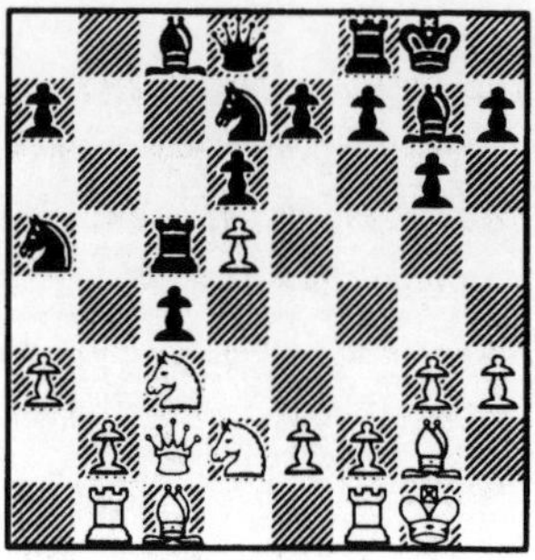

DIAGRAM 96. POSITION AFTER 16 . . . ♖c5

15 ♖b1	c4!
16 ♘c3	♖c5 (Diagram 96)

Black has the better position, according to onlooking masters, and Byrne himself afterwards. But as I said above, it's just a matter of time before the lion shows his strength.

17 ♘a2	♖c7

Too passive. ♕b6 is much better to keep moving ahead.

18 ♕a4	♖c5
19 ♘b4	♘b6
20 ♕d1	♗b7
21 ♘e4	♖c8
22 ♗e3	♘b3
23 ♘c3	♕d7
24 ♘c6	

DIAGRAM 97. POSITION AFTER 24 ♘c6

24 . . .	♗×c6?

Black starts downhill. A bold sacrifice of the exchange is called for or Black will be smothered. 24 . . . ♘×d 25 ♗×d ♖×c! 26 ♗×c ♕×c 27 f3 d5 28 ♗f2 f5 29 e3 e5 with the threat . . . d4.

25 d×c	♕d8
26 ♘b5	♘a4
27 ♘×a	♘×b
28 ♕c2	♖c7
29 ♘b5	♖c8
30 ♖×b	♗×b
31 ♕×b	♕a5
32 ♗h6	Resigns

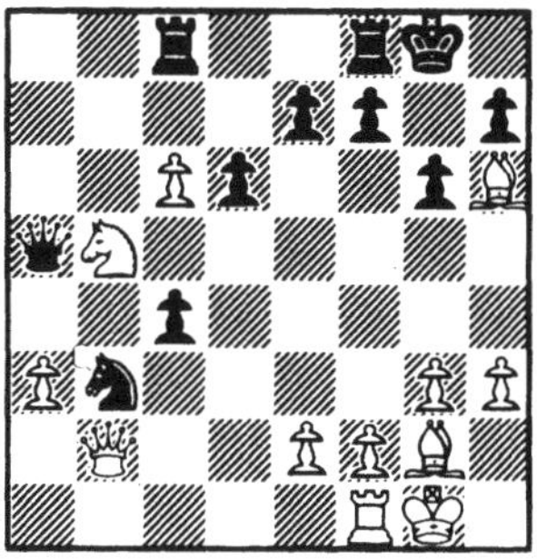

DIAGRAM 98. POSITION AFTER 32 ♗h6

It's a matter of taste when to resign. (A good loser is one who knows when to resign.)

4.5 *The Mysterious Rook Pawn Move*

Nimzovich was famous for his mysterious Rook moves, placing a Rook on a file already jammed with pieces and pawns. For me, the main mystery has been the way masters play with the Rook Pawn. Well do I remember a group of us studying endings, the best of us being two experts. In positions like this (See Diagram 99) they would comment, 'when White goes h4, Black always goes h5, for some reason'. It was automatic with them, not requiring explanation. Only when I began to study Fischer's games did I decide to look into this Rook-Pawn play further. Over and over Fischer would play a Rook Pawn up to the fourth even in the middle game. What did it mean? Aren't you supposed to play in the center?

Everybody knows that when Black has fianchettoed his King Bishop on the h8–a1 diagonal, the a-Pawn push—a5, a4, a3—is aimed at b2 to gain complete control of said diagonal. Also in the King's Indian we, as Black, play a5 to protect our Knight on c5 from being driven off by b4. In the Rauser attack of the Dragon Sicilian, White plays h4 and h5 to open up a file against Black's castled King. In the following position from the Queen's Gambit accepted, (Diagram 100), Black has played 4 . . . b5 to try to keep the Pawn on c4. White's best reply is 5 a4! to shatter Black's Pawn structure. For example:

DIAGRAM 99.

DIAGRAM 100. POSITION AFTER 4 . . . b5

5 a4	c6
6 a×b	c×b
7 b3	c×b
8 ♗×b+ and ♕×b	

or if

7 . . .	♗e6
8 b×c	b×c
9 ♘e5 wins back the pawn	

Here the move 5 a4 exemplifies the principle of 'Attack his Pawn Structure', a theme fully explored in Soltis' *Pawn Structure Chess.*

Another opening example of Rook Pawn play is Botvinnik–Gligoric (1956).

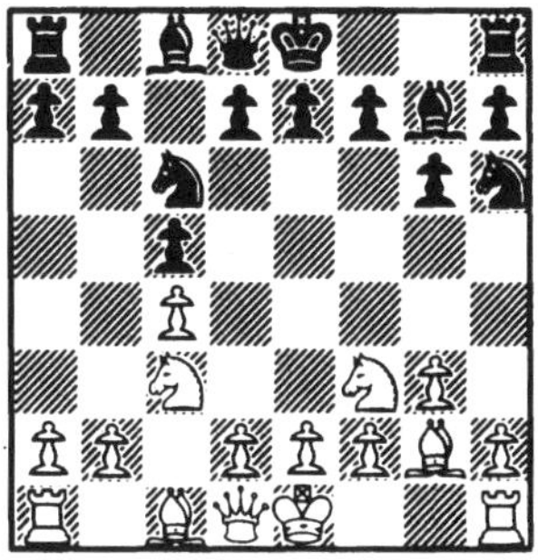

DIAGRAM 101. BOTVINNIK-GLIGORIC, 1956
POSITION AFTER 6 . . . ♘h6

Botvinnik immediately attacked with the Rook Pawn:

6 h4!	d6
7 d3	♖ab8
8 h5!	♗d7
9 ♗×h6	♗×h6
10 h×g	h×g
11 ♕c1!	

and Black has a difficult position to defend.

What few patzers realize is that a Pawn on g3, g6, b3 or b6 is considered *weak.* (I always thought a King castled behind a fianchettoed Bishop was nice and safe.) But the advance of the opponent's Rook Pawn to your third rank Pawn is a definite threat. Blocking it with your own Rook Pawn creates weaknesses also, but in general it is the lesser evil. Soltis, a Dragon expert, always plays h5 in response to h4 by White.

Now we come to the initial mystery. Why in the ending does a master respond with his Rook Pawn to the fourth rank when the opponent moves his to his fourth rank? It all relates to the attack and defense of the Pawn structure which, when broken up, allows the King to penetrate and lunch on a few Pawns. ('Mangiare' in Italian means to eat as well as to 'take' in chess.) Knowledge of how to attack and defend with the Rook Pawn is most helpful. For example, in a classic ending (Duras–Capablanca, New York, 1913).

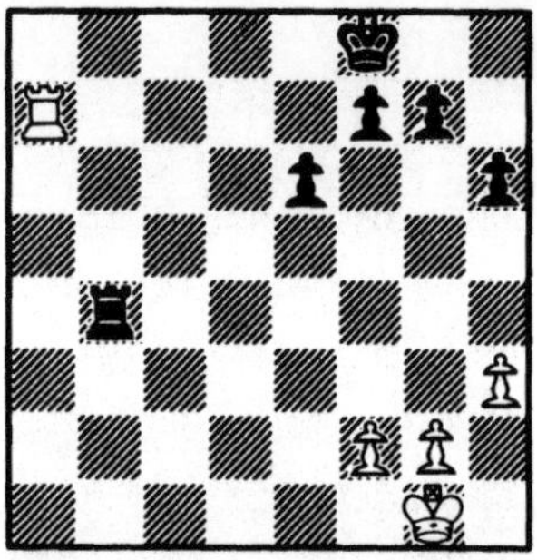

DIAGRAM 102. DURAS–CAPABLANCA, NEW YORK, 1913

White, being a Pawn down, should defend this type of position by h4 because Black will eventually have to play g5, whereupon h×g simplifies the ending to 3 Pawns against 2. But here h4 would simply lose a Pawn. Black attacks with the Rook Pawn.

1 . . .	h5
2 g3	h4!

If White plays 3 ♔g2 then 3 . . . h×g 4 ♔×g leaves White with isolated Pawns. If 4 f×g then Black's King Pawn becomes passed.

3 g×h	♖×h
4 ♔g2	e5
5 ♔g3	♖d4
6 ♖a5	f6 (Diagram 103)
7 ♖a7	♔g8

Here White should have seized the chance to play h4 to simplify the defense.

8 ♖b7	♔h7
9 ♖a7	♔g6
10 ♖e7	♖d3+
11 ♔g2	♖d5
12 ♔g3	f5
13 ♖a7	

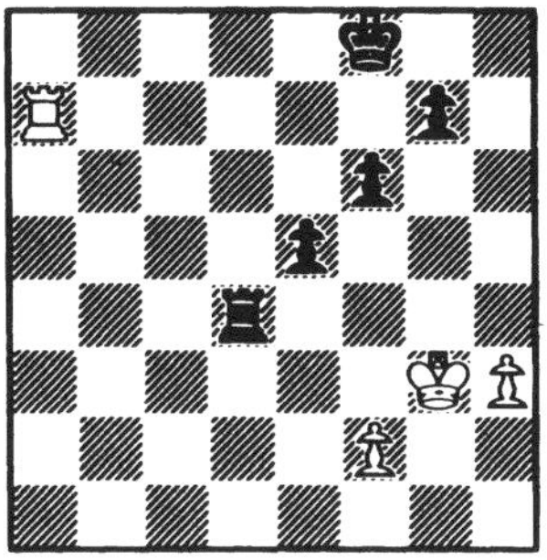

DIAGRAM 103. POSITION AFTER 6 . . . f6

White could draw with 13 f3! but let's look at White's last chance to draw with the Rook Pawn.

13 . . .	♖d3+
14 ♔g2	e4 (Diagram 104)

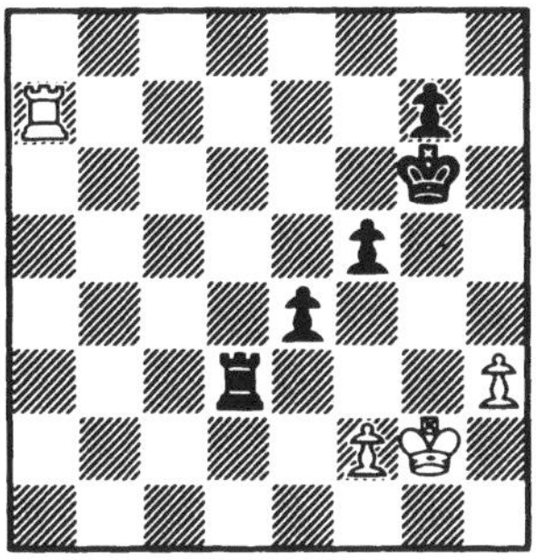

DIAGRAM 104. POSITION AFTER 14 . . . e4

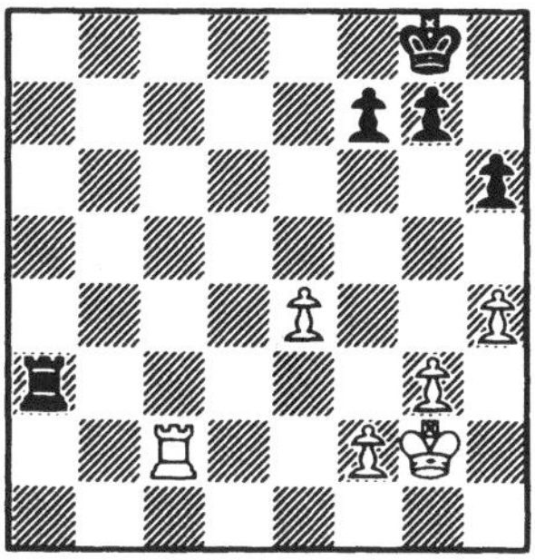

DIAGRAM 105. KORSCHNOI–ANTOSHIN, 22nd USSR CHAMPIONSHIP

Again, White should play 15 h4! to hold. Instead he played 15 ♖a4? and lost.

The correct way to utilize the Rook Pawn for attack and defense is illustrated by Diagram 105 (Korschnoi–Antoshin). If it were Black's move, he should play 1 . . . h5 to simplify down to 3 Pawns versus 2 when White plays g4. If it is White's move, he should play 1 h5! to prevent the Black plan of simplification. Korschnoi did so and won.

Also in Taimanov-Kopylov (Diagram 106), Black played 1 . . . h5 threatening h4 and h3. Hence White replies 2 h4! Again, in Aronin–Kotov (Diagram 107):

1 ♔f2	♔g8
2 h4	

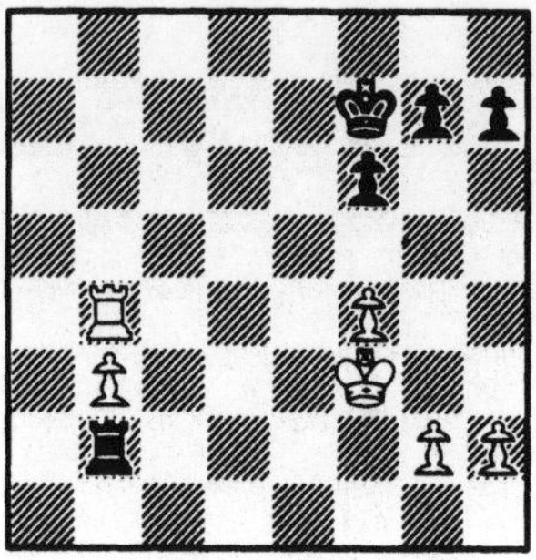

DIAGRAM 106.
TAIMANOV-KOPYLOV

DIAGRAM 107.

and guess what Black played. Yep! 2 . . . h5! to stop the King-side breakthrough. Now these Rook Pawn moves should be less mysterious in the ending. It still leaves a few mysteries in the middle game, however.

In the fifth game of the Fischer–Spassky match, the following position was reached (Diagram 108). Spassky (White) played 16 a4 and Fischer immediately replied 16 . . . a5! It looks like he gives himself a backward b6 Pawn on an open file, but he didn't want White to go a5, and the position is now blocked against White's two Bishops.

Maybe Fischer learned to play a5 in response to a4 the hard way as in the following game against Benko (Diagram 109). Here Benko (White) played 8 a4 and Fischer should have responded with 8 . . . a5 but chose instead 8 . . . ♘bd7 whereupon 9 a5 followed and Fischer lost in 40 moves.

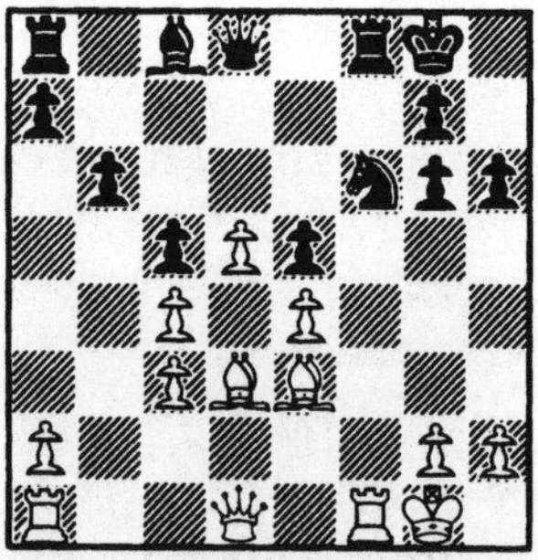

DIAGRAM 108, SPASSKY-FISCHER, WORLD CHAMPIONSHIP MATCH, 1972

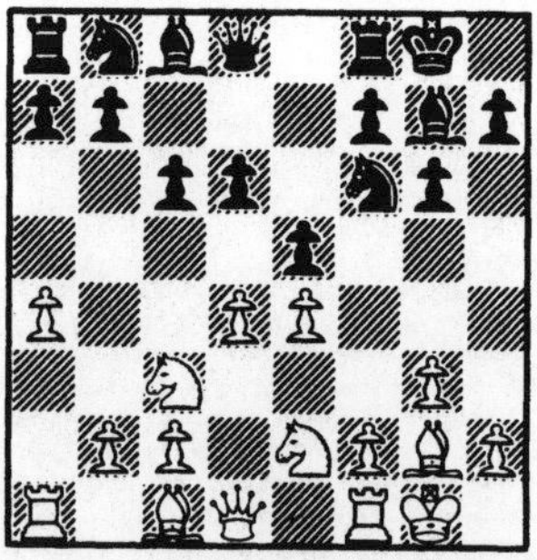

DIAGRAM 109. BENKO-FISCHER, CURACAO, 1962 POSITION AFTER 7 . . . c6

Finally, the Rook Pawn is played up to free the Rook as in Keres–Fischer (Candidates Tournament, 1959) (Diagram 110).

20 . . .	h5!

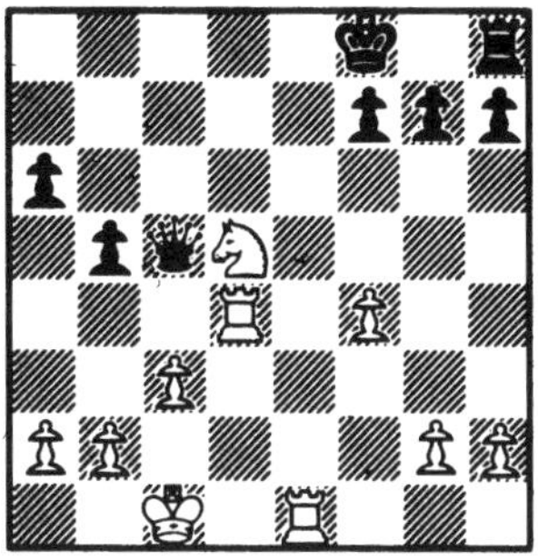

DIAGRAM 110. KERES–FISCHER, CANDIDATES TOURNAMENT, 1959
POSITION AFTER 20 c3

21 f5 ♖h6!

and Black gets his Rook into play sideways.

These examples from all three phases of the game should be sufficient to enlighten you about how to play with the Rook Pawn and how to meet mysterious Rook Pawn moves.

The champion of the mysterious RP moves must be Larsen. (See Diagram 111 Larsen–Gligoric, Vinkova, 1970.) Here he has both RPs on the 6th rank and won in another 36 moves or so.

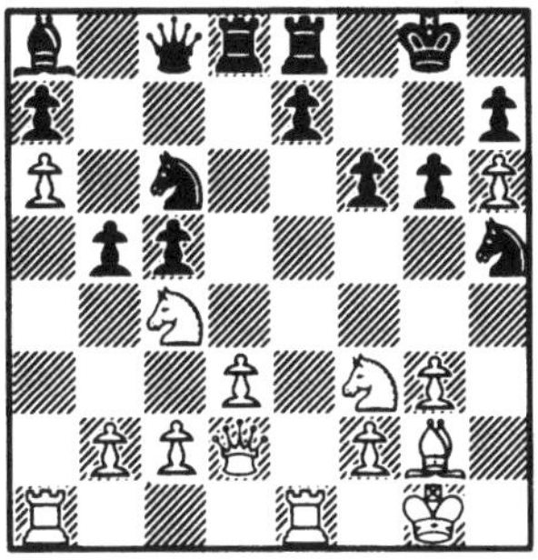

DIAGRAM 111. LARSEN–GLIGORIC, VINKOVA, 1970

4.6 *Curiosa*

Progressing from patzer to grandpatzer entails a host of surprises and curious happenings. Surprise is an emotion which results from an overthrow of belief. After several years as a beginner playing social chess, it was a great surprise to me to learn that the chessboard is not a square. It indeed looks like one and the laws of geometry should hold, but when you consider the number of moves, (and they are what matter), you can get the King from a1 to a8 in 7 moves by going straight up the a-file. But you can also get there in 7 moves by going away from the a-file along the diagonal to d4 and then over towards the a-file on the g1–g7 diagonal. That it is the moves and not the distance which matters is illustrated by this miraculous example of Reti's, which was so counter-intuitive to me, I couldn't believe it at first sight. All masters know it, but few patzers seem to.

DIAGRAM 112.

1 a4 . . .

Chasing the Pawn is obviously hopeless, so Black must trot along the a1–h8 diagonal to go to the aid of his own Pawn while keeping an eye on the a-Pawn. It is counter-intuitive to move *away* (in distance) from a Pawn you want to capture.

1 . . . ♔b2
2 a5 ♔c3

If 3 a6, then ♔d2 and Black also Queens in two.

3 ♔g3 ♔d4!

Again if 4 a6 ♔e3 and Queens in two. Hence:

4 ♔×f ♔c5

And captures the Pawn. My only modest contribution to this trick, which is of the greatest practical importance in the ending, is that if the White King is at h2, White wins.

Another shocker to me was that White can win the following position because it looks like Black wins the Pawn to draw (Diagram 113).

But 1 ♗d5!! ♔×d 2 ♔b5 and wins.

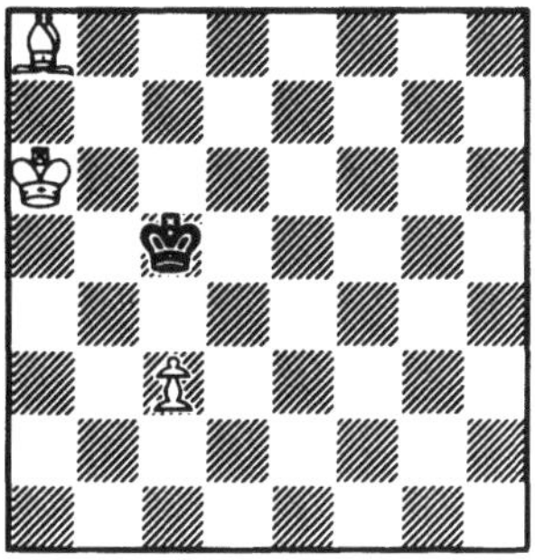

DIAGRAM 113.

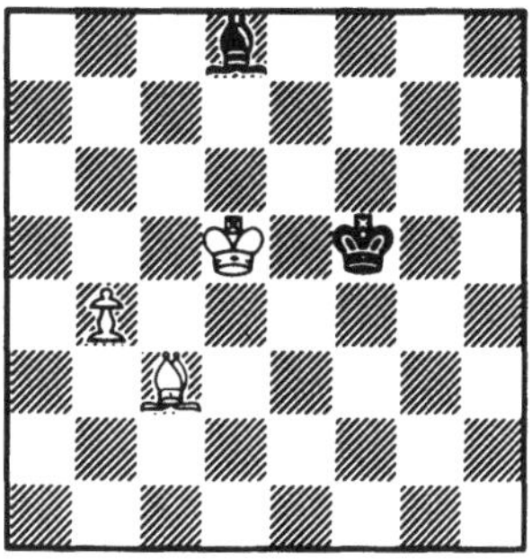

DIAGRAM 114.

An old-time but super-dramatic example of a counter-intuitive surprise, in which the King moves away from the action, is Capablanca–Janowski, New York 1916. In Diagram 114 Black resigned. But he can draw by bringing the King around behind!

1 . . . ♔f4!!
2 ♗d4 ♔f3!!
3 b5 ♔e2!!

Have you ever seen three double exclamations in a row? More to come.

4 ♔c6 ♔d3
5 ♗b6 ♗g5
6 ♔b7 ♔c4
7 ♔a6 ♔b3!!
8 ♗f2 ♗d8
9 ♗e1 ♔a4!! (Diagram 115)

Which prevents the Bishop's diagonal from being cut.

Speaking of contributions to the ending, I once thought I had

DIAGRAM 115. POSITION AFTER 9 . . . ♔a4!!

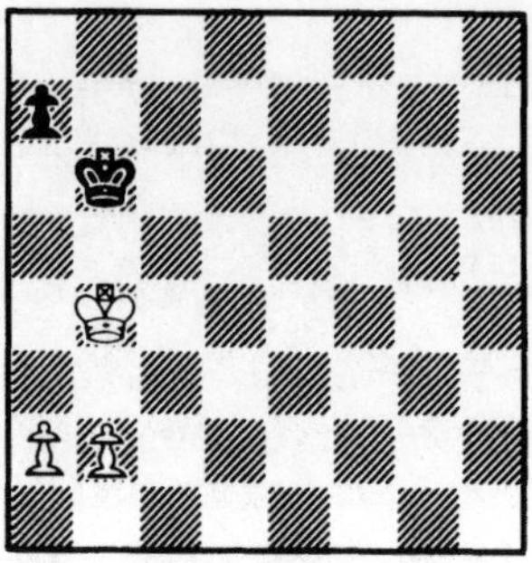

DIAGRAM 116.

discovered a new principle in the ending of two Pawns against one (Diagram 116).

My principle for White said = 'When the Kings are even (i.e. in opposition), make the Pawns uneven (i.e. not side by side)'; which of course implies that when the Pawns are even, take the King out of opposition. This is a good principle for the weaker side to know, because if White makes a mistake, Black can draw.

If Schlechter had known of this rule, he could have beaten Marshall in this position.

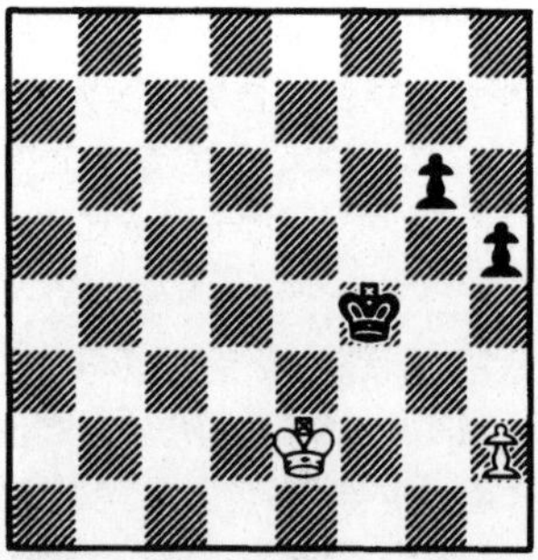

DIAGRAM 117. MARSHALL–SCHLECHTER, SAN SEBASTIAN, 1911.

1 . . .	♔g4!
2 ♔f2	♔h3
3 ♔g1	. . .

White's moves are forced, but now that the King's are uneven, the Black Pawns are kept even and White is helpless.

3 . . .	h4
4 ♔h1	g5

5 ♔g1	g4
6 ♔h1	g3
7 h×g	h×g

and wins.

I was saving all this as a secret until one day I bought Averbach and Mazelis' book on *Pawn Endings* and found that this had all been worked out in 1936 by someone named Bähr. Thus in Diagram 118 the Pawns are even, but the Kings are uneven, so if White moves g6, the game is drawn. If Black moves to h8, the Kings are even and now White makes the Pawns uneven by g6 and wins. Bähr's formulation is in terms of colors instead of my concept of 'evenness'. If you want to draw, when the connected Pawns stand on opposite colored squares, the Kings should also be on opposite colored squares; if the connected pawns are on same-colored squares, the Kings should also stand on same-colored squares.

DIAGRAM 118.

It may be that things like this are discovered and forgotten many times over. One can have originality without necessarily having priority.

Among the curiosa of the game are some of the players (including me). Some really strange types are attracted to the game. A few players seem dominated by the paranoid mode of thought, probably because the problem of shame-humiliation is so characteristic of the game.

Morphy, Steinitz, Lasker, Nimzovich and Botvinnik were thought to be afflicted by the paranoid mode at one time or other (Schonberg, 1972). Suspiciousness mounts to hilarious proportions in World Championship matches, as illustrated by Fischer-Spassky, 1972, when the Soviets had the chairs x-rayed and taken apart. In the second game of the Karpov–Korschnoi match, 1978, played in the Phillipines, Karpov was served a cup of yogurt. Korschnoi protested that this was a signal from the Soviet delegation to offer a draw. Korschnoi complained: "a yogurt after move 20 could signify 'we instruct you to offer a draw' or a sliced mango would mean 'we order you to decline a draw'; marinated quails' eggs could mean 'play Knight to Knight-five at once'. The possibilities are limitless." But how would Karpov remember the code for limitless food items? And suppose the quails's eggs were *un*marinated? The Korschnoi camp also announced they had a special ray detector to make sure their man was not being zapped. (Nobody seems to be more than four years old.)

Once I played a young guy who did not trust clocks. He insisted on using two clocks. Of course when some discrepancy arose, it added to his pressures, because how could he tell which clock was wrong? He had so much trouble concentrating on the game and on operating and suspiciously watching the clocks, that I lost, being myself so busy observing and reflecting about all this.

When to resign is a matter of taste. Some opponents just don't resign (especially computers) so you have to watch out for them. Here is a bizarre example.

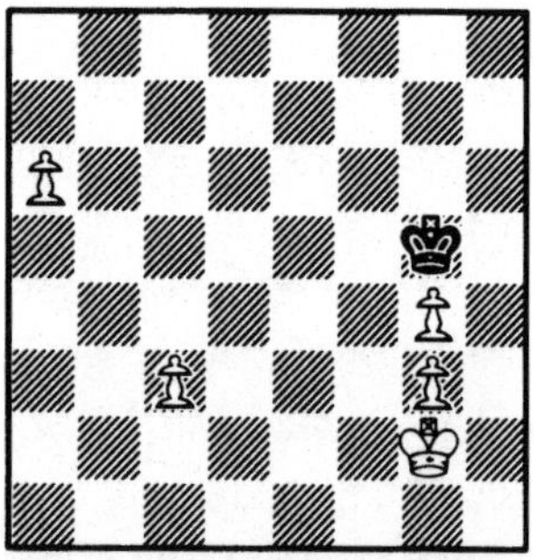

DIAGRAM 119. DR. G–A PLAYER

In this position as White, I expected Black to resign, because two of three Queens would be enough to win without stalemate. But we played on for another 8 moves until the mate. After the mate, my wild-eyed, long-bearded opponent leaned over the table, fixed me sternly in the eye, and said to me with a hushed voice—'I would have resigned earlier but in my last game I was a Rook down and still won'. A raw beginner, you say? He was a 1400-rated patzer.

Players move the pieces around differently. Some insist the Knights' heads be pointed in the same or opposite directions, and some slop them around any old way. A friend of mine who ran a chess club noted that in the course of a year, the Black Knights wore out first. They get slammed down defiantly a lot. Also the c6 square on wooden tables is the one that first requires repainting (the Ruy Lopez?). There must be something more agnostic about being Black, in chess as elsewhere.

Meeting before their match for the World Champtionship, Tarrasch said 'To you, Dr. Lasker, I have only three words, check and mate'. Naturally Lasker won easily 8 to 3 with five draws.

Nimzovich did head stands, knee bends, and calisthenics during a game. He claimed his doctor said exercise was good for him. Bernstein objected to letting an amateur, the then unknown Capablanca, enter a tournament. They met in the first round and Capablanca won the game, the brilliancy prize for that game and the tournament. There is something engaging about such nuttiness in chess.

V

The Greatest Grandpatzer of Them All

Who is it? A Great Grandpatzer Machine, of course. That is, a chess-playing computer.

5.1 *Artificial Intelligence*

The idea of modeling and 'mechanizing' human thought processes has attracted and repelled people for a long time. Much depends on one's metaphysics and one's image of, and beliefs about, machines. Over time, the way words fit the world shifts and our concepts of a machine change as new machines are invented. A century ago a machine was something with gears, sprockets, pulleys, levers, etc. When my grandfather said, 'let's take a ride in the machine' he meant an automobile. To my mother, a machine was a sewing machine. To my wife, it is an automatic washer-dryer. My friends and colleagues in artificial intelligence call their computer systems 'the machine'. A computer is a very special kind of machine in contrast to our other machines because we have created this machine in our own symbol-processing image. In artificial intelligence 'mechanism' means computational (rule-following) procedures, not physical mechanism.

Are people machines? Some biologists believe all living organisms are machines because they have a design and a purpose to them. If so, then people are special kinds of machines of extremely complex designs and purposes. If not, then people or their parts and processes might be like machines in certain respects, e.g. the heart is like a pump. Most people accept the latter analogy. It is when higher mental processes of thinking, feeling, and planning are considered, that the issue becomes controversial. Many people reject 'mechanizing' these processes because they take it as implying that they are machines and hence will be treated like machines. (Some people treat machines with greater respect than they do people. Actually people want to be treated as individuals rather than as members of a class, whether of people or machines.)

Artificial intelligence involves the study, understanding, modeling and the computational mechanization of processes which we say involve 'intelligence' when people utilize them. The combination of terms 'artificial intelligence' may seem both contradictory and pretentious. ('Nothing artificial can be intelligent, only humans are intelligent'.)

Working scientists do not spend much time on precise definitions of their domains of inquiry. Biologists get on with their work without defining 'life' and psychologists do not define 'mind'. For our purposes, let 'artificial' mean man-made computers (people are born of woman) and let 'intelligence' mean selecting the best action for a particular situation. The rest of the terms I will leave undefined and they will have to look after themselves.

A computer is a machine quite unlike previous machines because it translates, stores, processes and transforms symbols rather than energy. It uses energy but its real work is symbolic. It has a compiler which translates symbolic programs written in a high-level programming language into low level machine code which has a one-to-one correspondence with physical states of magnetic fields. The symbols are assigned meanings by humans who use this machine as an instrument to achieve certain purposes. This is possible because there is a dependable correspondence between controllable input and useable output. Man has made computers in the image of his own symbol-processing mind, and thus it is a very special kind of machine, quite different from sewing machines and sports cars which do not transform symbols using compilers and programs. Some (not all) human mental functions can be carried out by computer systems. They store and transform information using computational processes, i.e. a step-by-step execution of rule-following, purposive procedures which can be carried out by a set of physical mechanisms such as a computer. The computer can be made of anything that computers are made of. The physical realization of the computational processes is not the concern of the programmer. He knows nothing of the properties of silicon or the function of magnetic fields—these are the concerns of hardware experts. An analogy with the human mind-brain leaps immediately to mind, cognitive theorists being concerned with symbolic programs and neural theorists being concerned with the wetware of the brain, which incidentally is 80% water. Is the computer only an analogy or is it true that human minds function by using computational mechanisms? Computers may not think but we know people do compute, especially chessplayers.

5.2 *Mechanical Chessplayers*

Non-computer chess-playing machines go back at least 200 years. A fine survey of them, and an excellent discussion of how chess-playing computers operate can be found in Levy's *Chess and Computers*. These early automatons involved what magicians call 'cabinet illusions' and contained a contortionistic human inside them. The best story I can add is that one of these automatons, called 'Ajeeb', contained Harry Nelson Pillsbury, one of the United States' greatest players, along with a quart of whisky which he needed in his last years. He died at 34. This machine beat everybody because Pillsbury could beat almost everybody.

Here is Pillsbury at Hastings 1895, playing Gunsberg in the last round to win the tournament ahead of Lasker, Tschigorin, Steinitz, and Tarrasch. I offer this particular game because Gunsberg also worked in another automaton chess player called 'Mephisto'. 'Machine' against 'Machine' in 1895!

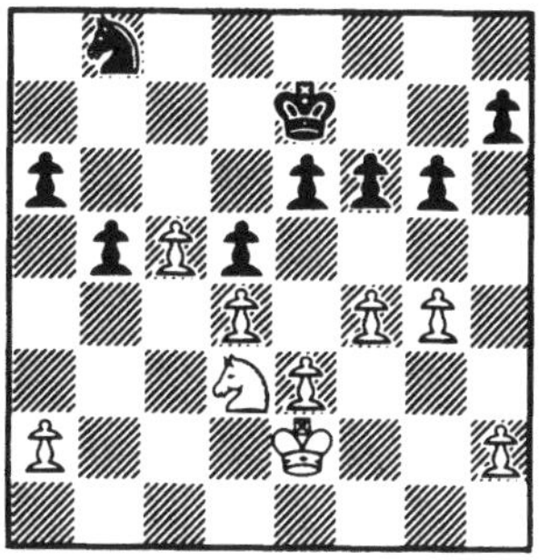

DIAGRAM 120. PILLSBURY–GUNSBERG, HASTINGS 1895

27 f5! . . .

The idea is to go after the Pawn on d5.

27 . . . g5

If 27 . . . g×f 28 g×f e×f 29 ♘f4 would still get d5.

28	♘b4	a5
29	c6!!	. . .

More surprising than it looks. Sacrificing the Knight is obvious.

29	. . .	♔d6
30	f×e	♘×c
31	♘×c	♔×c

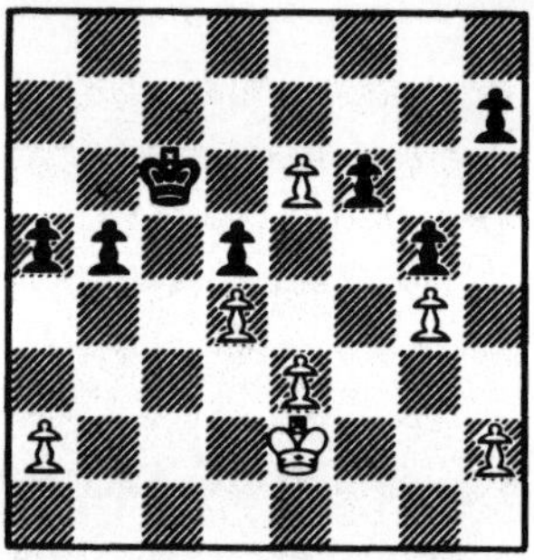

DIAGRAM 121. POSITION AFTER 31 . . . ♔×c

32	e4!	d×e
33	d5+	♔d6
34	♔e3	b4
35	♔×e	a4
36	♔d4	h5

Mephisto is no slouch either. But Ajeeb sees all!

37	g×h	a3

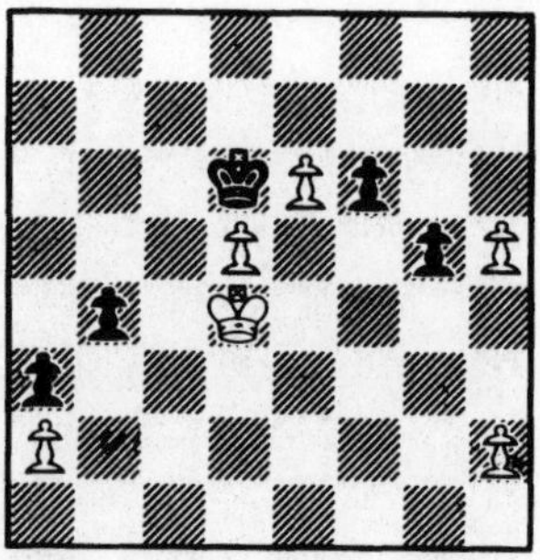

DIAGRAM 122. POSITION AFTER 37 . . . a3

38	♔c4	f5

39 h6	f4
40 h7	Resigns

Current chess-playing computers do not contain a physical person, only the symbolic embodiment of a person's ideas about how chess is best played in the form of a computer program. When you are playing against a computer, you are playing against its programmers once removed plus the brute speed a computer is capable of. The early chess-playing programs of the 1950's were quite weak by human standards.

But the fact that they could do it at all was impressive. A philosopher critic of artificial intelligence, H. Dreyfus, who held that it was impossible for a machine to think, was easily defeated by a chess program. He nimbly retreated to the position that this demonstrated only that one does not have to think in order to play chess. (It is futile to try to catch slippery critics like this.) Gradually the programs have become stronger and stronger (where do they get the money to work on these things?) until 1967 when the Greenblatt program (MacHack, VI) at M.I.T. achieved a USCF rating of 1640 in tournament play. The machine was definitely on the move towards the heights of grandpatzership. The first win of a computer in tournament play is of historical importance.

White: MacHack VI   Black: Human (1510)

Massachusetts State Championship, March 1967

1 e4	c5
2 d4	. . .

Not a bad move in the days of the Smith–Morra Gambit, which this is not to be, however.

2 . . .	c×d
3 ♕×d	♘c6
4 ♕d3	♘f6
5 ♘c3	g6
6 ♘f3	d6
7 ♗f4	. . .

Until here it's a Sicilian–Dragon, but White's 7th move is a weirdo.

7 . . .	e5
8 ♗g3	a6
9 0–0–0	b5

Black appears to be a disdaining patzer determined to wipe this dumb machine off the board without developing or castling.

10 a4	♗h6+
11 ♔b1	b4 (Diagram 123)

You can't charge ahead like this against a coming grandpatzer. Watch this!

12 ♕×d! . . .

If 12 . . . ♕×d 13 ♖×d and the Rook forks both Knights.

12 . . . ♗d7
13 ♗h4 ♗g7
14 ♘d5 ♘×e

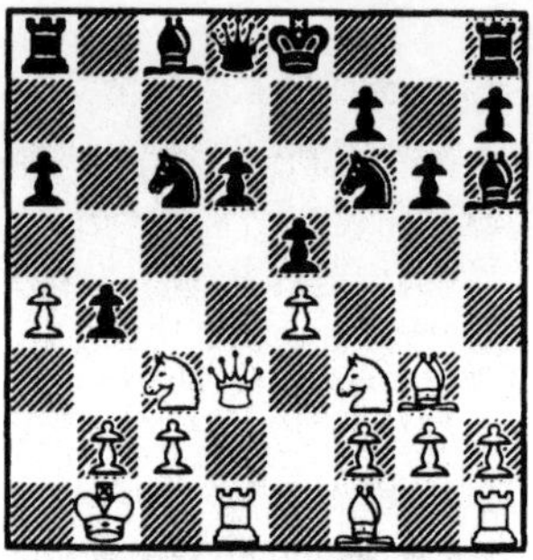

DIAGRAM 123. POSITION AFTER 11 . . . b4

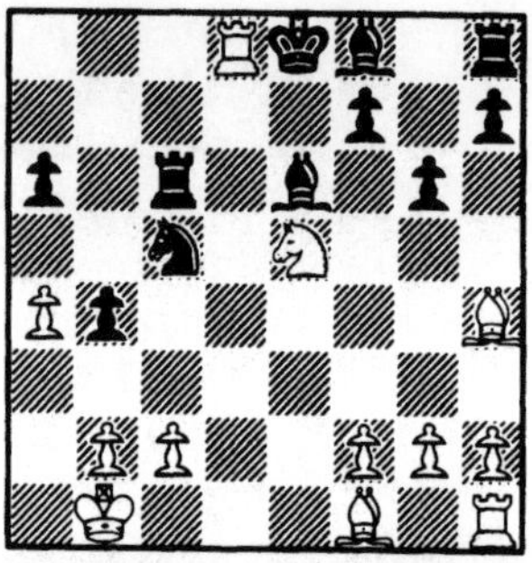

DIAGRAM 124. FINAL POSITION

Black does not believe that White can 'see' anything. '''Computers don't have eyes, so how can they see?'''

15 ♘c7+ ♕×c
16 ♕×c ♘c5

It's too embarrassing to resign to a mere machine. Maybe it will blunder back the Queen.

17 ♕d6 ♗f8
18 ♕d5 ♖c8
19 ♘×e ♗e6
20 ♕×c6+ . . .

Aha! I knew it would lose the Queen sooner or later.

20 . . . ♖×c
21 ♖d8 mate Ahem, er, uh, um . . . (Diagram 124)

Current chess-playing programs are much stronger than MacHack VI and now constitute a serious threat to any aspiring grandpatzer trying to get a rating above 1700. One of the best programs was Chess 4.5 from Northwestern University. It won the Class B section of the Paul Masson Chess Classic in California, July, 1976 with a perfect score of 5–0. To produce this score against opponents averaging a rating of 1735 meant its performance rating was estimated to be 2136, a threat even to masters. Here is one of its games from this tournament. Note again the opponent's problem of the ego game, 'I am smarter than a dumb machine', on the 8th move.

White: Chess 4.5	Black: Arnold (1704)
1 e4	c5
2 ♘f3	d6
3 d4	c×d
4 ♘×d	♘f6
5 ♘c3	a6
6 ♗e2	e5
7 ♘b3	♗e7
8 0–0	. . .

All book so far. But now Black makes a strange move, hoping to blast White's King rapidly, but it loses a Pawn and the open file is worth little.

8 . . .	g5? (Diagram 125)
9 ♗×g	♖g8
10 f4!	e×f
11 ♗×f	♗h3

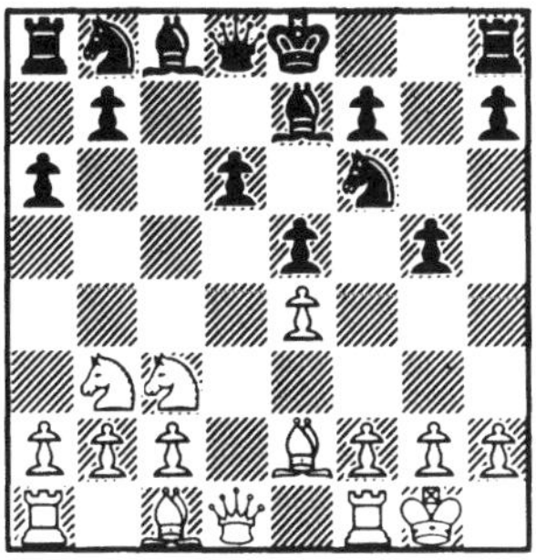

DIAGRAM 125. POSITION AFTER 8 . . . g5?

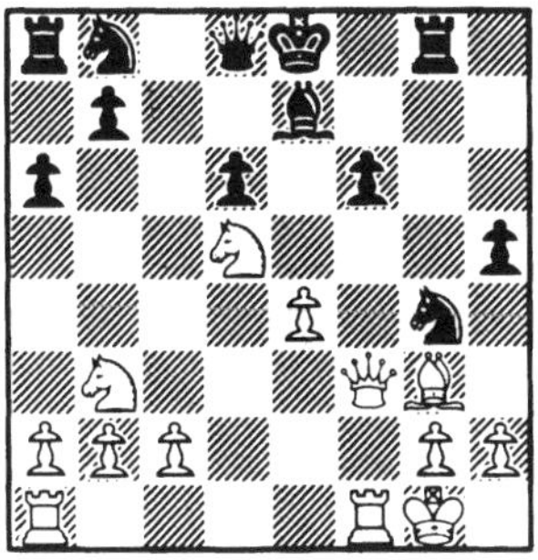

DIAGRAM 126. POSITION AFTER 15 . . . f6

Black must think '"it won't see it."'

12 ♗g3!	♗g4
13 ♘d5!	. . .

Black is undeveloped and uncastled. White now plays like a grandpatzer should.

13 . . .	h5
14 ♗×g	♘×g
15 ♕f3	f6 (Diagram 126)

Notice that White does not exchange his good Knight for the sorry Bishop on e7. Most commendable.

16 h3	h4

17 ♗×h	♘e5
18 ♕h5+	♔d7
19 ♗×f	♘bc6
20 ♖ad1	♔c8
21 ♘×e+	♘×e
22 ♗×e5	Resigns

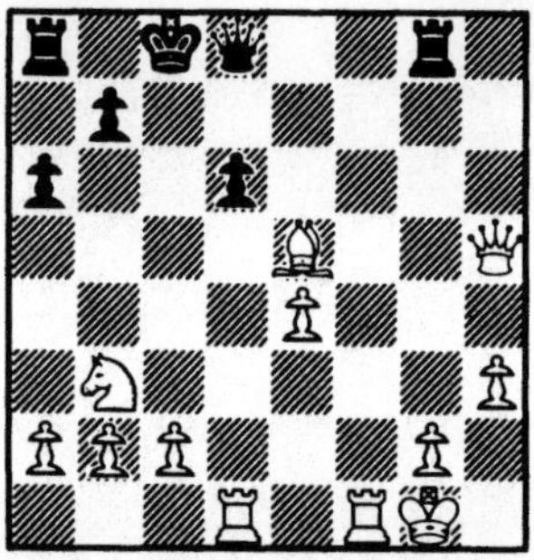

DIAGRAM 127. POSITION AFTER 22 ♗×e5

This quick demolition should gave pause to all current patzers and grandpatzers. Maybe a computer will never become world champion, but that is not the grandpatzer's problem. His worry is, can he defeat one of these things?

Another example:

White: White (1742)	Black: Chess 4.5
1 e4	♘c6
2 d4	d5
3 e5	f6

Some exotic moves here on both sides.

4 f4	♗f5
5 ♘f3	e6
6 a3	♘h6
7 ♗d3	f×e
8 f×e	♗e4 (Diagram 128)

This is getting to look like a typical patzer-grandpatzer mess. (Verpatzen = to make a mess.)

9 0–0?	♗×f
10 ♖×f	♘×d
11 ♗g6+	h×g
12 ♕×d	c6
13 ♕d3	. . .

DIAGRAM 128. POSITION AFTER 8 . . . ♗e4

Hoping the machine will not 'see' it. White should develop his pieces instead of coffee-housing.

13 . . .	♘f5
14 g4?	♗c5+
15 ♔f1	♘h4
16 b4	♘×f
17 ♕×g+	♔d7
18 b×c	

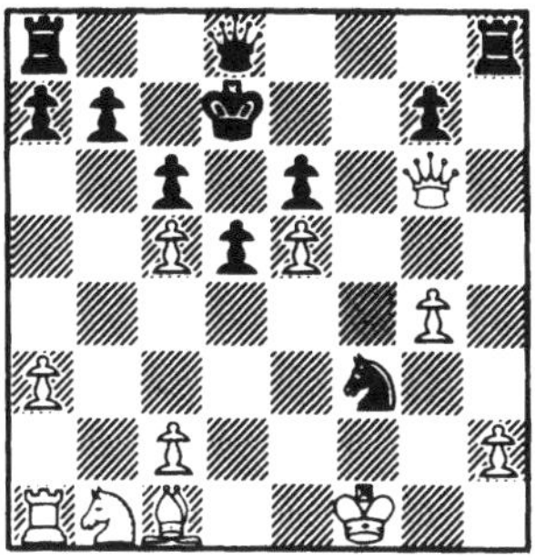

DIAGRAM 129. POSITION AFTER 18 b×c

18 . . .	♕f8!
19 ♗f4	♖×h

Black does not grab the Bishop because of ♕×g+ and ♕×h+. He proceeds methodically and steadily. Notice that White's Queen Knight is still undeveloped.

20 ♘c3	♘×e
21 ♕g5	♘f7
22 ♕g6	♖h1+

23 ♔g2 ♖×a

Grandpatzers do not resign easily and computers do not resign at all. The only question now is, how will Black be able to mate?

24 ♘e2 ♖×a
25 ♘d4 ♖e8

These are powerful moves anybody could be proud of. Notice how one gets an uncanny feeling of 'humanness' about these machines. Why shouldn't we? They are designed to perform just like we do at our best.

26 g5 ♘h8!
27 ♘×e ♖×e
28 ♕h7 ♕×f
29 ♕×g+ ♖e7
30 ♕×h ♖e2+
31 ♔h1 ♕f1 mate

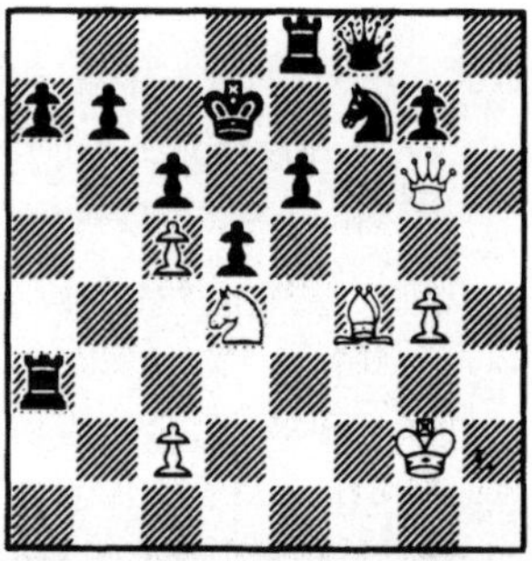

DIAGRAM 130. POSITION AFTER 25. . . ♖c8

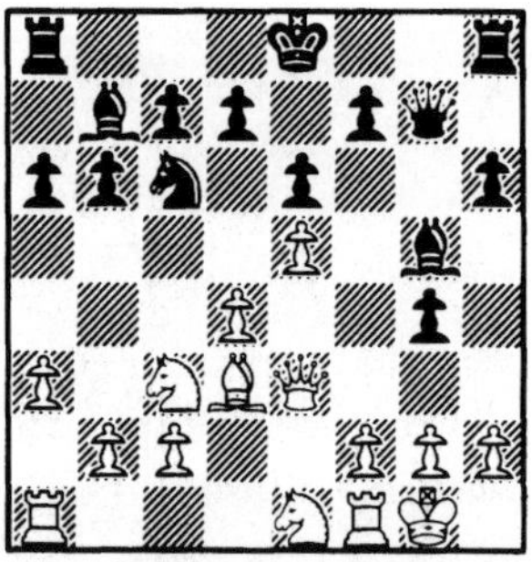

DIAGRAM 131.

The machine may not 'see' everything but it sure sees mates.

It even sees traps. Consider Diagram 131 (White: Chess 4.5; Black: Chu (1784) Here White went:

16 f4 ♗e7

with a trap in mind. He should have played simply g×f.

17 f5! e×f
18 ♗×f ♘×d

A cheap trap to pin and win the Queen.

19 ♗×d+ ♔×d

Black panics. He should play ♔f8 and perhaps survive.

20 ♕×d+ ♔c8
21 ♘d3 . . .

See how the machine 'saw' the pin?

21 . . . ♔b8 (Diagram 132)

22 ♕d7!	♕g5
23 ♖×f	♕e3+
24 ♔h1	♗d8
25 ♕×g	♔a7

Black is all tied up and the passed Pawn is a major threat.

26 e6	♗g5
27 ♖e1	♖hg8?

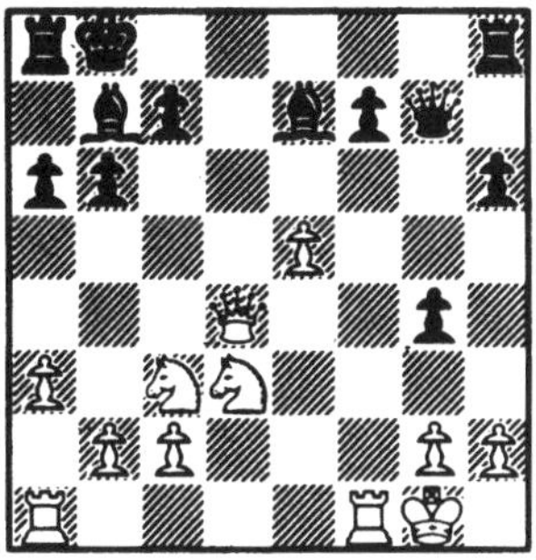

DIAGRAM 132. POSITION AFTER 21 . . ., ♔b8

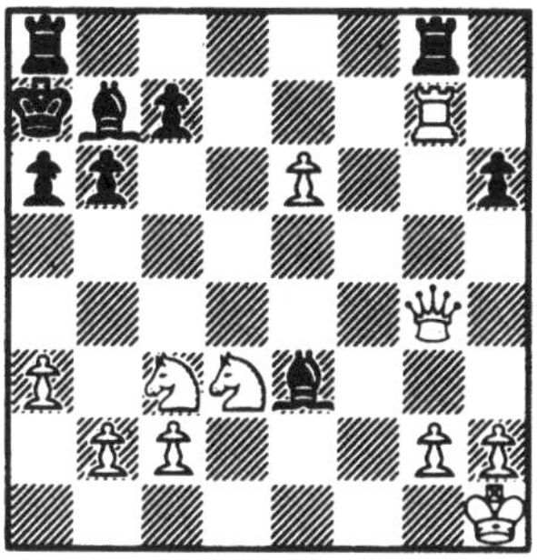

DIAGRAM 133, POSITION AFTER 29 ♖G7

Black is still counting on White not 'seeing' a mate threat. But we know better, no?

28 ♖×e	♗×e
29 ♖g7	. . .

Isn't that a cute move? Black figures he might as well go for the mate but after

29 . . .	♖af8
30 h4	. . .

he resigns against this all-seeing opponent.

Throughout, I have stressed the word 'see' because when I come to discuss how to play against computers, you will see that the problem of the ego-game becomes paramount in such contests.

5.3 *The Russians are coming, the Russians (Soviets) are coming*

A chess program is only as good as its heuristic programmers can make it. I knew some of the programmers of the early chess computers, and they were patzers even weaker than me. They hoped to bootstrap the program up until it played better than they did which it can because of brute speed, applying its evaluation function to hundreds of thousands of potential positions which a human cannot do.

When Botvinnik retired from tournament chess and began working on computer chess, things looked very hopeful for chess programs. A 3-time World Champion Grandmaster and one of history's greatest players must know something special he can contribute to a chess program. And this was not a 57-year-old guy with fading powers. In 1968 he played the most beautiful game of the year against a world-class player.

White: Botvinnik Black: Portisch

Monaco, 1968

1	c4	e5
2	♘c3	♘f6
3	g3	d5
4	c×d	♘×d
5	♗g2	♗e6
6	♘f3	♘c6
7	0–0	♘b6

As one might unedifyingly say, we have a Sicilian–Dragon Reversed for White (Diagram 134).

8	d3	♗e7
9	a3	a5
10	♗e3	0–0
11	♘a4	. . .

White wants to quickly occupy c1 with his King's Rook.

11	. . .	♘×a
12	♕×a	♗d5

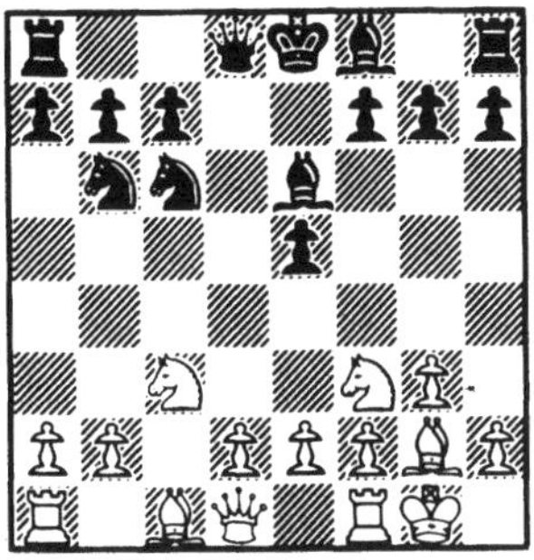

DIAGRAM 134. BOTVINNIK-PORTISCH, MONACO, 1968 POSITION AFTER 7 . . . ♘b6

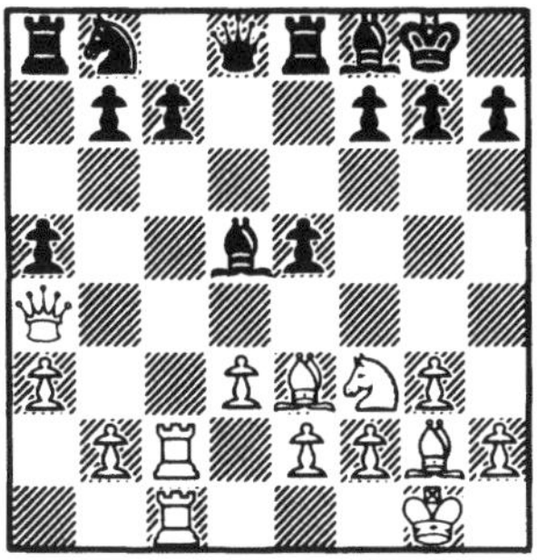

DIAGRAM 135. POSITION AFTER 15 . . . ♘b8

13	♖fc1	♖e8
14	♖c2	♗f8
15	♖ac1	♘b8 (Diagram 135)

Obviously White cannot play 16 ♖×c7 because ♗c6 would lose the exchange. Portisch took a stroll around the room and returned to this stunner:

16	♖×c7!	. . .

Here is what makes a great grandmaster great. Anybody can see that 16 . . . ♗c6 wins the exchange but looking further and further, White sees he can get two Pawns for the exchange and maybe . . .

16	. . .	♗c6
17	♖1×c6	b×c
18	♖×f!!	. . .

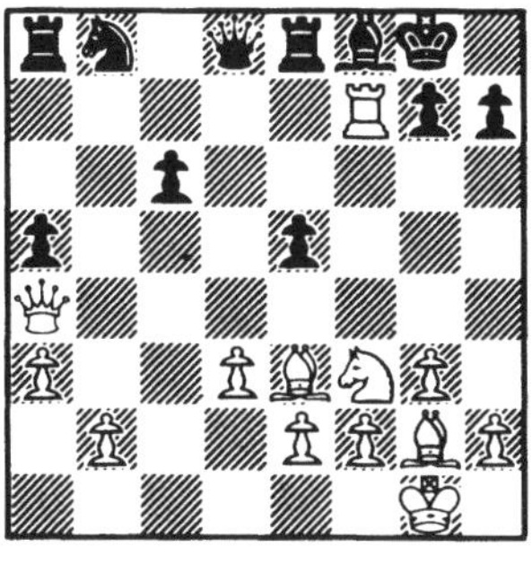

DIAGRAM 136. POSITION AFTER 18 ♖×f!!

sacrifice the whole Rook to irrevocably shatter Black's King's field. Black cannot take the Rook because of 18 . . . ♔×f 19 ♕c4+, ♖e6 20 ♘g5+, etc. or 19 . . . ♔f6 20 ♗g5+, etc.; or 19 . . . ♔g6 20 ♘g5 leading to mate.

18 . . .	h6
19 ♖b7	♕c8
20 ♕c4+	♔h8
21 ♘h4	. . .

He doesn't need that Rook to mate.

21 . . .	♕×b
22 ♘g6+	♔h7
23 ♗e4	. . .

A slight threat of 24 ♘e7+ and ♕g8 mate.

23 . . .	♗d6
24 ♘×e+	g6
25 ♗×g+	♔g7

Why is Black hanging around to watch all this? It must be some sort of bird-and-rattlesnake fascination with being crunched.

26 ♗×h6+	. . .

DIAGRAM 137 FINAL POSITION

Brilliant to the end. Black cannot take the Bishop so he resigns.

Any chess program should be able to profit from such a wonderful player. But it takes two sorts of talent to write a superior chess program, high-level programmers as well as high-level chess players. The story goes that Botvinnik could not get along too well with his first programmers.

A Soviet program called KAISSA won the first World Computer Championship in Stockholm in 1974, winning all four games against other chess programs. Some believe it is unfair to pit humans against computers. Perhaps computers should play only one another. They do. Here is an exhibition game KAISSA played against CHESS 4.0, then the strongest of the USA programs.

White: CHESS 4.0	Black: KAISSA
1 e4	d5

Evans recommends this center counter opening for Black in *The Chess Opening For You* because it forces White into unfamiliar terrain. Your Grandpatzer mentor maintains that grandpatzers should avoid it because it opens up the game too rapidly, with White ahead in development.

2 e×d	♘f6
3 d4	♘×d
4 ♘f3	g6
5 ♗e2	♗g7
6 0–0	0–0

It all looks somewhat humanoid up to now but the next moves on both sides are indeed puzzling.

7 ♖e1	♗f5
8 ♘h4	e5?
9 ♘×f	g×f
10 d×e	♘b4 (Diagram 138)
11 ♕×d	. . .

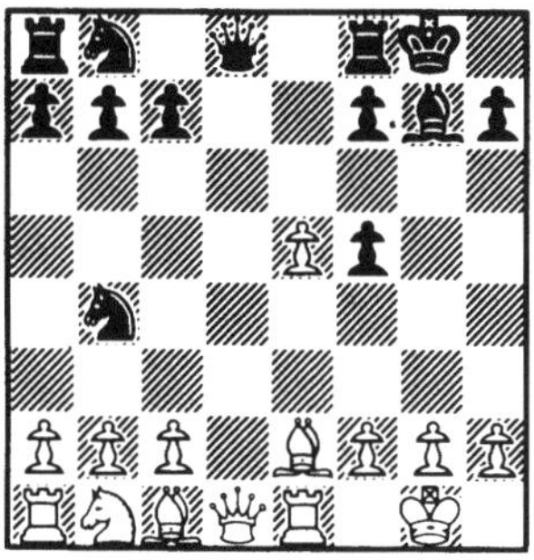

DIAGRAM 138. POSITION AFTER 10 . . . ♘b4

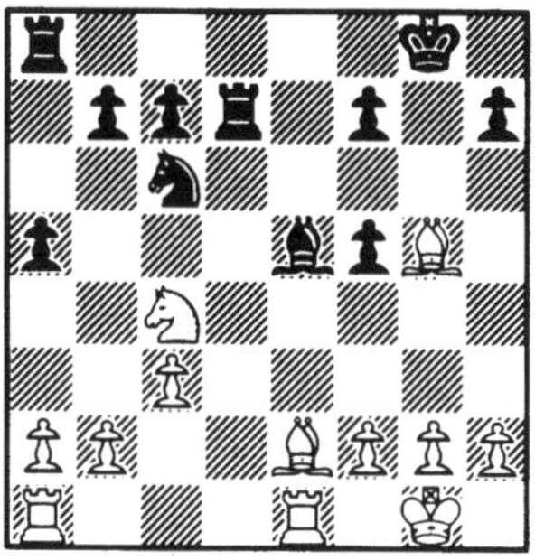

DIAGRAM 139. POSITION AFTER 15 . . . a5

Going into the ending to play against the doubled, isolated Pawns?

11 . . .	♖×d
12 ♗g5	♖d7
13 ♘a3	♗×e
14 c3	♘b5c6
15 ♘c4	a5 (Diagram 139)

The position is very messy and patzerish. Why doesn't White take the Bishop and give himself the two Bishops? The advantage of two Bishops is that they control squares of *both* colors.

16 ♗f3	f6
17 ♗h6	a4
18 ♖ad1	♖×d
19 ♖×d	♔h8 (Diagram 140)

Very mysterious. White is superior, controlling the d-file.

20 ♗×c	♘×c
21 f4	b5
22 f×e	b×c
23 e×f	♖d8

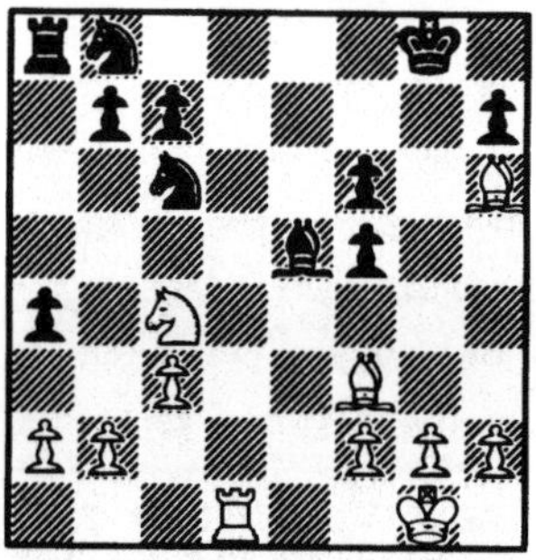

DIAGRAM 140. POSITION AFTER 19 ♖×d

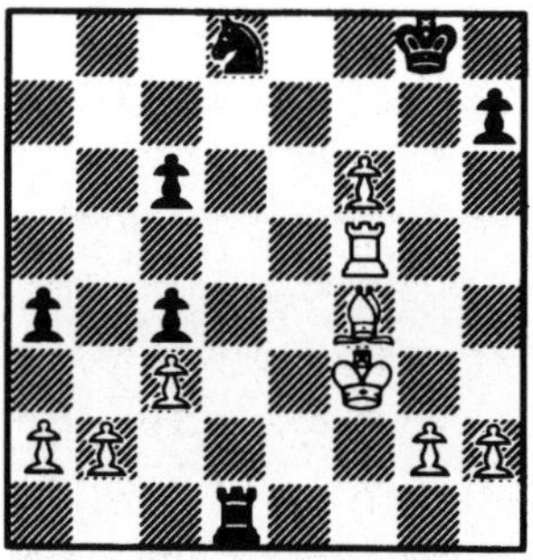

DIAGRAM 141. POSITION AFTER 28 ♔f3

Now Black has four Pawn islands consisting of three isolated Pawns and a set of doubled, isolated Pawns. The Pawn structure favors White who doesn't seem to know quite what to do about it, and so he drifts and wanders.

24 ♖f1	♔g8
25 ♖×f	♖d1+
26 ♔f2	♘d8
27 ♗f4	c6
28 ♔f3	. . . (Diagram 141)

White swims around just making moves without a plan. The game drones on to the 65th move and was adjudicated a draw by Levy. Although it looks like White was superior in the opening and middle game, both programs in this game appeared to lack positional judgement and plans.

Here is another game between two chess programs in which the first reported positional sacrifice by a program occurs on move 16.

White: Chaos Black: Chess 4.0

First World Computer Chess Championship 1974

1 d4	d5

2	c4	d×c
3	♘f3	♘f6
4	e3	e6
5	♗×c	c5
6	♕e2	a6
7	0–0	b5 (Diagram 142)
8	♗b3	♗b7
9	♖d1	♘dd7
10	♘c3	♗d6
11	e4	c×d
12	♘×d	♕b8
13	g3	b4
14	♘a4	♗×e4

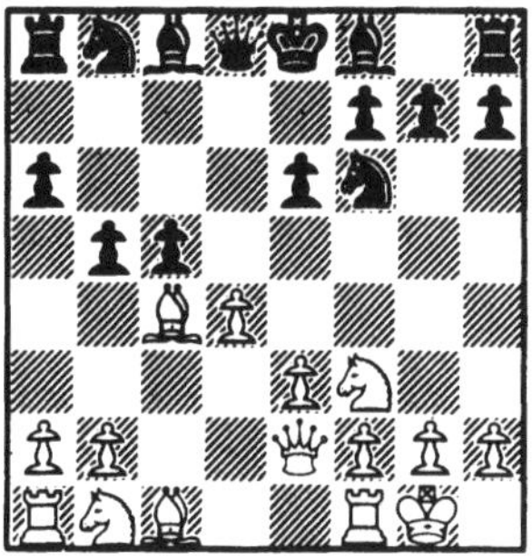

DIAGRAM 142. POSITION AFTER 7 . . . b5

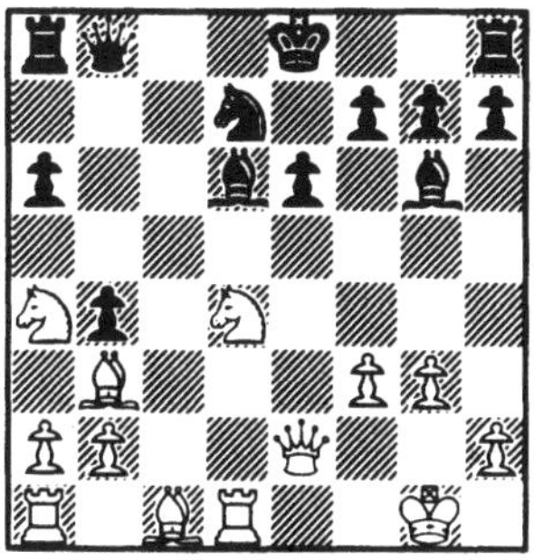

DIAGRAM 143. POSITION AFTER 15 . . . ♗g6

Grabbing a Pawn before castling is a no-no even for humans.

15	f3	♗g6 (Diagram 143)
16	♘×e!	. . .

This is well known to masters as the Capablanca 'positional' sacrifice on e6, giving up a piece to take advantage of the exposed King. It is 'positional' because there is no clear forced win in sight and Black's position is horrible.

16	. . .	f×e
17	♕×e+	♗e7
18	♖e1	♕d8
19	♗f4!	. . .

Threatens a small case of mate or loss of the Queen with ♗c7.

19	. . .	♔f8

Black uncannily sees the threat.

20	♖ad1	♖a7
21	♖c1	♘g8

22 ♖cd1 a5
23 ♗d6 ♗×d
24 ♕×d+ ♘e7
25 ♘c5 ♗f5
26 g4 ♕e8
27 ♗a4

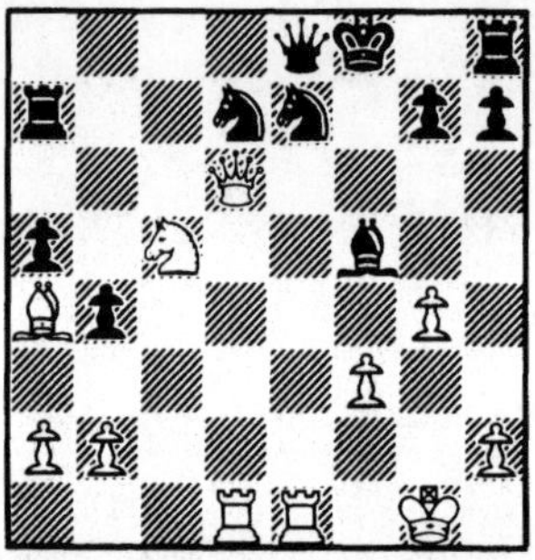

DIAGRAM 144. POSITION AFTER 27 ♗a4

Black is dead lost but will White begin to swim?

27 . . . b3
28 g×f b×a
29 ♗×d a1 = ♕

A very patzerish swindle attempt!

30 ♖×a ♖a6
31 ♘×a ♕d8
32 ♔f2 . . .

White does swim a little but soon gets over it.

32 . . . ♔f7
33 ♕e6+ ♔f8
34 ♕×e+ ♕×e
35 ♖×e ♔×e

Two pieces up. White won it easily.

5.4 *How to play the Grandpatzer Machine*

Hans Berliner, a master and former World's Correspondence Chess Champion, (it takes 8–10 years to win the World's Correspondence Chess Championship!) has written extensively about the problems of chess programs. His Ph.D. thesis in Computer Science at Carnegie-Mellon University, one of the world's leading centers for Artificial Intelligence, was devoted to the topic. Berliner knows what he is talking about. Consider this inspired and subtle ending from the finals of the World's Individual Correspondence Chess Championship, 1968. Estrin, a Soviet grandmaster, is the current 1977 World's Correspondence Champion.

White: Estrin Black: Berliner

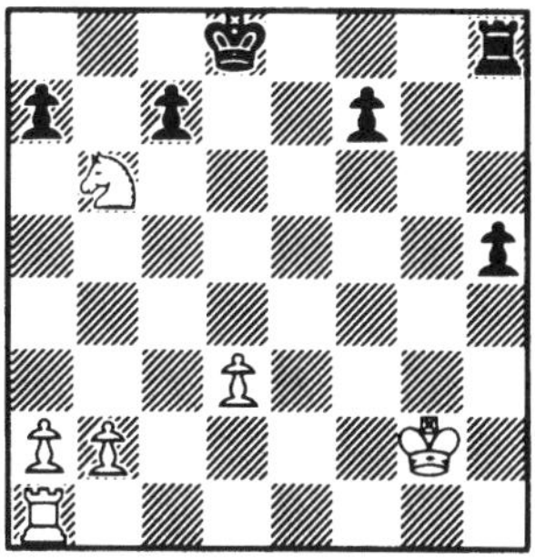

DIAGRAM 145. ESTRIN–BERLINER
WORLD'S INDIVIDUAL CORRESPONDENCE CHAMPIONSHIP, 1968

28 . . .	c×b!!

To keep the Queenside Pawns from being liquidated

29 ♖f1	♔e7
30 ♖e1+	♚d6!

Although it looks to the patzer that Black must try to win on the King-side where he has two passed Pawns, our World's Champion sees that these

Pawns are to be used only as decoys and the crucial action will take place on the Queenside.

31 ♖f1 ♖c8!!

Berliner remarks, 'one of the best moves I have ever made'.

32 ♖×f ♖c7
33 ♖f2 ♔e5
34 a4 . . .

Lots of things can happen here but Black has a plan and sticks to it (see Rule 3 on page 53).

34 . . . ♔d4
35 a5 ♔×d
36 ♖f3+ ♔c2!

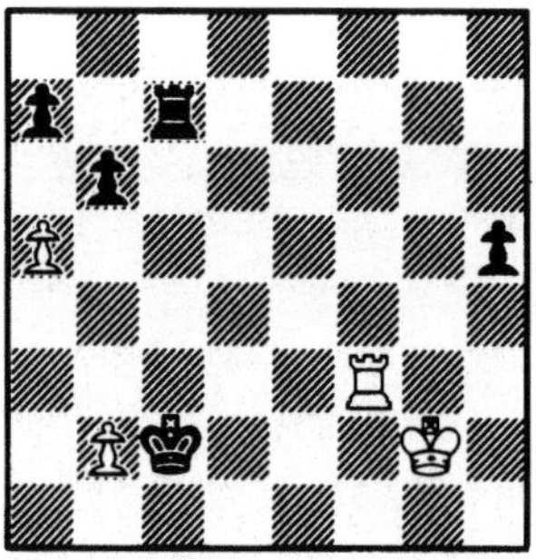

DIAGRAM 146. POSITION AFTER 36 . . . ♔c2!

37 b4 b5!
38 a6 ♖c4
39 ♖f7 ♖×b
40 ♖b7 . . .

After 40 ♖×a ♖a4 wins easily.

40 . . . ♖g4+
41 ♔f3 b4
42 ♖×a b3

White resigns. A super-brilliant Rook and Pawn ending.

Berliner lets us in on a secret limitation of chess programs which he calls the Horizon Effect. Consider Diagram 147 with White to play:

Suppose the search is limited to 3 ply (3 half-moves). White will move 1 ♗b3 c4 2 Any, and now it is time to evaluate. If he moves 1 ♗b3 he will lose the Bishop, hence he seeks something better, finds 1 e5 so that if 1 . . . b×♗ 2 e×f ♗×f 3 ♗b3 and there is no capture of the Bishop. Thus he

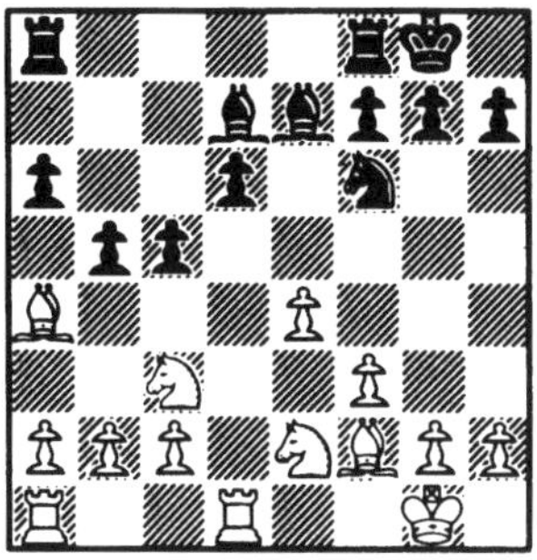

DIAGRAM 147.

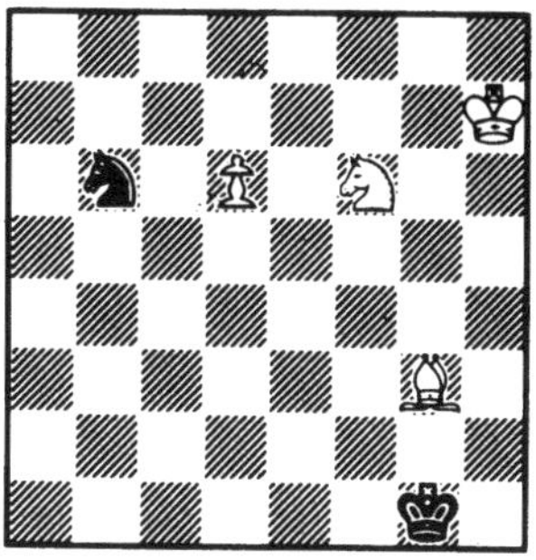

DIAGRAM 148.

doesn't see that 3 . . . c4 wins the Bishop. Berliner terms this the negative Horizon Effect.

The Positive Horizon Effect consists of grabbing too soon when a more effective move could be made. Consider Diagram 148 with White, the program, to move and limited again to 3-ply.

If the program plays 1 d7 Black must play 1 . . . ♘×d to prevent the Pawn Queening and then 2 ♘×d leaves White with a very difficult Knight and Bishop mate. The leisurely 1 ♗e5 and ♗d4 forces the Pawn through and makes the win much easier. The trouble here is that there is a consequence on the horizon which the program tries to realize immediately within the horizon, otherwise it does not realize that it exists.

Extending the number of ply is of course being worked on and now programs are up to 7–8 ply. In some situations Berliner believes they should have at least 14-ply capacities. However, the main problem is how to improve the evaluation function rather than how to do more computational searching. As described previously, the big difference between a master and a grandpatzer is not the depth or breadth of analysis but at the terminal-nodes of the analysis. The master says to himself, 'that looks good for me' *without further analysis*. Whereas the grandpatzer might say, 'I don't know if that's good or bad' or worse 'that looks bad for me'. It is this evaluation judgement of the position by terminal-node pattern-matching, after analyzing a sequence of moves, to a quiescent position, that characterizes the master's strength. Masters know hundreds of thousands of patterns and Berliner believes world-class players may know a million of them.

Berliner gives us a simple but forceful example of the value of pattern-matching over analytic searching (Diagram 149).

It would take a program a 27-ply search to discover 1 ♔e3, a move which every grandpatzer would make immediately because he knows

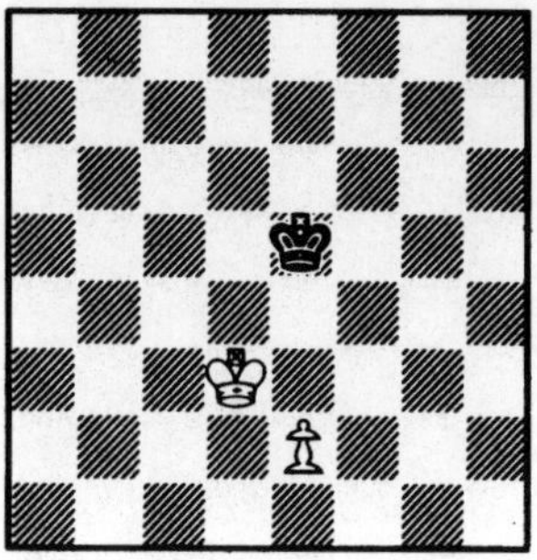

DIAGRAM 149.

White must take the opposition. Pattern recognition means to see a given position as a token, an instance of particular type. A program that noted that a potential move exists which would produce a position matching this King's-in-opposition pattern would not have to engage in elaborate searching. (Of course, it doesn't make any difference if the right move can be found in a fraction of a second. Brute speed is brute speed.)

In February of 1977, Chess 4.5 won the Minnesota Open Championship scoring 5–1 against expert and class A players and receiving a performance rating of 2271. In five minute chess, it scored 2–2 against David Levy and twice beat Hans Berliner, now a 2354 player, who admits he is not best at blitz chess. Chess 5.0 has now beaten two grandmasters (Stean and Hübner (!)) at 5 minute chess and defeated Walter Browne in a simultaneous exhibition. (Would our greatest 5-minute player, Fischer, dare take on chess 5.0?) This jump in performance from B player to master level in a short period of time has been achieved by extending the lookahead capabilities from a mean longest branch of 4–6 ply to 7–8 ply play. Thus, what looks like a mutation or emergent property on the surface is simply a consequence of quantitatively pushing an underlying ability an average of 2–3 steps farther. This may have implications (what are they?) for the evolution and emergence of human intelligence and language.

Here is Chess 4.5 beating a rated expert in the Minnesota Open:

White: Chess 4.5	Black: Fenner (2016)
1 e4	c5
2 ♘f3	e6
3 d4	c×d
4 ♘×d4	a6
5 c4	♘f6
6 ♗d3	♕c7
7 0–0	♗c5

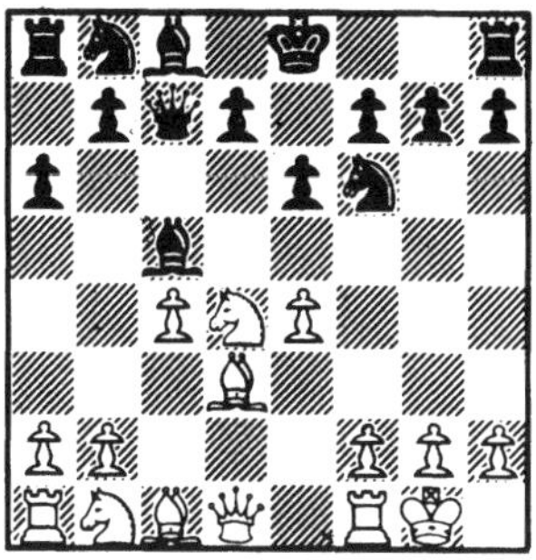

DIAGRAM 150. POSITION AFTER 7 . . . ♗c5

The opening is a little unusual for a Sicilian.

8	♘b3	♗a7
9	♘c3	♘c6
10	♗g5	♘e5
11	♗×♘	g×♗
12	♕e2	d6
13	♔h1	. . .

White gets ready to push f4 and to open the f-file.

13	. . .	♗d7
14	f4	♘×♗
15	♕×♘	0–0–0
16	♖ad1	. . .

White should have played 16 f5 with the threat of f×e and winning the Pawn on f6.

16	. . .	♗c6
17	f5	♗b8

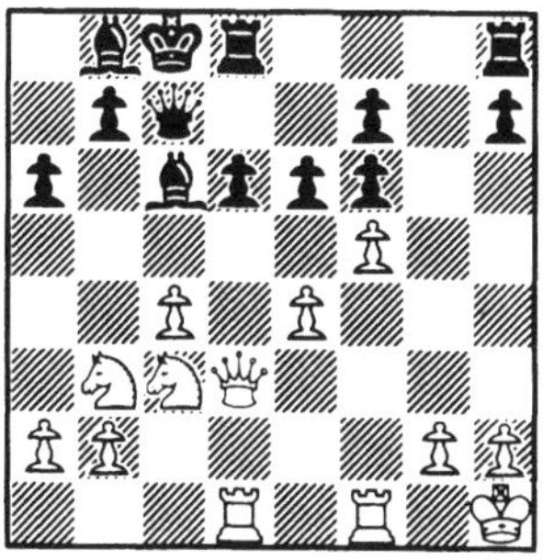

DIAGRAM 151. POSITION AFTER 17 . . . ♗b8

I cannot believe an expert would make this move against a human. The cheap threat to mate at h2 is too obvious. Maybe he just wanted to see what the machine would do.

18 g3	h5
19 f×e	h4
20 ♖×f	h×g
21 ♕×g	♖dg8
22 e×f!	. . .

Here is a beautiful combinational move. Would you have seen it?

22	♕×f

If 22 . . . ♖×♕ 23 ff8=♕+ ♖×♕ 24 ♖×♖+ ♔d7 35 ♖f7+ wins.

23 ♖×♕	♖×♕
24 ♘d5	. . .

Here Black, quite lost, offered a draw.

24 . . .	♗e8

Again going for a cheap trap. You cannot do this against the Great Grandpatzer Machine.

25 ♘b6+	♔d8
26 ♖×b	♗c6
27 ♖×♗+	♔c7

Not even Hans Berliner, in reviewing this game, saw White's next move.

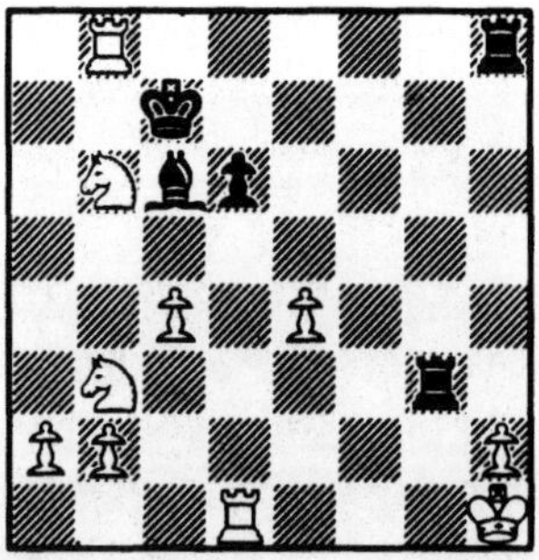

DIAGRAM 152. POSITION AFTER 27 . . . ♔c7

28 ♖c8+!!	♖×♖
29 h×♖	♗×e+
30 ♔g1	♖h8
31 ♘d5+	♔c6
32 ♘a5+!	Resigns

If 32 . . . ♔c5, 33 b4 mate! If 32 . . . ♔d7 33 ♘f6+ wins the Bishop. Did you see that mate?

Chess 4.6 (USA) won the 2nd World Computer Championship at Toronto, Canada 1977. Kaissa (USSR) tied for 2–3 with Duchess (USA). In the position of Diagram 153, White (Duchess) has just checked Black (Kaissa). Black played ♖e8, White took the Rook and won. At the site of the tournament, both Botvinnik and Levy commented on Black's poor move allowing a Rook to be captured instead of playing the King to g7. Kaissa, when asked why she did not play ♔g7, pointed out the mate:

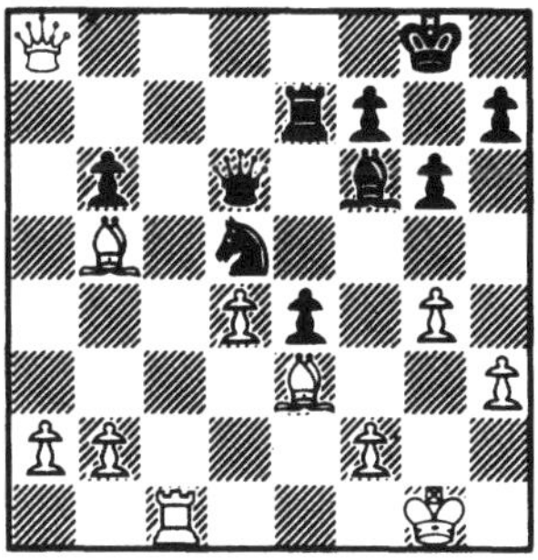

DIAGRAM 153. DUCHESS (USA)-KAISSA (USSR)
SECOND WORLD COMPUTER CHAMPIONSHIP, 1977

1	♕a8+	♔g7
2	♕f8+	♔×♕
3	♗h6+	♔ any
4	♖c8 and mates	

Note again how the computer evaluates *every* check, no matter how absurd, which the humans Botvinnik and Levy did not. To play like a computer you must examine *every check and capture*, and analyze to quiescence no matter what the situation because time and again I have observed that the patzer assumes the chess program will not see something. (Incidentally, this is also one advantage of the blindfold master over the patzer.) Against computers, humans tend to play more weakly than usual because they believe the machine will not see threats and they attempt to coffee-house their way through. Human vanity is what must be controlled here. Play positional chess objectively and play the position, not a 'stupid' machine. It does not get tired, it does not get sick with colds or the flu and is not wracked by emotional tensions of anger, fear, surprise, or despair. Nor is it swayed by seeing you in these states. It does not celebrate victories or bemoan losses. It does not play the ego game; it does not loathe itself for mistakes. It can look ahead at hundreds of thousands of positions (sometimes 1.5 million!), and calculate *accurately*. Therefore, it has many advantages over you which you only increase by contemptuously underestimating it.

My second recommendation involves planning. Programs suffer from Horizon Effects because they do not (as yet) formulate or follow extended plans. In one sense, they do not actually play a game of chess; they solve a series of independent chess problems, finding the best move in each position with the moves being mainly independent of one another. Chess programs are masterly at the combinational middle game when the opportunity arises, but they do not bring about these opportunities as consequences of positional plans. They simply take advantage of weaknesses in your plans. So play patient positional chess with no cheap and transparent traps. Strive for continuity and depth of plan.

Levy, an International Master with a 1977 rating of 2325, had a bet of about $5000 with some members of the artificial intelligence community (not *me*!) that no chess program will be able to beat him in a match under tournament conditions by 1979. In August 1978, Levy won against Chess 4.7, $3\frac{1}{2}$–$1\frac{1}{2}$. I will predict that in 1979 a chess-playing computer will be a most formidable grandpatzer, and that masters and grandmasters will have trouble with it at 5 minute chess (but only if they consent to play it).

Players of the future may begin to use chess programs during adjournments, which should bring an end to our long-standing absurdity of having several consultants help out a player with adjourned games—of which there would be few if we speeded up the game and allowed only a short period before resumption of adjourned positions. After all, Queens and clocks were introduced to speed up the game (naturally over resistant opposition), but we take them as sensible now. Watch out for future opponents making several phone calls during a game—they may be consulting a chess program. With the advent of microprocessors (small, portable computers), a player who leaves the room several times during a game might be suspect. Postal chess may soon become obsolete or simply consist of man and computer against man and computer with the man with the better computer program winning most of the time. Will a computer ever play grandmaster level chess under present tournament conditions and become World's Champion? I don't know, but Dr. G is confident that a computer is about to become the *Greatest Grandpatzer of Them All.*

Bibliography

1. Averbach, Y. and Maizelis, I. Pawn Endings. Chess Digest, Inc., Dallas, Texas, 1974.
2. Euwe, M. and Meiden, W. The Road To Chess Mastery. David McKay Company, Inc., New York, 1966.
3. Euwe, M. and Hooper, D. A Guide To Chess Endings. Dover Publications, Inc. New York, 1976.
4. Evans, L., Gligoric, S., Hort, V., Keres, P., Larsen, B., Petrosian, T. and Portisch, L. How To Open A Chess Game. RHM Press, New York, 1974.
5. Evans, L. The Chess Opening For You. RHM Press, New York, 1975.
6. Fine, R. Basic Chess Endings. David McKay Company, Inc., New York, 1941.
7. Fine, R. The Middle Game In Chess. David McKay Company, Inc., New York, 1952.
8. Hooper, D. A Pocket Guide to Chess Endgames. G. Bell and Sons, Ltd., London, 1970.
9. Keres, P. Practical Chess Endings. Doubleday and Company, Inc., New York, 1974.
10. Kotov, A. Think Like a Grandmaster. Chess Digest, Inc., Dallas, Texas, 1971.
11. Levenfish, G. and Smyslov, V. Rook Endings. Chess Digest, Inc., Dallas, Texas, 1971.
12. Levy, D. Chess and Computers. Computer Science Press, Inc. Woodland Hills, California, 1976.
13. Morrison, M. E. (Ed.). Official Rules of Chess. David McKay Company, Inc., New York, 1975.
14. Pachman, L. Modern Chess Strategy. Pitman and Sons, Ltd., London, 1963.
15. Reinfeld, F. 1001 Brilliant Chess Sacrifices and Combinations. Sterling Publishing Company, Inc., New York, 1955.
16. Schonberg, H. C. Grandmasters of Chess. Fontana /Collins, Glasgow, 1972.
17. Soltis, A. Pawn Structure Chess. David McKay Company, Inc., New York, 1976.

Printed in Poland
by Amazon Fulfillment
Poland Sp. z o.o., Wrocław

54166326R00087